AF412163

DISTRIBUTED

David Blamey & Brad Haylock (Eds.)

Open Editions

45 Handforth Road
London SW9 0LL
United Kingdom

+ 44 (0)20 7820 9779
info@openeditions.com
www.openeditions.com

First published in London 2018

British Library Cataloguing in Publication Data:
A catalogue record for this book is available from the British Library

ISBN 979-0-949004-09-3

Printed and bound in Europe

DISTRIBUTED

Occasional Table

Open Editions

Ahmed Ansari
Stuart Bertolotti-Bailey
David Blamey
Justin Clemens
Alex Coles, Neil Arthur & Jonathan Lindley
David Cross
Neil Cummings
Sean Dockray & Benjamin Forster
Susan Hawthorne
Brad Haylock
Robert Hetherington
Gareth Long
Jens Maier-Rothe & Markus Miessen
Billie Muraben
Rathna Ramanathan
Patricia Reed
Adrian Shaughnessy
Martine Syms & Pip Wallis
Jake Tilson
Eva Weinmayr

David Blamey & Brad Haylock (Eds.)

Table of Contents

AFTERWORD

David Blamey & Brad Haylock

BRAD HAYLOCK   This is the seventh book in the 'Occasional Table' collection that you have worked on as series editor. Since this is, in part, a book about books, it seems fitting that we should reflect on our motivations and our experiences of editing and publishing. You work across several spheres of practice, of which publishing is but one. I do the same, so I know that this is an activity often undertaken for reasons other than money. In the face of what is probably better judgment, why publish?

DAVID BLAMEY   I don't regard the subject of publishing to be restricted to the production and dissemination of books. If publishing has, at its core, something to do with making information available to a public, my interest starts to become piqued the moment we move beyond the boundary of the book *per se*. By this I mean in no way to disrespect the legions of book lovers that I am hoping to attract to our publication on the subject of distribution – which, oddly enough, takes the form of a book – but on the specific question of why publish, my justification is only marginally linked to books. A mixtape shared between three friends is publishing. The Bayeux Tapestry is publishing. A Soviet bootleg Beatles record pressed onto an x-ray is publishing. I'd even go so far as to suggest that a poseur is a publisher, as would be a biker covered in tattoos. In a sense, everything I do that isn't private is publishing: the exhibitions, writing, lectures, films, sound works, music mixes, performances, etc. I publish, *therefore I am*.

However, like several of the contributors included here, I also confess to having a romantic attachment to the book object. It's partly a generational thing, linked to the way I was educated, perhaps, but I do respect the commitment required to consign one's intellectual exertions to a physical form of multiplicity. Ink on paper still has a presence in the world that feels permanent and more open to scrutiny than the short bursts of keyboard activity needed to generate a web post.

You are right to imply that bringing a new book into the world is something of a fool's errand these days. As some of the chapters here attest, it is increasingly difficult to financially justify publishing books. The sums no longer add up. This book will take years to sell. Most of the money earned will go to printers, paper manufacturers, designers, bookshops, distributors and the Inland Revenue. The people who have actually made the content are the lowest paid. I'm considering quitting and starting an online sound project after this. I have finally come to the feeling that I'd rather work on something that's free at the point of use and where no one gets paid, than struggle under the current conditions where everyone seems to pay, or get paid, completely disproportionately to their actual involvement.

But let me ask you something, since the proposal to do this book initially came to me from you. Why are you interested in the subject of distribution, and does what we've published meet your expectations?

BRAD HAYLOCK   I hold the view that ideas have a considerable power to shape our world. The distribution of knowledge is therefore a political problem, and one that is inseparable from the practicalities of dissemination. These are questions that I have long been concerned with. Where I grew up, in regional Australia, the prevailing cultural climate was conservative and homogeneous. European settlement in Australia is characterised by violent dispossession, but this history was not taught in schools. Through books, but also through music, visual art, zines and magazines, I found stories and ideas that helped me to begin to make sense of what I saw around me. This is why I hold what I would now call a commitment to epistemic pluralism. But because the social and political impact of knowledge is dependent upon its circulation, I am necessarily also concerned with the question of distribution.

Does what we've published meet my expectations? Yes – we've captured a wide range of perspectives, with insights running the full gamut, from the importance of the photocopier to cultural analyses of the everyday and hard-hitting critiques of epistemology itself. We're in a period of extreme channel proliferation, so distribution, as an object of study, may shift gears again in the next few years, but this collection has drawn out many important angles on the topic as it stands.

DAVID BLAMEY   Something that I feel we should comment on in relation to this notion of subject complexity is our commitment to presenting a wide range of viewpoints and our willingness to allow that diversity to be reflected in the fabric and tone of individual chapters. In presenting voices that come from the heart alongside more cerebral modes of expression, we are able to not only reflect the plurality of the world that our writers and readership inhabit, but also address head-on the issue of academic writing being commonly viewed as wilfully obscure.

It has been perplexing to note that over the years, whenever reviewers are gracious enough to appraise these anthologies, they have had some very kind words, but on occasion have offered the opinion that the writing is uneven. At first I was taken aback to hear this, but on reflection I've concluded that it's a better challenge to engage a diversity of perspectives, even if the resulting mix is too expansive for some tastes. Critics with a scholarly background have tended to commend chapters with abundant footnotes, while critics who also consider themselves artists often despair of painstaking prose. The optimum position for me lies somewhere in between. After all, isn't it equally uninteresting to read someone who just writes about him or herself as someone who has nothing personal to say?

BRAD HAYLOCK   These related questions of form, content and audience are pressing. I work in a university. Academic writing is often maligned as unintelligible by readers who don't spend much time with it. At its worst, it is an obscurantist performance that can mask an absence of anything worth saying, and academic writing of this type deserves every criticism coming its way. The Sokal affair, which Patricia Reed discusses in this volume, perhaps best reveals what the worst of academic writing makes possible. But academic writing takes the form it does for a reason. At its best, it allows a great deal of conceptual territory to be covered very quickly. Academic writing is written by academics for academics. Regardless of formal differences from one discipline to the next, it is an instrumental form of writing: it serves a purpose and, for the most part, it serves this purpose well. The problem lies simply in the fact that many of the codes that permit its efficiency and efficacy can make the writing indecipherable – or at least extremely unpleasant to read. The issue at hand is this: ideas in academic writing shouldn't be buried by form. In recent years, academics and other taxpayers alike have rightly pointed out that the output of knowledge workers in state-funded universities ought to not be concealed behind the paywalls of commercial journal publishers. What is true of channels may also be true of form: shouldn't the intellectual products of state-funded universities be communicated in a form that the public can read? The figure of the public intellectual has long fulfilled the role of translator and disseminator of academic knowledge for a wider audience, but changes are afoot in the UK, Australia and elsewhere that will require universities to better demonstrate the societal impact of their research, and such changes to the criteria by which public funding is distributed within the sector may mandate a situation in which more academics become public intellectuals.

All of this is a long-winded way of saying that I like the in-between position you're advocating. I value intellectual rigour and clarity of communication equally. But your call for widely intelligible prose won't mean much if the text isn't available to readers in the first place. Should we have published this volume as an e-book, or as a blog? Or, heaven forbid, on Twitter?

DAVID BLAMEY   Actually, I don't see the various platforms that you mention as being mutually exclusive. This book will, I hope, be reviewed on a blog at some point in the future. We will publicise it on Twitter and Facebook as a matter of course. Furthermore, I can predict with some certainty that one of these days an unauthorised copy of the full text will find its way into circulation as a PDF file. We will publish this volume into a mixed economy of circulatory paths.

But let me respond to your invitation to comment on the burgeoning choice of reading platforms by noting that the culture for writing has changed since the advent of digital media. I was recently asked to contribute a text for an online publication on a subject that greatly interested me. When I enquired about the number of words required, the answer was 90. It was an interesting challenge. I worked as hard as I could, but my final text weighed in at a morbidly obese 120. Writing for the page is different from writing for the screen. If the stage for your words is a book, craft skills are required to construct a reasoned argument that are in addition to those that will get you by online. With each new title in this anthology series I have to gird up my loins a notch higher in anticipation of the number of unsuitable manuscripts that are handed in as printable copy. Language is fluid, and writing styles ebb and flow, but almost certainly there would have been less sub-editing work if we'd published all of this online.

BRAD HAYLOCK   Editing is a subtle art. So much work goes on behind the scenes: countless conversations and versions of texts shared between editors, authors, copy-editors and, later in the process, designers and proofreaders. Part of it is about craftsmanship; my brain likes details, so I find it easy to dive into the mechanics of a text. But the higher-level questions are the more demanding: how does any one text in a volume relate to the others? How does an essay fit into current debates in a given field? What does the reader expect? The process has to be a cooperative one – a cycle of push and pull between authors and editors, to be sure, but with common goals and a concern for the reader in mind. It is a process of user-centered, collaborative design.

DAVID BLAMEY   I usually meet potential contributors to talk through their ideas and almost always come away feeling optimistic, expectant and energised. In fact I'd go a step further than that. When I meet contributors to talk about their interests and how they might play a part in giving birth to a new book, I kind of fall in love a bit. Does that sound extreme? The meeting of minds, exchange of viewpoints and development of a plan to bring a new piece of work into the world forms a bond. If the promise of that exchange isn't fulfilled by the text it's heartbreaking.

BRAD HAYLOCK   I can absolutely relate to the feelings of energy and expectation that you describe. I enjoy curating exhibitions; editing a multi-authored volume gives me the same kind of buzz. Clearly, there are a great many parallels between the two types of practice, but, while the discipline of curating has received much attention in recent years, the aesthetics of editing is too rarely discussed. It is an inestimable privilege to be able to formulate an angle on a topic or question that one is passionate or curious about and to ask people whose work one admires to respond. Some of the most exciting insights emerge.

You and I each invited a number of authors to submit proposals for this book. Some of the authors I approached were past collaborators or old friends; some I had met once or twice, in person or online; others I knew only by reputation. The social aspect of publishing as a practice is best expressed, I think, by the title of a book produced on the occasion of a 2006 exhibition of Roma Publications titles, and its sentiment is true of the editorial process, too: *Books Make Friends*. The quality of the finished work is obviously important, but the conversations along the way can be as enjoyable as the satisfaction of a job well done. I have no shortage of optimism when embarking on projects such as this.

DAVID BLAMEY   But what's missing? Are there avenues that you'd hoped to explore but haven't? Although we were never intending to produce a definitive book on the subject of distribution, I would have maybe hoped to find more writers willing to comment on the dark side. Subjects such as the exploitation of indigenous peoples' intellectual property by multinational corporations, or the misappropriation of aid distribution, for example, are facets of our topic that I had in mind at the outset.

BRAD HAYLOCK   I do agree that we should have looked at intellectual property more scrupulously, or at specific cases of abuse in this domain. As Neil Cummings discusses in his chapter in this volume, intellectual property laws are a technology for the annexation of knowledge and its instrumentalisation, typically in the service of capitalism. As such, they expressly serve to limit the distribution of knowledge and therefore warrant much critical attention. For my part, I think it was remiss of us to not interrogate the blockchain more closely. We tried, but couldn't find the right author in time. I recently read a news item about Dogecoin, a cryptocurrency that is modelled on Bitcoin but takes its name and mascot from the internet meme 'Doge', which features images of a Shiba Inu superimposed with short linguistic constructions that are grammatically incorrect in a very particular way. Dogecoin started as a joke in 2013, but a few weeks ago it reached a market capitalisation of two billion US dollars. The blockchain will usher in new forms of distribution entirely. But perhaps it would have been premature to attempt a critique of it in this volume – we are yet to understand what horrors may lie in wait in that technology.

DAVID BLAMEY   Let's keep that up our sleeve for another day, then. Any shortcomings in the current offering will give us just cause to return to the subject again.

COMMON

Neil Cummings

Is sunlight distributed? No. Is air? No. Water? No. Freedom? No. Language? No. Is creativity distributed? No. Of course, these vital common resources can be exchanged, but for a resource to be distributed it needs a vector. Technically, a vector is any value given magnitude and direction. Vectors distribute. Vectors turn common resources into values, give them magnitude and direction. Vectors can be owned, and through their ownership they convert values into potential revenue streams. So, I pay a company that claims ownership of a vector that distributes energy from the sun as electricity to my home.

It goes something like this. The energy stored in coal that fuels the power station was formed aeons ago through photosynthesis in early plants. Or the oil and natural gas the power stations burn is produced from dead, decomposed and compressed sea creatures who ate phyloplankton. Phyloplankton flourished by converting energy from the sun through photosynthesis. This stored sunlight, stockpiled for millions of years as hydrocarbon, is turned into electricity via a dense hybrid network – of plants, animals, mines, oil and gas fields, ships, pipelines, furnaces, turbines, cables, knowledge, skills, people, finance, forms of organisation and software – and distributed. I flick a switch and a little sun illuminates my room.

Electricity is the common of sunlight, turned into a vector and distributed. The same thing happens with water, or creativity, or rights enshrined in laws, or languages, or public research, or affective ecologies, or a whole host of other common resources and common values. Although, interestingly, what is not accounted for in these vectors of distribution are what are historically termed 'externalities'. For example, the carbon dioxide produced in the distribution of sunlight as electricity is returned to the common, as pollution in our biosphere. In economic practices, pollution is not deemed to be part of the property of those who claim rights over the distribution of energy. It's external to the vector. So are the adverse health effects on humans and all the other entities, all the plants, animals and bacteria that make up our worlds. Same with the damage caused by the extraction of energy by mining, drilling or fracking, or the disposal of waste into water systems, or spills from pipelines, or long-term storage of toxic substances.[1]

1.　　Each year in the UK, around 40,000 deaths are attributable to exposure to outdoor air pollution. There are also links to cancer, asthma, stroke and heart disease, diabetes, obesity and dementia. Royal College of Physicians, *Every Breath We Take: the Lifelong Impact of Air Pollution*. Report of a working party (London: RCP, 2016). https://www.rcplondon.ac.uk/projects/outputs/every-breath-we-take-lifelong-impact-air-pollution (accessed 20 October 2017).

The violence and damage of distribution is returned to the common, and is mostly unaccounted for. This has to change.

The work of economist Elinor Ostrom is part of this change.[2] Ostrom, through a lifetime of research, has demonstrated that there are no externalities. Our extraction and distribution of carbon, or fish, or creativity, has been enabled because economic practices, scientific disciplines and political discourse fail to account for all of the costs in what she has termed 'social-ecological systems' (SESs). Ostrom's SESs begin to model inter-related networks of animals, bacteria, plants, minerals, labour and energy, and explore how governance affects all of the components that produce our commons of air, energy, water and soil.

Distribution

'The common' is a term used to denote cultural and, more traditionally, natural resources accessible to members of a given community: for example, the rights to graze animals, collect firewood, harvest fruit or catch fish. I would suggest that resources and values held in common need not be distributed: they can freely circulate, be used and exchanged outside of conventional property relations, without ownership. This may not be true for everything, but for many things, and I suggest that resources held in common enrich rather than deplete the possible.

As with the example of electricity, there is always enormous and often hidden violence necessary to make common resources a vector, a value for distribution. This violence has been ongoing since at least the beginning of the nineteenth century when 'industrial capitalists' competed on a global scale to monopolise energy, minerals, land, processes and the manufacturing and distribution of previously common things,[3] even knowledge and ideas. It's the foundation of what McKenzie Wark, in his book *A Hacker Manifesto*, names 'the vectoralist class':[4] a class that has

2.   In 2009, near the end of her life Elinor Ostrom shared the Nobel Prize in Economic Sciences for her 'analysis of economic governance, especially the commons'. See: https://www.nobelprize.org/educational/nobelprize_info/ostrom-edu.html

3.   Since 1750 there has been a forty percent increase in the atmospheric concentration of carbon dioxide, from 280 ppm to 403 ppm in July 2017. Ed Dlugokencky and Pieter Tans, 'Trends in Atmospheric Carbon Dioxide', Earth System Research Laboratory, National Oceanic and Atmospheric Administration, U.S. Department of Commerce. https://www.esrl.noaa.gov/gmd/ccgg/trends/global.html (accessed 10 October 2017).

4.   McKenzie Wark, *A Hacker Manifesto* [version 4.0], n.d. http://subsol.c3.hu/subsol_2/contributors0/warktext.html (accessed 20 October 2017).

the power to claim the rights to the vectors that distribute resources, to that which would otherwise be common.

It's no surprise that the formation of the vectoralist class coincides with the enclosure movement. A series of acts of parliament – the majority of which, some 4,000 acts, were passed between 1730 and 1839 – enclosed previously open fields, forests, water and common land in England and Wales, creating property rights for resources that had previously been common. Already rich landowners were using their control of parliament for their own private benefit, to consolidate farms, concentrate land value and expropriate resources. The process also accelerated the creation of a rural poor, who became labour for the emerging urban industries. Vectoralists insist that enclosure is necessary for development: to encourage investment, innovation and the more efficient distribution of resources.

Vectoralist logic is routinely applied to all common resources. Parallel to the enclosure movement, a similar process turned the common of creativity into a value for distribution. The principal vector for enclosing creativity is copyright law; this evolved to enable individuals to profit financially from the distribution of texts after the advent of cheap reproduction, cheap printing, in the early eighteenth century. The Statute of Anne of 1710 was the first iteration of a copyright law in England. Its intended use was to stop other printers printing a text and distributing it. The statute granted rights of restriction from unauthorised distribution for fourteen years, after which time the published work would return to the commons, where anyone could copy, modify and re-publish it. A delicate balance was struck – between enabling producers to make a temporary vector to benefit financially from a distributed text and enriching the common of creative resources.

This delicate balance has long been abandoned. The three-hundred-year labour of copyright has been to slowly construct an ideological nexus as the source of creativity: the figure of the individuated author or artist, a singular, bounded subject, secure in time and space. The birth of the author has been at the expense of the death of the common as source and resource. It's no surprise to me that the words 'authorial' and 'authority' have the same root, linked by power and the legal right to exert that power. A power to enclose and a power to exclude. The author anchors vectors through the force of the law. Copyright was extended in 1928 to thirty years, then quickly extended to the natural life of the designated author; then the life of the author plus thirty, then fifty years, and in 1997 it was extended to the life of the author plus seventy years. I'm sure lobbyists from the vectors of distribution, the 'creative industries', are currently seeking extensions. Let's be clear, it's not authors or artists who are being rewarded by distribution, but rather the vast content and rights, secondary rights and derivative rights management industries. The vectoralists.

Currently, all creative acts are born into property forms ready for distribution by the vectoralist class. Any instance of a thing assembled in the world that is sufficiently different from anything else before it – be it any object, image (still or moving), words collated as a text, sequence of sounds, archive metadata or gene sequence – is defined as a property and legally belongs to someone: a person, or a legal entity like a corporation.

In these already dense networks of distribution, we experience creativity and we reproduce creativity, or electricity, or water, or generosity, as individuated, as a property, usually someone else's property and scarce, or precious: precious, as a revenue stream. As a consequence, we inhabit a creative culture riven with anxiety about plagiarism and copying: we constantly worry about rights, image rights, terms and conditions and permissions. 'Can I photograph that, please?'

Attitudes towards distribution are always ideological. Any discussion of common resources is usually accompanied by the knowing counter-refrain 'Oh, the tragedy of the commons', with the assumption that common resources will be mismanaged, wasted and eventually destroyed. This weary refrain is a reference to 'The Tragedy of the Commons', the title of an article published in *Science* magazine in 1968 by Garrett Hardin.[5] Basically, Hardin, a biologist influenced by systems research, believed that as more self-interested herdsmen with more self-interested sheep grazed on common land, it would become depleted. His solution to this theoretical problem was to reinforce the power of vectoralists: 'The tragedy of the commons as a food basket is averted by private property, or something formally like it'. The tragedy of the commons is the ideological substrate of the vectoralists.

Unlike Ostrom, Hardin doesn't seem to consider the possibility that people – like other hybrid ecologies with finite resources – might communicate, share and collectively manage access to the resource.

5.   Garrett Hardin, 'The Tragedy of the Commons', *Science* 162, no. 3859 (December 13, 1968). DOI: 10.1126/science.162.3859.1243 http://www.garretthardinsociety.org/articles/art_tragedy_of_the_commons.html (accessed 19 October 2017).

Since Hardin's infamous text was published, the vectoralists have slowly added information, data, interfaces and platforms to their portfolios: they mine our needs and desires, our affective and emotional lives, to produce new vectors.

Now, as I said earlier, copyright works by exclusion. In the world of material goods, this makes some physical, if not common, sense. Physical things are relatively slow moving, and have a material presence. They are bounded in time and space. Think of a simple wooden chair – handmade, artisanal; it exists in one place, at one time, more or less. To make a copy of it would be very laborious. It would take an investment in materials and labour and, although different, the copy would always refer back to the previous version. Like a footnote. Of course, these linear relations of original and copy are rendered redundant by things made for reproduction, where there is no source: things like books, prints, photographs, sculptures, readymades, ideas and anything digital. That's why vectoralists have produced and legally enforce the idea of an intellectual property: so they can claim rights over immaterial things, or things that have no origin, or things that can be reproduced with little effort.

Copyright is a vector to enclose and distribute creativity. Like the burning of hydrocarbons, its effects are toxic. It poisons our creative biosphere.

The Return of the Common

Let me introduce to you a writer in computer languages, a genius programmer called Richard Stallman. In the late 1970s, Richard was collaboratively writing programmes for early general-purpose machines when he realised that companies and individuals were starting to claim property rights – intellectual property rights – over the code. Languages collaboratively developed and assembled into programmes were being enclosed. Richard felt that all languages, including programming languages, are shared and of necessity non-owned, a commons of resources. And that a meaningful utterance is only possible by drawing upon, modifying and sharing resources that are freely distributed within a community of speakers and listeners, or writers and readers. Restrictions in language limit the possible. This is why we value freedom of expression.

Software codes are special kinds of language. They do what they say. They are expressions that are executable, performable: they initiate actions. 'Jump!' Richard could see that any language that issues commands to machines was going to have a profound effect on our emerging worlds. He had also experienced the fact that all the 'individual' contributions to programming languages could be configured – no, worse! – would be born into property, as an intellectual property: and indeed they are.

In 1983, Richard started writing the thousands of lines of code necessary to build a complete operating system, called GNU, which would be 'free', like spoken language and outside of property – like a common.[6] To gain support for the project Richard wrote a GNU Manifesto, which contained three essential freedoms: freedom to run a programme for any purpose; freedom to access the code and modify the programme; freedom to share the modified version. To enact and protect these freedoms, Richard then went on to write the General Public License (GPL) in 1989. The GPL is a piece of legal code that is able to license contributions to 'software' out of copyright and intellectual property restriction, and enshrines the right to copy, modify and share assembled languages. The genius of this idea was to encode in the licence a viral heart. The rights to copy, modify and share are passed on through all subsequent versions of the software, and any and all derivatives. GPL-protected resources are resources that can never be legally enclosed. They are a new common.

By 1991, despite a vast collaborative effort, the GNU project was still not a complete operating system. It was missing a vital part: the kernel. The kernel communicates between a programme and the hardware it sits in and on. Coincidentally, and independently, a Finnish software engineer, Linus Torvalds, had written a kernel he called Linux; the two projects merged and were released as GNU/Linux under the GPL version 0.12 in 1992. This was the first Free, Libre or Open Source Software (FLOSS) operating system: anyone can access the source code, install it in a machine and use it. Anyone. If you have the skill and inclination, you can adapt, modify and improve the operating system – to enable a particular task or function, or move it to a different hardware configuration – and you can share these modifications with others, too. Many anonymous people, located around the globe, are collaborating and doing just that. The GPL has enabled FLOSS software to flourish at an astonishing rate into a vast software commons.

6.   'GNU' as a name is a geek joke. GNU is a recursive acronym – 'Gnu's Not Unix' – because GNU's design is like the Unix operating system, but different and 'g-new'. GNU Operating System, https://www.gnu.org/gnu/manifesto.en.html (accessed 8 November 2017).

Over the last twenty years or so, the GNU/Linux operating system has mutated into myriad distinct distributions, or 'distros' for short. The most popular are Debian, Fedora, Mint and Ubuntu, together with commercial versions such as Red Hat. Each is optimised for different tasks, whims or fashions, but all have GNU/Linux in common. The machine I am using to write this text functions because of Ubuntu. I downloaded it from a repository on the Internet for free and installed it on a generic laptop. It runs beautifully. I'm also writing using LibreOffice, which is a FLOSS version of a popular proprietory administrative software. Again, I downloaded it legally for free and it works perfectly.

You can never own proprietory operating systems or software. When you click 'Agree' on the long and impenetrable terms and conditions, you agree to merely license their utility from a vectoralist. Nor can you 'own' FLOSS software. As I said, it is a commons of resources, but you have all the freedoms of ownership and more. You are free to use, modify and share any improvements you make with others, and you also benefit from all the improvements and modifications made by the thousands, possibly millions, of 'others' using the same software. In digital, knowledge-based and immaterial ecologies, the 'tragedy of the commons' is inverted: the more people using the resource, the better. Scarcity is overwritten by abundance. The GPL functions like a planetary-scale ratchet, all the time enriching rather than depleting the common of available resources.

So, while it began as an operating system, FLOSS software has subsequently been modified to produce an incredible range of resources. It runs the majority of servers that support the Internet, mostly through running Apache software, written and supported by a decentralised community of open-source developers.[7] FLOSS, and specifically Linux, enables most mainframes and supercomputers to function in research, science, development, space and military environments. Mutated versions of Linux also run on embedded systems – devices whose operating system is typically built into the hardware. Digital watches, traffic lights, toasters, heart pacemakers, smart TVs and pretty much anything else with the prefix 'smart' in the name is enabled by FLOSS software, as are autonomous

7.   From Netcraft's September 2017 Web Server Survey: 'Apache remains far ahead in the lead with 2.88 million web-facing computers giving it a 42.3% share of the market.' The report goes on to ask: 'Which underlying operating systems are used by the world's web facing computers? By far the most commonly used operating system is Linux, which runs on more than two-thirds of all web-facing computers.' Netcraft, 'September 2017 Web Server Survey', https://news.netcraft.com/archives/2017/09/11/september-2017-web-server-survey.html (accessed 20 October 2017).

vehicles, all blockchains, including Bitcoin, environmental sensors and process control and supply chain networks. The much-heralded 'Internet of things', when it arrives, will be running on common resources. Of course, most smartphones and portable devices function because of Android, software based on Linux and released with an Open Source Licence.[8] In only twenty-six years, FLOSS software has gone from an aspiration to the common substrate that enables our world.

The thing is, the GPL has also inspired different kinds of licences that function in different contexts – perhaps the Creative Commons licences are the best known – that protect not only software, but also an astonishing range of resources from enclosure.[9] Things like images, sounds, moving images, texts, books and objects. This is what this text is protected by.

Also, the ethic of FLOSS is mutating to produce collaborative and common resources like *Wikipedia*, the free encyclopedia that anyone can contribute their knowledge to. Since its launch in 2001 it has gone from being the butt of jokes to the most visited resource on the Internet.[10] Similar resources include the gigantic archive of out-of-copyright films, books, audio, TV programmes and websites, www.archive.org, or the Open Music Archive, a collaborative project initiated by artists Eileen Simpson and Ben White to source, digitise and distribute out-of-copyright sound recordings.[11] The archive distributes these recordings freely, and also becomes a vehicle for future collaborations and exchange. These are just a few of the common resources inspired by the ethic of the GPL.

We could also redescribe hashtags and tags as contributions to the common of knowledge. Hashtags make a vector for specific knowledge. They link, connect, classify and categorise, but they can never be claimed as a property. Never be distributed. Maybe we could enlarge the common to include standards like the pitch of threads on screws, or the length of a metre, the dimensions of shipping containers and the TCP and IP commu-

8.   The Android core is protected by the Apache License Version 2.0. Like other FLOSS licences it allows the user of the software the freedom to use the software for any purpose, to distribute it, to modify it and to distribute modified versions of the software under the terms of the licence. 'Apache License', *Wikipedia*, https://n.wikipedia.org/wiki/Apache_License (accessed 20 October 2017).

9.   Creative Commons, 'Creative Commons Licenses', https://creativecommons.org/licenses (accessed 25 October 2017).

10.   There are about 71,000 active contributors working on more than 46,000,000 articles in 299 languages. 'About Wikipedia', *Wikipedia*, https://en.wikipedia.org/wiki/Wikipedia:About (accessed 24 October 2017).

11.   Open Music Archive, http://www.openmusicarchive.org (accessed 25 October 2017).

nications and software protocols.[12] None of these resources could be said to be distributed; they are common standards held by consensus and implemented, or used. The collaboratively sequenced human genome, the project to trace and map all the genes that make up human DNA, was declared a common in 2001. Use and re-use enrich the wealth of the common.

Bonus Level

It's true that we could celebrate distribution as the vectors of a powerful financial and political economy that produced the agricultural and industrial revolutions. Distribution is a means of exchange that has increased standards of living and education, built creative and knowledge-based industries and enabled the transformation of energy and matter on an unprecedented scale. This celebration would be for the vectoralists.

Vectors of distribution are always in dialectical conflict with the common. Yet we can no longer afford the constant expropriation of value and resources, or fail to value that which is common and outside of distribution. What FLOSS software has shown, and what principally feminist economists have argued, is that we could reimagine and remake our world in common.[13] If the common is characterised as resources generated through the free cooperation of its users, Ostrom has insisted that we account for the contributions of 'other' entities and assemblies of 'other' entities as users, too. Different ecologies of animals, bacteria, plants, minerals, labour and energy produce our traditional commons of air, energy, water, forests and soil, and all these users should have mutual access and rights to the resources produced. The feminist economic geographers J.K. Gibson-Graham have called for attention to be paid to our affective and emotional commons, and for us to be sensitive to

12.   TCP is the Transmission Control Protocol and IP the Internet Protocol. These common protocols provide the structure for global communication, by specifying how data should be packeted up, addressed, transmitted, routed and received.

13.   J.K. Gibson-Graham is a name shared by feminist economic geographers Julie Graham and Katherine Gibson. Their first book, *The End of Capitalism*, was published in 1996. J.K. Gibson-Graham, *The End of Capitalism (As We Knew It): a Feminist Critique of Political Economy* (Cambridge, MA; Oxford: Blackwell, 1996). The two women also founded the Community Economies Collective (CEC), 'international collaborative networks of researchers who share an interest in theorizing, discussing, representing and ultimately enacting new visions of economy': Community Economies, 'About Community Economies', http://www.communityeconomies.org/Home

embodied knowledge, the labour of care and values we value, like trust, love, generosity and equity. These are common, vital values that circulate, that enable relations and communities to form and dissipate.

Distribution has produced tremendous violence and inequity, and even threatens the long-term viability of our biosphere – not only for us humans, but all the myriad entities and assemblies of myriad entities that coproduce our worlds. We need to limit activities that enclose the common, deplete resources or poison our biosphere. To do this, better management of the vectors of distribution will be necessary. They'll have to be repurposed to maximise diversity, produce surplus and distribute it generously. Everywhere and to everyone. We will need to enrich the common if we are to remain resilient in the Anthropocene.

Is sunlight distributed?

NEVER LET ME GO

David Cross

Never Let Me Go is the title of a 2005 novel by Kazuo Ishiguro. In an institution that prepares a class of young people for serving others, the process of education cultivates self-expression through creativity and enables students to develop personal qualities of tolerance, courage and empathy. But this is done in a way that forestalls their critical understanding of their situation, so that their unwitting consent is secured for giving with no expectation of receiving. Accepting the limits of their awareness and the brevity of their existence, their insights spring instead from the struggles of loyalty divided between obligation, friendship and love.

Distribution is key to the global financial and ecological crises. Relating the concept of distribution to the principle of equity, I will describe the attempts that I have made with other people to activate resistance to economic and ecological debt in the university where I work. Through cycles of action and reflection, these attempts have drawn attention to the structures and practices in the university that distribute value and risk, authority and power. I propose that the critical manifestation of distribution in my university is the separation of academic activities from executive functions, which compounds the ideological effects and psychological affects of neoliberalism in the academy. I will also outline my idea for an experimental system for redistributing attention, energy and value. But first, let me describe my starting point and rationale.

Since 2007, I have been a Reader in Art and Design at the University of the Arts London (UAL), where I have continued my long engagement with the relationship of visual culture to the contested ideal of 'sustainable development'.[1] Seeing sustainability as a reconciliation of ecological, economic and social justice issues, I view the obstacles to achieving it not as scientific or technological, but ideological and psychological: belief structures, especially individualism, the separation of people and the environment, and the fantasy of cornucopia frame choices that converge on crisis. Conversely, the critical tendencies of art bring a reflexive and emancipatory impulse that could lead beyond passive spectatorship towards active social agency.

1.   From 1992 to 1997 I was a Research Fellow at the Royal College of Art. Connecting academic activities with the practical operations of the College, I established energy efficiency measures that cut CO_2 emissions and saved around £50,000 annually in 1993.

So for a long time, you were kept in the shadows, and people did their best not to think about you. And if they did, they tried to convince themselves that you weren't really like us.[2]

The ecological aspect of the crisis, like the 'hyperobject' posited by Timothy Morton,[3] seems almost unthinkable in its complexity. Scientific models of the anthropogenic transformation of the planet include feedback loops in the ecosystem, such as those accelerating climate damage, which bring risks of uncontrollable losses, from mass extinction to ecocide.[4] But, despite the existential threat, when causes and effects are so separated by delay and dispersal that their relationship appears random, most people focus on more immediate concerns. To connect environmental issues to social behaviour, Mathis Wackernagel developed the method of ecological footprint calculation, which applies a spatial analysis to the impacts of consumption, allowing different consumption patterns to be mapped and compared.[5] Andrew Simms devised the concept of 'Earth Overshoot Day', which applies a temporal analysis, relating ecological footprint (the rate at which resources are consumed and waste is produced) to 'biocapacity' (the rate at which ecosystems renew themselves).[6] With the New Economics Foundation, Simms also co-authored *The Great Transition*, a comprehensive programme of radical economic and social reform.[7] Yet the private media avoid such systemic thinking, preferring to frame the symptoms of ecological collapse as separate instances of the manageable degradation of the environment. Meanwhile, countless commercial messages attribute almost supernatural powers of healing and renewal to 'nature', sustaining the fantasy of an eternal place outside consumer culture that can serve as both resource pool and waste sink.[8]

2.	Kazuo Ishiguro, *Never Let Me Go* (London: Faber & Faber, 2005), 258.
3.	Timothy Morton, *Hyperobjects: Philosophy and Ecology after the End of the World* (Minneapolis, MN: University of Minnesota Press, 2013).
4.	See Polly Higgins, *Eradicating Ecocide*, http://eradicatingecocide.com (accessed 27 October 2017).
5.	Mathis Wackernagel et al., *Global Footprint Network* www.footprintnetwork.org (accessed 27 October 2017).
6.	Earth Overshoot Day, http://www.overshootday.org (accessed 27 October 2017).
7.	Stephen Spratt, Andrew Simms, Eva Neitzert and Josh Ryan-Collins, *The Great Transition: A Tale of How it Turned Out Right* (London: New Economics Foundation, 2010).
8.	Sally Weintrobe (ed.), *Engaging with Climate Change: Psychoanalytic and Interdisciplinary Perspectives* (London: Routledge, 2013), 201.

The economic aspect of the crisis is experienced by the vast majority of people as an endless struggle with poverty or lack, while a correspondingly small minority of 'high-net-worth' individuals continually increase their wealth. Yet, extreme inequality is not inevitable. As the Bank of England has shown, the 'logic' of accumulation (and therefore of depletion) is encoded in the way that money is created — as debt to be repaid with interest.[9] While rent transfers value to people who own property, *from* people who use it, interest is a feedback mechanism that compounds inequality by transferring value to people who lend, *from* people who borrow. Codifying surplus and deficit, debt articulates the distribution of economic power, which at the global scale involves a net transfer of resources from the poorest people to the richest, and on an unprecedented scale.[10] Because money is created as debt, there can never be enough money to repay the capital and the interest.[11] This is why debt drives the endless pursuit of economic growth, despite the finite capacity of the earth.

Historically the most important of all finite resources, fossil fuels form a key intersection between the economic and ecological crises. Since the Industrial Revolution, fossil fuels have powered the material production that has driven social transformation and given rise to the consumer society. With their unique potential to amplify the productivity of labour power, fossil fuels are a prime commodity, a 'meta asset' under-lying all other asset classes. Today, the global financial system is so closely connected to the fossil fuel industry that in some respects they function as a single entity.[12] Yet fossil fuels embody a paradox. Although they have fuelled exponential growth for nearly two centuries, hydro-carbons exemplify the 'law' of diminishing returns: as deposits of easily accessible and higher quality fuels are exhausted, more energy is needed to extract the fuel that remains, so even while fuel production rises, the net energy yield declines towards zero.[13]

9.   Michael McLeay, Amar Radia and Ryland Thomas, 'Money Creation in the Modern Economy', Bank of England Monetary Analysis Directorate, *Quarterly Bulletin* (2014), 15. www.bankofengland.co.uk/publications/Pages/quarterlybulletin/2014/qb14q1.aspx (accessed 31 October 2017).

10.   Matthew Salomon and Joseph Spanjers, 'Illicit Financial Flows to and from Developing Countries: 2005-2014' (Washington DC: Global Financial Integrity, May 2017).

11.   David Graeber, *Debt: The First 5000 Years* (New York: Melville House, 2011), 365.

12.   Mark Carney, 'Breaking the Tragedy of the Horizon – climate change and financial stability', speech given at Lloyds, London, 29 September 2015.

13.   Nafeez Ahmed, *Failing States, Collapsing Systems: BioPhysical Triggers of Political Violence* (Cham: Springer, 2017).

Fossil fuel finance is a gamble that the 'logic' of accumulation will outperform the 'law' of diminishing returns. So divesting from fossil fuels is both a prudent act of financial risk management[14] and a practical step towards ending dependency on hydrocarbons. But divesting is about more than self-interest. Reducing the impact on human health and longevity of air pollution from burning fossil fuels,[15] avoiding the destruction of the global climate[16] and easing the pressure for military conflict are vital ways to oppose the inequitable distribution of risk and harm, around the world and between the generations.[17] Divesting from fossil fuels is both a prudential and an ethical imperative.

However, I want to focus on the ideological contradictions of infinite growth on a finite planet and to propose that letting go of fossil fuels is a cultural project.

My gallery. You must mean my collection. All those paintings, poems, all those things of yours I gathered over the years. It was hard work for me, but I believed in it, we all did in those days. So you think you know what it was for, why we did it. Well, that would be most interesting to hear. Because I have to say, it's a question I ask myself all the time.[18]

To change the channels that money flows through is to redistribute social power. When I was invited in 2012 to give a presentation on sustainability to our university's community of readers and professors, I summarised UAL's considerable achievements in sustainability in the curriculum and some areas of the estates. But I showed how these were vastly overshadowed by the environmental impact of our banking relationship. Using research by Mika Minio-Paluello, I proposed that UAL should switch banks from the Royal Bank of Scotland (RBS), which was heavily invested in extreme fossil fuels.[19] I contrasted RBS with

14. James Leaton, *Unburnable Carbon – Are the World's Financial Markets Carrying a Carbon Bubble?* (London: Carbon Tracker Initiative, 2011).
15. Heather Walton et al., *Understanding the Health Impacts of Air Pollution in London* (London: Kings College, 2015).
16. 'Counting down to climate change', Editorial, *The Lancet*, 390, no. 10107 (4 November 2017).
17. *IPCC, 2014: Climate Change 2014: Synthesis Report. Contribution of Working Groups I, II and III to the Fifth Assessment Report of the Intergovernmental Panel on Climate Change* [R.K. Pachauri and L.A. Meyer (eds.)]. (Geneva: IPCC, 2014), 13.
18. Ishiguro, *Never Let Me Go*, 248.
19. Mika Minio-Paluello, *The Oil and Gas Bank: RBS and the Financing of Climate Change* (BankTrack, Friends of the Earth Scotland, New Economics Foundation, People & Planet and PLATFORM 2007, 12 March 2007). https://www.banktrack.org/ncwo/the_oil_gas_bank

Triodos Bank, which works to avert economic/ecological collapse by only financing organisations that benefit the environment and society.[20] Unlike RBS, Triodos is so well capitalised that it avoids exposure to the 'big three' credit ratings agencies: Fitch, Moody's and Standard & Poor's, which were implicated in the sub-prime mortgage scandal that led to the global financial crisis. I proposed that whichever bank we use, we should critically engage with it through practice-led research into broad themes such as 'Value and Exchange'. Although my colleagues thanked me kindly, they gave no feedback and the meeting moved smoothly down the agenda.

Yet, several months later, I was invited again to speak about sustainability to this group. This time, I proposed that UAL should divest from fossil fuels and reinvest in renewable energy and I was encouraged by my colleagues' positive response. When, in February 2013, UAL Vice Chancellor Nigel Carrington signed the People & Planet Green Education Pledge, I wrote to him and his executives, welcoming the move but advising that UAL should act quickly to avoid opening up a gap between expectations and actuality. I alerted them to the global movement to divest from fossil fuels and advised them of the reputational risks of banking with RBS. Throughout that year, I sent them updates on the public disapproval and government scrutiny[21] of RBS for its dishonest, irresponsible and predatory banking practices.[22] I described research into stranded assets by the University of Oxford's Sustainable Finance Programme showing that the global fossil fuel divestment movement had learned from the campaigns to divest from tobacco companies and apartheid regimes, and was moving faster.[23] I proposed that UAL could be the first university in Britain to divest from fossil fuels. This time, I was called into a meeting to discuss divestment. But in the meeting, I found its only purpose was for the university's Head of Sustainability to tell me to stop contacting the Vice Chancellor and his executives about climate change and fossil fuel divestment.

20.	See www.triodos.co.uk/en/about-triodos (accessed 25 October 2017).

21.	Matt Scuffham and Kirstin Ridley, 'RBS fined $612 million for rate rigging', Reuters, 6 February 2013. www.reuters.com/article/us-rbs-libor/exclusive-rbs-fined-612-million-for-rate-rigging-idUSBRE91500B20130206 (accessed 18 October 2017).

22.	*RBS and the Case for a Bad Bank: The Government's Review* (London: HM Treasury, November 2013).

23.	http://www.smithschool.ox.ac.uk/research/sustainable-finance/publications/Stranded-Assets-and-Scenarios-Discussion-Paper.pdf

During 2013 and 2014, I gave lectures across UAL and beyond, connecting art, climate change and finance, explaining why UAL should divest from fossil fuels and reinvest in energy that is not only renewable, but also decentralised, diversified and democratically controlled. Georgia Brown, a BA Sculpture student at Wimbledon College of Arts, came forward, and together we initiated a campaign for UAL to divest from fossil fuels. We were then joined by other students including Amy McDonnell, a PhD candidate, and Ana Oppenheim, Campaigns Officer of the Students' Union, and we had valuable support from academics, especially Kyran Joughin.

The Fossil Free UAL campaign held discussions and displays, launched a petition, staged a performance and submitted a Freedom of Information request. Beyond the university, the global divestment movement started by Bill McKibben and 350.org was an astonishing success, with the total divested from fossil fuels growing exponentially, from millions to billions and then trillions of dollars.[24] However, there was still no response from the Vice Chancellor or his executive board.

The problem, as I see it, is that you've been told and not told. You've been told, but none of you really understand, and, I dare say, some people are quite happy to leave it that way. But I'm not. If you're going to have decent lives, then you've got to know and know properly.[25]

A key function of a university is to distribute authority and power. Authority can be understood here as the ability to produce legitimacy by obtaining people's consent, while power is the ability to control their actions.[26] A university distributes its authority and power internally by mediating the relationship between its academic activities and its administrative, or management, activities.

As an organisation, UAL comprises six art schools with distinct identities joined by overarching structures of administration, management and governance to form a higher education corporation. The unauthorised formula 'university/art school' could describe UAL, the forward slash connoting a joining but also a fault line potentially

24. Damian Carrington and Emma Howard, 'Institutions worth $2.6 trillion have now pulled investments out of fossil fuels', *The Guardian*, 22 September, 2015.
25. Ishiguro, *Never Let Me Go*, 79.
26. There is a large debate around these issues in political philosophy. I have taken my definition from D.D. Raphael, *Problems of Political Philosophy* (London: Macmillan, 1982).

vulnerable to the pressure of debt. The formerly autonomous art schools and the university of which they are now parts can be distinguished by the historically different relationships between their structures and their cultures. While the art schools tend towards horizontal networks of material creativity, open discourse and critical enquiry, the university operates as a hierarchy, a centralised system of decision-making, ratification and management within an ostensibly neutral ethos of efficiency and compliance with legislation.

Yet it is impossible to comply with socially divisive laws in a neutral way. Similarly, the value of efficiency depends on whose interest it serves. For example, education can efficiently distribute social opportunity, or efficiently concentrate it: the former purpose can serve the common good; the latter can favour private interests. So although an organisation's internal structure and practices might remain constant, its social function can be transformed by changes in the external political and economic context.

It never occurred to me that our lives, until then so closely interwoven, could unravel and separate over a thing like that. But the fact was, I suppose, there were powerful tides tugging us apart by then, and it only needed something like that to finish the task.[27]

Following the global financial crisis of 2007–8, the UK bank rescue package gave out £500 billion of public money to the private banks that had caused the crisis, in a move that was 'designed to restore confidence in the banking system'.[28] This increased the public-sector deficit to the extent that it became possible for politicians to gain popular consent for state funding cuts that instituted an historic redistribution of social power in favour of private interests. As David Graeber has shown, cuts in public spending exactly correspond to the rise in private debt. But it is crucial to recognise that the cuts do not simply shift debt from public to private. The Panama Papers[29] and Paradise Papers[30] revelations show that vast tax avoidance is legal. Thus, by increasing the fiscal deficit to bail out the

27.   Ishiguro, *Never Let Me Go*, 194.
28.   'Darling on Bail-out Measures', BBC News Channel, broadcast 8 October, 2008 bbc.co.uk/1/hi/uk_politics/7659130.stm (accessed 30 October 2017).
29.   'Panama Papers', records of financial transactions anonymously leaked to *Süddeutsche Zeitung*, 2015.
30.   'Paradise Papers', confidential electronic documents obtained by the German newspaper *Süddeutsche Zeitung* and shared by the International Consortium of Investigative Journalists, reported in *The Guardian*, November 2017.

banks while maintaining a system that enables wealthy individuals and corporations to avoid paying tax, the government shifts the burden of debt onto those least able to pay it.[31]

In the 2010 UK Government Spending Review, the public funding of education was cut from £7.6 billion to £3.4 billion over five years, a reduction of sixty percent.[32] Within this cut, art and design education were especially hard hit. Also in 2010, the Browne Review recommended that state funding for higher education be replaced by undergraduate student fees of up to £9,000 a year.[33] This led to the total withdrawal of public funds for the undergraduate teaching of art and design in Britain. The 2015 UK Government Spending Review pressed further still, aiming to eliminate the fiscal deficit by focusing on economic and military security while protecting core public services, a category that does not include either higher education or the arts and humanities.[34]

The inequitable and regressive redistribution of wealth formerly branded as 'austerity' looks set to continue: following cuts of £12 billion to welfare services, the Government required its departments to identify where a further £20 billion of cuts could be made by 2019–20.[35] This wholesale withdrawal of social opportunity increases pressure on universities' charitable status, while the disproportionate impact of the cuts on black, Asian and minority ethnic people, and on disabled people, conflicts with universities' ability to deliver on their policies for widening participation. Added to these conflicts are the internal contradictions of the Higher Education and Research Act 2017, which enshrines universities' ethos of public service and academic freedoms[36] while undermining them through its main purpose of exposing universities to destructive competition from deregulated commercial 'educational

31.   David Graeber, 'Britain is Heading for Another 2008 Crash: Here's Why', *The Guardian*, October 28, 2015.

32.   HM Treasury, *Spending Review 2010*, Policy paper (UK Government July 2015), 11.

33.   John Browne et al., *Securing a Sustainable Future for Higher Education: an Independent Review of Higher Education Finance*, independent report (UK Government, 2010). Retrieved from www.gov.uk/government/publications/the-browne-report-higher-education-funding-and-student-finance (accessed 26 October 2017).

34.   See HM Treasury, *A Country that Lives Within its Means: Spending Review 2015*, UK Government, July 2015.

35.   Ibid., 3.

36.   *Higher Education and Research Act 2017*, UK Government, http://www.legislation.gov.uk/ukpga/2017/29/section/14 (accessed 27 October 2017).

providers'.[37] Doing little to oppose the political shift towards a market-oriented conception of education, the executive and management teams of most UK universities may have remained largely unaware of these conflicts and contradictions. But this seems unlikely, given that they seem to have been actively transforming universities from places for the social production and distribution of knowledge into engines of capital accumulation.

I nodded slowly. 'So that's why they took away our art...' [38]

Andrew McGettigan has shown how the marketisation of British higher education redistributes risk and reward.[39] While promising to empower students as consumers, marketisation transfers power away from those who value universities as public institutions towards the unaccountable executives and the private banks to which they are indebted. At every level and scale, from student loans to mortgages secured on family homes and institutional property speculation, the debt and financialisation that spring from marketisation produce ideological effects that correspond to psychological affects.

For example, the government's designation of higher education in art, design and the humanities as not worthy of public funding doesn't simply reduce the available resources – it has the ideological effect of lowering the perceived social value of these activities. People whose work is implicitly portrayed as superfluous or irrelevant are likely to feel indignation, resentment, loss of confidence, or a deeper disillusionment. Also, as many practitioners and academics have spent their working lives dedicated to their field, and are more closely associated by name with their 'outputs' and achievements, the psychological affects may be especially intense.

Putting students in debt by making them pay tuition fees perverts the nature of the educational relationship from learning as an inherently social process within a framework of education as a public good to a

37.   Ibid., www.legislation.gov.uk/ukpga/2017/29/notes/division/3/index.htm (accessed 25 October 2017). See note 28 on Deregulation of higher education corporations.
38.   Ishiguro, *Never Let Me Go*, 173.
39.   Andrew McGettigan, *The Great University Gamble: Money, Markets and the Future of Higher Education* (London: Pluto Press, 2013).

personal transaction, a private investment in 'cultural capital'[40] and professional skills.[41] Far from feeling empowered by this, students may find it unbearable to acknowledge the debt as real – I have often heard students speak of their debts as distant or abstract, and joke about escape by declaring themselves bankrupt or assuming a false identity. Ignoring the bleak humour of its 'customers', the university/art school mediates a set of transactions in which students first contribute economic capital by paying fees, and then invest and develop their social capital of interpersonal skills, imagination and creativity. In return, students are awarded the cultural capital of grades and, hopefully, a recognised qualification which may bring advantage in the increasingly competitive employment market.

I'm not saying that everything was fine before the cuts. Even when education was publicly funded there were tensions between the ideal of transformative education, in which staff and students work together in an emancipatory pedagogic relationship, and the actual power dynamic of requiring students to submit work for assessment. Long before the bailout of the banks, the 'audit culture' that aimed to improve accountability in the public sector burdened academics with bureaucracy, including the rigid imposition of flawed assessment criteria. Still, the marketisation of education may never entirely reduce academic employment to a trade of cognitive and affective skills in return for payment. Similarly, although the university may be completely dependent on fees, the pedagogic relationship is unlikely to become a simple exchange of payment for grades.

Nevertheless, there is relentless pressure towards a narrow instrumentalisation of art and design education through measures such as the National Student Survey (NSS) and the Teaching Excellence Framework (TEF). The NSS implicitly invites students to evaluate their course, their tutors and their university from the position of consumers of education as a service, rather than co-producers of, and participants in, the experience of learning. Correspondingly, the TEF combines student satisfaction statistics from the NSS with other factors, including dropout rates and graduate employment rates, in order to calculate 'bronze'

40.   See Pierre Bourdieu, 'The Forms of Capital', in *Handbook of Theory and Research for the Sociology of Education*, ed. John G. Richardson (New York: Greenwood Press, 1986), 241-258.
41.   See Council for the Defence of British Universities, http://cdbu.org.uk, and Timothy Ingold et al., *Reclaiming our University*, https://reclaimingouruniversity. wordpress.com.

'silver' or 'gold' awards that are used to determine the fees that universities can charge. The National Union of Students staged a boycott of the NSS, challenging its legitimacy. Meanwhile, opposition to the TEF ranged from the Russell Group's[42] diplomatically expressed scepticism of the validity of the metrics to a more principled resistance from the Council for the Defence of British Universities, which denounced the exercise as 'simplistic, arbitrary and inadequately tested'.[43]

Struggles around the distribution of risk and reward comprise problems that are not 'closed' or technical, like those of mathematics or accountancy, but 'open', meaning they cannot be reconciled within a single set of preferences. For the university, funding cuts pose 'wicked problems'[44] that exacerbate the inequitable distribution of power within its own walls and in its relationship to society. These problems implicate us in decisions which risk irreversible harm to the institution that we inherited from our predecessors, share with others today, and have an obligation to pass on to those who come after us. In a context of heightened anxiety around severe budget cuts, an intellectually incoherent programme of academic restructuring could be rushed through, shielded from legitimate and much-needed critique by the real and perceived threat of redundancy. Clearly, this would impact on people differently depending on whether they were tenured or precarious, homeowners or tenants. The inequitable distribution of risk and reward is an instrument of governance: in a move reminiscent of *The Prince*,[45] academic staff with relatively secure employment contracts could be divided from their colleagues whose precariousness would be disproportionately increased by such restructuring. This poses a particular danger for universities whose cultural capital is based on a reputation for creativity and risk-taking in a supportive environment of respect, trust and goodwill.

Under the combined influence of funding cuts and debt, academic principles and activities are becoming subordinated to the financial operations of the organisation, limiting the ability of creative and critical

42.   The Russell Group is an association representing the interests of 24 leading British research universities: www.russellgroup.ac.uk (accessed 17 November 2017).
43.   Dorothy Bishop, 'TEF and the Reputation of UK Higher Education', Council for the Defence of British Universities, http://cdbu.org.uk/tef-and-the-reputation-of-uk-higher-education (accessed 27 October 2017)
44.   Horst Rittel and Melvin Webber, 'Dilemmas in a General Theory of Planning', *Policy Sciences* 4 (1973): 155–69. https://doi.org/10.1007/BF01405730
45.   Niccolò Machiavelli, *The Prince* [1531–2], trans. George Bull (London: Penguin, 2004), 40–5.

thinking to inform the university strategy in relation to a deeply retrograde social transformation. To the extent that the university/art school accepts 'the deficit', and the 'austerity' that is held to be its corollary, it normalises an instrumental conception of cultural practice. Perhaps more insidiously, the concentration of economic power brought by financialisation is emboldening members of the university executive to go beyond their operational control of teaching, learning and research and seek to define the very purpose of art and design education. In a blandly teleological closure, this purpose is described as 'promoting enterprise and employability' in the service of 'the creative industries'.[46] A forced union of divergent impulses, the very concept of 'creative industries' is conflicted: whereas creativity entails a willingness to break with convention, the 'creative industries' harness such unruly impulses within the established order of economic growth that is almost certainly unsustainable in its processes, and inequitable in its distribution. The notion of the creative industries doesn't explicitly challenge or oppose the critical and emancipatory potential of cultural practice; it simply forgets them.

So I didn't have the head to go into why it mattered so much. And though I did just drop it and carry on with the discussion we'd been having, the atmosphere had gone chilly, and could hardly have helped us get through the difficult matter in hand.[47]

Debt is not a neutral mechanism, but a key part of the value system in which people are figured as human resources, the future is worth less than the present and the biosphere is valued as 'natural capital'.[48] This barren and stultifying worldview diminishes our sense of what is possible by imposing a gulf between what we are capable of and what we accept. Debt is a power relation of concealment and disguise that brings not only a corrosive anxiety about entrapment and exposure to risk, but also uncertainty at the level of inequity, which affects one's sense of self in social situations.

46.   Nigel Carrington, *The Role of Higher Education in Supporting the Creative Economy* (London: Policy Forum, 17 June 2015).
47.   Ishiguro, *Never Let Me Go*, 187–8.
48.   EF Schumacher developed the concept of 'natural capital' in *Small is Beautiful: Economics as if People Mattered* (London: Blond and Briggs, 1973). The concept has since been used to support the monetisation and privatisation of ecological systems.

While the number of wealthy art students grows, chronic financial constraint condemns many others, especially those living and working in London, to an insecure existence of balancing study with underpaid part-time employment. For students and staff alike, the stresses of multiple demands on time, financial uncertainty and vulnerability can test not only their ability to plan and their stamina to deliver, but also their loyalties and friendships. In *Breaking the Silence*, Rosalind Gill has revealed how, in academia, neoliberalism produces divisive competition that prevents colleagues from discussing their anxieties, so that, by unspoken agreement, the structural issues remain beyond the frame of official discourse.[49] The larger the loan that the institution takes on, the more acceptable becomes the idea that everyone should pursue economic growth. Correspondingly, the deeper that students and staff go into debt, the less time they have to practise the freedoms of academic enquiry and creative expression. In a destructive feedback loop, dissent is marginalised while emancipatory and reflective critique gives way to instrumental innovation, until a regime of compliance based on inequality of access to information and resources is tacitly accepted as rational and inevitable.

I've thought about those moments over and over. I should have found something to say. I could have just denied it, though Tommy probably wouldn't have believed me. And to have tried to explain the thing truthfully would have been too complicated. But I could have done something.[50]

Although debt may not prevent knowledge from being used for the public or common good, it greatly increases the pressures and incentives for knowledge to serve private interests instead.[51] With its promise of financial reward for originality, the concept of intellectual property gains currency in an indebted and financially constrained environment. Because intellectual property is a privatisation of knowledge, it undermines the ideal of a creative community in which influences are shared

49.   Rosalind Gill, 'Breaking the Silence: The Hidden Injuries of Neo-liberal Academia', in *Secrecy and Silence in the Research Process: Feminist Reflections*, ed. R. Flood and Rosalind Gill (London: Routledge, 2010), 228–244
50.   Ishiguro, *Never Let Me Go*, 192.
51.   See David Cross, 'A Placement for Everyone', in *Transformative Pedagogies and the Environment: Creative Agency Through Contemporary Art*, ed. Marie Sierra and Kit Wise (Champaign, IL: Common Ground, forthcoming).

and ideas are co-produced. As financialisation captures and concentrates value from the public and the commons, the resulting inequality weakens the bonds of community, so people become isolated, and may internalise problems that should be addressed in public. As debt reduces people's freedom to speak out, it increases their complicity, causing a sense of guilt and a habit of denial.[52]

Today, the student's journey to becoming an artist combines learning as a conscious process of identity formation with the hidden forces of economic inequality under neoliberalism. Within 'the art world', these forces take on a particular psychological intensity. Perhaps to a greater extent than more collaborative forms of cultural production, such as architecture, film-making, music or theatre, contemporary art is especially closely identified with its creators. The focus on names is reinforced by the institutions – the gallery, the biennial, the museum – and their outputs – the art object, the solo exhibition, the artist's monograph – which perpetuate the canon of established artists, usually individuals with a unique 'signature style'. Competition between artists for resources is not simply amplified by public funding cuts, but distorted by the uneven distribution of personal debt. State funding for the arts once redistributed opportunity, providing alternative ways for emerging artists to advance their careers beyond the private gallery network. So the withdrawal of funding erases many of the public co-ordinates of success, causing disorientation that disproportionately impacts on artists with the least social and economic capital. Art school should be a place for encounters with social and cultural differences, in such domains as gender, ethnicity and class. As a symptom of class difference, economic inequality is cloaked in embarrassment, envy and resentment, giving it an invisibility that allows it to escape critical interrogation.

And when things go badly, of course I'm upset, but at least I can feel I've done all I could and keep things in perspective.[53]

Compounding the problem, a new orthodoxy of positive thinking in the university, the art school and beyond encourages people to suppress negative thoughts and feelings, accept what is being done, and share

52.   See *Bonds: Guilt, Debt and Other Liabilities*, Berlin: Haus Der Kulturen Welt, 2012, hkw.de/en/programm/projekte/projekt_80117.php (accessed 27 October 2017).
53.   Ishiguro, *Never Let Me Go*, 204.

forward-looking narratives. In 2015, as major 'budget shortfalls' in the university became apparent, the idea of 'resilience' rose to official prominence at UAL. Unlike sustainability, which entails an ethical obligation to others that both draws on and nurtures a critical and emancipatory impulse, or ecosophy, which offers a model of dynamic interrelationships, 'resilience' subordinates critical thinking to practical expediency by focusing on small-scale, local, reactive solutions that address the symptoms rather than the causes of systemic crises. As Mark Neocleous has shown,[54] this perfectly serves neoliberalism, which draws people into accepting contradictions that enable private interests to benefit from and operate against both public service and the common good. Moreover, in the context of the entrenchment of social inequality, the dismantling of the welfare state and the militarisation of law enforcement, encouraging people to apply their creativity to resilience as a response to 'austerity' carries risks. When open problems are misconstrued as closed problems, and public issues are misrecognised as personal issues, they may become intractable, engendering a sense of paralysis and complicity in which mental health issues can proliferate.

The rise of institutional initiatives to support 'wellbeing', such as the introduction of 'Mental Health First Aid' (MHFA),[55] doubtless sprang from the best of intentions, and may be of great relief and comfort to many people. Yet, as I have tried to show, the ideological effects of neoliberalism on higher education risk producing a defective relational environment that cognitive behavioural strategies may be unable to address. Moreover, in offering mental health advice to help staff and students cope with a traumatic social transformation in which it is actively participating, the institution may be inadvertently recruiting people to 'collude in their own repression'.[56] Nevertheless, the Vice Chancellor of UAL has written: 'Everyone is somewhere on the mental health spectrum, so this is a business productivity issue which should be dealt with alongside other health and safety considerations. Creating

54.   Mark Neocleous, 'Resisting Resilience', *Radical Philosophy* 178 (March/April 2013). www.radicalphilosophy.com/commentary/resisting-resilience (accessed 27 October 2017)

55.   See Jay Watts, 'The Mental Health First Aid Programme is a Pet Project', *Independent*, July 15 2017. www.independent.co.uk/voices/mental-health-first-aid-theresa-may-depression-anxiety-nhs-underfunded-services-turned-away-a7842571.html (accessed 27 October 2017)

56.   Victor Burgin, 'Art, Commonsense and Photography' [1976], in *The Camerawork Essays*, ed. J. Evans (London: Rivers Oram Press, 1997), 76.

a positive environment for mental health demonstrably costs less than failing to do so'.[57]

Anthropologist and systems theorist Gregory Bateson coined the term 'double bind'[58] to describe a psychological problem that can occur in family and organisational relationships:

> *The first proposition from which the hypothesis is derived is that learning occurs always in some context which has formal characteristics. [...] Further, the hypothesis depends on the idea that this structured context also occurs within a wider context—a metacontext if you will—and that this sequence of contexts is an open, and conceivably infinite series.*[59]

Here, I am focusing on the interactions between people within a sequence of contexts that includes the art school, the university, UK higher education, the global financial system and the planetary ecosystem. In line with Bateson's assertion that the observer must be included within the focus of observation,[60] I have described elsewhere how I designated my academic job as an artist's placement, in order to question the arbitrary separation of art and life and to critically situate myself in relation to the institution at a time of systemic change.[61] Collapsing the distinction between my art practice and my paid employment has been a way to engage with the university/art school as a set of interrelated contexts for identity formation and cultural production, especially in relation to the unfolding economic and ecological crisis.

> *A falling leaf, the greeting of a friend, or a 'primrose by the river's brim' is not 'just that and nothing more.' Exogenous experience may be framed in the contexts of a dream, and internal thought may be projected into the contexts of the external world.*[62]

Could the distribution of power and authority in the university produce the conditions in which double binds might arise? Bateson refers to the 'theory of logical types', which asserts that 'no class can, in formal

57. Nigel Carrington [blog] http://blogs.arts.ac.uk/vice-chancellor/ (accessed 5 November 2017).
58. Gregory Bateson, *Steps to an Ecology of Mind* [1972] (Chicago: University of Chicago Press, 2000), 271–8.
59. Ibid., 245.
60. Ibid., 246.
61. Cross, 'A Placement for Everyone'.
62. Bateson, *Steps to an Ecology of Mind*, 272.

logical or mathematical discourse, be a member of itself'.[63] Academic and executive functions are members of the class 'university', so, following Bateson, we could say that if part of the university acts in a way that implicitly claims it is the whole university, then it has conflated different logical types. The mistake may originate from the external context, in which the category 'society' has been wrongly subordinated to the category 'economy'.

Arising through habitual interactions, rather than traumatic events, double binds form when a primary negative injunction conflicts with a secondary injunction, which may be at the level of metacommunication – nonverbal signals about the type of message. For example, a person may say that they care about someone or something, but their actions and/or the context of power relations in which they are communicating may contradict what they say. A double bind can be completed by a tertiary negative injunction prohibiting the victim from leaving the field.[64] If the field is neoliberalism, then debt is the prohibition. That being so, the risk is that:

> *The bind becomes mutual. A stage is reached in the relationship in which neither person can afford to receive or emit metacommunicative messages without distortion.*[65]

So, how might double binds in the university/art school be undone? If the executive staff themselves were open to the transformative education they aim to deliver, they might use their power to counter the divisive and contradictory influence of neoliberalism. But that is both unlikely and problematic, as economic power enables those who wield it to exempt themselves from critique. Instead, we must look to the university's sources of social and cultural value, from which economic value is extracted: the academic networks of practice-based, intellectual and pedagogic interactions. In these, the capacity of art to aestheticise contradiction as paradox resonates with the ability of artists to inhabit divergent tendencies or impulses, both between subject positions and within them. Moving between abstract concept and material form, between action and reflection, academic staff and students posit contributions to knowledge, which are made contingent on articulating particular positions in defined

63.   Ibid., 280.
64.   Ibid., 206.
65.   Ibid., 237.

situations. Aiming to tolerate ambiguity and difference, and to support dissensus, artists, designers and educators practise their skills of observation, integrate theory and practice, cultivate critical thinking, disrupt the symbolic order, resist the closure of meaning and hopefully develop a sense of proportion.

These may help to resist 'double binds'. But to reverse the extractive colonisation of art education by finance, action is also needed that connects the internal and external contexts.

Although UAL never acknowledged the divestment campaign run by its own staff and students, in November 2015 the university announced that it would divest its endowments of £3.9 million from fossil fuels and sign the United Nations Principles for Responsible Investment. As campaigners, we were delighted, seeing it as a signal that staff and students could work together and that academic research can have an actual effect. For a brief, exhilarating moment, our campaign overcame the deadening structural separation between the academic and operational aspects of the university. Having glimpsed our organisation's 'operating system', it seemed possible to imagine a redistribution of attention, effort and reward. Divestment from fossil fuels is a 'letting go' that is more than financial: connecting the university's aims of becoming sustainable and delivering transformative education could germinate emancipatory forms of interpersonal and institutional change which can hardly be managed, much less imposed by executive order.

For divestment from fossil fuels to be a meaningful response to global warming, reinvestment must follow in renewable energy that is diversified, decentralised and democratically controlled. Yet, in the two years following UAL's pledge to divest, no information was released about how, or whether, divestment had been carried out. When in October 2016 we asked for evidence that UAL had actually divested, we were told that a long list had been drawn up of fund managers who may be commissioned to handle the divestment and reinvestment. We asked to see the list, but UAL refused, claiming commercial confidentiality. In October 2017, we enquired again and were told that UAL is 'in the process' of appointing fund managers and that it would report on its progress in 2018.

The explicit content of the message – that the divestment process was under way – implied that the university is committed to sustainability. Yet, by rejecting the campaigners' request for transparency and refusing dialogue, at the level of 'metacommunication', UAL signalled that the distribution of information and power remains unchanged. This undermines UAL's strategy of 'delivering transformative education', which promises to involve staff and students in rigorous critical questioning, working together to challenge orthodoxies and taking creative risks.[66]

Although the case for divestment didn't result in prompt action by our university, our bank has not been slow to act: research by the Rainforest Action Network and others[67] shows that, between 2014 and 2016, Royal Bank of Scotland cut ninety-five percent of its financing for extreme fossil fuels. Having previously proclaimed itself as 'The Oil and Gas Bank', and ignored calls to divest, RBS is now getting out of fossil fuels, leaving them as stranded assets in the hands of slower-moving investors, such as universities and public sector pension funds. This repeats a tactic from the US sub-prime mortgage crisis, when banks sold off assets that they knew were becoming worthless.

Moving beyond the impasse around divestment, towards prefiguring a zero-carbon society, I devised a proposal for Visible Energy, a teaching and research project that would connect the academic and operational sides of the university. Linking aesthetic practice to practical action, the idea is to build a new model for collaboration, based on sharing information and power between producers, consumers and investors in renewable energy.

The project aims to move from a centralised to a distributed structure. This might be unimaginable if not for a brilliantly simple diagram, drawn in 1964 by Paul Baran of the RAND Corporation,[68] in which a single configuration of points or co-ordinates is connected by lines to compare centralised, decentralised and distributed organisational structures. Baran used it to propose a computer network that could maintain communication despite damage from a nuclear attack. This model established the conceptual basis for the development of the Internet, in which computers evolved from being *terminals* in centralised structures to *nodes* in distributed structures. Today, as electricity grids are evolving from centralised to distributed structures, Baran's model offers a conceptual topography of a dynamic system, which brings new risks and opportunities in facing the ecological and economic crises.

66.   UAL has declared 'delivering transformative education' to be its top strategic area of focus to 2022. See www.arts.ac.uk/media/arts/about-ual/strategy-and-governance/documents/university-strategy/UAL_LTE_Strategy_2015_Web3.pdf (accessed 27 October 2017).
67.   *Banking on Climate Change*, Rainforest Action Network (June 2017) https://www.ran.org/banking_on_climate_change.
68.   Paul Baran, *On Distributed Communications* (Santa Monica, CA: RAND Corporation, 1964).

To be eligible for UK Energy Catalyst funding, the project had to involve collaboration between a university and a business. I was attracted to this condition, having previously proposed that UAL should critically engage with its providers of finance, insurance and energy.[69] I was both excited and anxious when UAL suggested collaboration with Bouygues, a multinational corporation with over €14 billion market capitalisation.[70] In February 2017, Bouygues was awarded a contract of undisclosed value for Facilities Management of UAL's energy systems, electrical, mechanical and fabric maintenance, cleaning, security and project management, including the relocation of London College of Communication and the transfer of London College of Fashion to the Olympic Park in East London.[71] I contacted Bouygues, proposing Visible Energy, a collaboration at the intersection of renewable energy, distributing value (possibly using blockchain technology), and co-operative ownership and control.

Over several months, I engaged in discussions with senior staff at UAL, drafting and revising a project funding bid. In these discussions, the UAL Head of Sustainability identified the reasons why the project couldn't happen: it would require 'sign-off' from the Head of College and UAL Legal; a 'private wire' might be needed; the quantities of electricity and money at stake were so small that the project would only be a game... But the objection raised most often was that a co-operative business model wouldn't fit with the institutional culture of UAL. Nevertheless, with the deadline imminent, a senior executive at Bouygues replied to my email invitation, expressing interest in the project. Within minutes, our dialogue was summarily cut off by UAL, effectively terminating the bid. I couldn't afford conflict, so I interpreted our clash as a misunderstanding of the kind that happens in transformational Action Research, which tests implicit assumptions about how people should act.

I don't mean I'm going to go round showing everyone exactly. But I was thinking, well, there's no reason why I should keep it all secret any more.[72]

69.   Cross, 'A Placement for Everyone'.

70.   'Bouygues', Markets, Bloomberg, www.bloomberg.com/quote/ENT:FP (accessed 27 October 2017).

71.   University of the Arts London, 'Bouygues Awarded New UAL Facilities Management Contract', blogs.arts.ac.uk/estates/2017/02/13/bouygues-awarded-new-ual-facilities-management-contract (accessed 27 October 2017).

72.   Ishiguro, *Never Let Me Go*, 186.

I presented the project at a symposium on the Anthropocene, convened by Gene Ray.[73] I described how the project would centre on a renewable energy system to visualise its own ecological and economic performance, probably through a mobile application. Given present unsustainable levels of consumption, the system would be unlikely to produce surplus energy. But it would enable members to see beyond the centralised energy corporations and banks and visualise new relationships between energy, ecology and value. I showed NASA satellite images of San Juan, the capital of Puerto Rico, in the nights before and after Hurricane Maria struck in October 2017, disabling the island's electric power grid and communications network. I cited Chamaala Klinger, Owen Landeg and Virginia Murray at Public Health England, who researched the impact on health of such power cuts from extreme weather events. The researchers listed what communities lose in a power cut: light, obviously, but also clean water, food storage, medication storage, life support devices, temperature control, safety mechanisms, sewage disposal, transport, communications, air quality and mental health.[74] Underscoring the emancipatory goal of the project I proposed, I asserted: 'Energy is power. As long as others control it, they have power over us. To the extent that we own and control our energy, we increase our ability to transform ourselves, and make the transition towards ecological and social justice'. So, a key aspect of the project is that it would be a co-operative: a democratic, member-run organisation that is the common property of its members. In this aim, I am much indebted to the Social Science Centre at Lincoln University in the UK. Joss Winn and Mike Neary, members of this cooperative, write: 'Our research seeks to develop a framework for co-operative higher education that is grounded in the social history of the co-operative movement, the practice of democratic governance and common ownership of social institutions, and the production of knowledge at the level of society'.[75]

A distributed structure may be not only more resilient, but also more resistant than a centralised structure to capture or co-optation.

73.   David Cross, 'Beyond Debt and Destruction?' in *The Anthropocene Atlas of Geneva, an International Symposium*, HEAD Geneva, Switzerland, 18 October 2017.
74.   Chaamala Klinger, Owen Landeg and Virginia Murray, 'Power Outages, Extreme Events and Health: A Systematic Review of the Literature from 2011–2012', *PLoS Currents* 6 (2014). DOI: 10.1371/currents.dis.04eb1dc5e73dd1377e05a10e9e dde673.
75.   Mike Neary and Joss Winn, 'Beyond Public and Private: A Framework for Co-operative Higher Education', *Open Library of Humanities* 3, no.2 (2017): 2, DOI: http://doi.org/10.16995/olh.195

However, the distributed renewable energy co-operative would be both a means to an end and an end in itself: its members would decide how big it should be, what it should look like, how far it might extend and what it is ultimately for.

Never Let Me Go is, at one level, a moving account of young people doing their best to understand and care for each other as they grow up in a difficult situation. Facing a bleak future together, they show resilience, develop compassion and achieve a semblance of peace. Although their tenderness is met with indifference and rejection, it never occurs to them to question the limit of their existence, which is bounded by an edge to their world.

WEIGHTLESS DATA:
THE NEW HEAVY FREIGHT

Adrian Shaughnessy

What does distribution mean in the digital age? In the networked era of Bluetooth, Dropbox, Elon Musk's plans for Hyperloop travel and air-conditioned data farms containing all the knowledge in the world, 'distribution' feels like a term in need of redefinition. In comparison to online distribution, moving physical goods by truck or van appears antediluvian.

I've recently moved to the country, but when I lived in London I worked from home two or three days a week. I sat at a window overlooking my street. All day long, delivery vehicles drew up and delivered – or attempted to deliver – packages. Often the recipients of these packages were not at home. I'd watch as drivers, invariably harassed-looking individuals, doubtless on zero-hours contracts, scanned the street searching for a likely neighbour to take temporary custody of a package. Sometimes I ended up with two or three boxes in my hallway. Later, at six or seven o'clock, as my neighbours returned from work, they'd call round to retrieve their parcels. Sometimes packages would sit for days. Sometimes I felt like I was a home delivery depot.

In the country, when a van turns up to deliver my online order of a book or a set of lights for my bike, I feel a spasm of guilt. I've caused a motor vehicle – usually diesel-powered – to add to atmospheric pollution. And since I'm some distance from the nearest town, I've probably caused the driver to lose money, or to be financially penalised for a late delivery. One driver told me he is also penalised for early deliveries. But any enterprise that seeks to put physical objects into people's hands must make use of motorised distribution. Supermarkets are replenished with constant deliveries from refrigerated trucks; shopping malls need restocking daily; even your friendly coffee shop is entirely dependent on deliveries of roasted beans.

As a publisher of physical books, it's an issue that confronts me constantly – how to get these material artefacts of ink, glue and paper into the hands of book buyers? And how is it best done at a time when the old world of hard matter is being eclipsed by a new immaterial world of vapour-like digital connectivity? Of course, this collision between hard and soft delivery methods goes beyond the world of books: politics, economics, health, even human happiness, are affected as the online delivery of everything from services to information supersedes traditional types of delivery.

How else can we explain the election of Trump? I recently watched a BBC documentary on the Silicon Valley oligarchs who hold sovereignty over our online lives (and, increasingly, our offline lives too). The most chilling fact to emerge from this investigation was that at the control centre of the Trump digital election campaign, in an anonymous building in San Antonio, Texas, employees of Facebook, Google and YouTube were seconded to make the 'delivery system' function using their on-line platforms. It's that phrase – 'delivery system' – that really chills the soul. What does it mean to the future of democracy, to the future of government? A senior official from the now-abandoned control centre was interviewed. In a moment of unexpected candour, she offered this alarming observation: 'We wouldn't have won it without Facebook'.

The type of control offered by Mark Zuckerberg's enterprise (which the designer Paula Scher calls 'the new suburbia') has been the wet dream of dictators for millennia. It's now possible, via Internet connectivity and smart algorithms, to control thought – or at least to control emotion. 'Internet profiling' – to use the benign-sounding terminology of Silicon Valley – means that Facebook can manipulate emotion and thus affect decision-making. Individual psychology can be altered merely by sending Facebook users positive or negative messages. What makes it worse is that it is facilitated by us, the users of the Internet. No force is involved. No coercion is needed. Instead, we give our consent the second we step into the digital terrain of the World Wide Web. Here – take everything, we say. It's yours. Go make trillions of dollars with it. Go win elections with it!

There are now two parallel distribution systems: the digital version is free to use in most cases (or at least it appears to be), which is why it is so seductive; the other, the one with vans and trucks and roads, is not free. But materiality and a desire to own objects (furniture, clothes, gadgets, books) remains stubbornly impervious to Ayn Rand–reading digital billionaires who want us to live in a frictionless world in which everything flows through their networks, but in which they take zero responsibility for the impact of their delivery systems and their effects on the health, well-being and happiness of the citizenry.

Whichever way we look at it, distribution is power. Distribution is a control mechanism that governs everything, from the food we eat to the entertainment we consume. The more you control the method of distribution, the more power you accrue. We only have to look at the music business to see how control is determined by distribution. I designed record covers for many years, and had dealings with numerous record labels, large and small. The small ones – which were usually the ones making the most interesting music – were always at the mercy of distributors. A failed distributor almost inevitably meant disaster for a tiny label. And so the Internet seemed to herald a utopian future for the little guy. Here was a low-cost way to get music into the hands of music fans around the world – from producer to consumer with a few clicks. Utopia!

Except, it hasn't worked out like that. Firstly, the Internet facilitated unpaid downloading, and the peer-to-peer exchange of audio files became the equivalent of a failed distributor. And now, paid-for streaming, of which I'm an avid user, has simply resulted in the cake getting smaller. Instead of control resting with cultural producers, it now rests with the new immaterial distributors – Spotify, Apple, Amazon, et al. It seems that we have meekly exchanged one set of gatekeepers for another. Music may now be cheap, and labels may no longer be at the mercy of distributors with trucks and warehouses, but the only thing that has changed is that the control has shifted to the owners of online distribution systems. Vinyl discs may be enjoying a welcome resurgence, but not on a scale that can adequately fund the makers of music, or sustain the music industry (although this is not a bad thing in the eyes of some).

Books have proved to be more resilient than music. E-books have not enjoyed the same success that MP3 files have for music, and the physical book retains its primacy in the publishing ecosystem. This is partly because copying a 300-page book is harder and slower work than copying sixty minutes of audio. But is it also because the book is an unimprovable artefact. As Umberto Eco states: 'Alterations of the book-as-object have modified neither its function nor its grammar for more than 500 years. The book is like the spoon, scissors, the hammer, the wheel. Once invented, it cannot be improved. You cannot make a spoon that is better than a spoon.'

While book lovers will rejoice over the printed book's dogged endurance, the question of distribution remains. Books, as with frozen peas and other essentials of modern living, have to be distributed; this means a return to the realm of vans and trucks, with all their attendant problems: poorly paid drivers, congestion and harmful emissions. There are no easy answers to the question of distribution, or so it seems. My own publishing company – a micro-practitioner in the publishing cosmos – uses a hybrid distribution regime. Our books are delivered from the printer by truck to a central distribution point. Orders are taken online from our website, and then books are dispatched to all corners of the planet by national postal services. It's hard to see how it could be any simpler, or with a smaller ecological footprint. We have no sales force travelling the country selling our books; we print small quantities of each title that mostly sell out, and we use the regular postal systems of the countries that our books are ordered from. But without the Internet we couldn't function this way. We'd be forced to use the distribution systems that conventional publishers use. The Internet has allowed us to forge a different model – one where we (almost) control the delivery system.

The Internet is the first system to challenge the traditional distribution networks that control so much of our lives. And although it has been largely taken over by the oligarchs of Silicon Valley, every system, every regime, has within it the seeds of its own subversion and its own corruption. The dark web, although seemingly a black hole of offensiveness, like an unofficial Amazon of the unacceptable, is an example of how systems subvert themselves. The networks that gives us cybercrime and online harassment also enable families, friends and colleagues to communicate with ease and intimacy. The infrastructure that allows our every online move to be tracked and used to sell us stuff also gives us the Paradise Papers and other unveilings of malpractice. The networks that have given us Trump have also given his opposition a voice to shout back at his loathsome racism and hateful jingoism.

Human beings may be struggling under new and pernicious stresses: there is little room for optimism when we contemplate the dystopias of eco-collapse, chronic income disparity leading to the new normal of permanent precarity, and the ever-present threat of nuclear war. But human resilience, as we've seen in the past, has a tendency to postulate utopias that counter prophesies of doom. At the same time as the Silicon Valley overlords are thinking about a tighter grip on the citizens of the world, others are putting forward new blueprints for living: loosely categorised as post-capitalist thinking, new ideas such as universal basic income, sustainable living practices and new technologies such as AI, if properly managed, might set us free rather than enslave us. All of this will require fresh thinking on how we deliver these new ideas, so we could start by rethinking distribution before we move on to knottier and more intractable problems.

TWO DISTRIBUTIONS, AND BOOKS AS EVENTS

Brad Haylock

Books are important. This is hard to deny – but also hard to substantiate. We generally understand that knowledge is good, and that more of it is better. Philosophy, the sciences and the academy in general are built on this assumption. Regardless of format – although the question of format is also undeniably important, as we will see – books are an historically proven means of circulating knowledge. But too rarely do we actually ask: how do books work in the world, and what impact might they have?

The oldest cave paintings – in places we today know as Indonesia, Spain, southern France and Australia, among others – date back to some 35,000 years ago. Their figurative markings reveal the roots of the higher-order consciousness that characterises modern humans.[1] We might today say that knowledge communities, or *publics*, assembled around these depictions of animals, rituals and deities, although the paintings predate even the Latin word *publicus*, the root of the modern 'public', by tens of millennia. Relatively recently – a mere five and a half millennia ago, approximately three millenia BCE – writing was invented, including the inscription of marks into tablets of moist clay in Mesopotamia, and the use of the pressed pith of the *Cyperus papyru*s plant as a writing substrate in Ancient Egypt.[2] For the first time, the non-oral communication of knowledge across time and space became possible. This is important because clay and papyrus remember things in a way that cave walls do but people don't, and it is much easier to move pieces of clay and dried grass to people than people to caves.

Parchment supplanted papyrus as the book substrate of choice around 200 BCE. Made from the untanned skins of cattle, sheep, goats and other beasts – or, in its finer form, vellum, from the skins of young animals, usually calves – parchment was favoured for its superior archival qualities and its resilience to the material trauma of the act of erasing.[3] While the act of writing on the desiccated arse of an ass sounds decidedly uncompelling to contemporary ears, parchment remained an important book substrate for over two millennia. (Indeed, British laws were still recorded on vellum until early 2017 – an incidental revelation on the back of the Brexit controversy.)[4] Papyrus and early parchment books took the

1.   David Lewis-Williams, *The Mind in the Cave: Consciousness and the Origins of Art* (London: Thames and Hudson, 2002).
2.   Philip B. Meggs, *A History of Graphic Design*, 2nd ed. (New York: Van Nostrand Reinhold, 1992), 7–11.
3.   Ibid., 38.
4.   James Tapsfield, 'Tory Fury as Historic Brexit Act Won't Be Printed for Posterity on Vellum Because the Centuries Old Tradition Has Been Quietly Ditched', *Daily Mail*, 21 March 2017.

form of scrolls, but the later material heralded another innovation, namely the codex form – a stack of sheets, folded and sewn down the middle to form pages.[5] Although binding methods have evolved, the codex is the form of printed book we still know and use; it is a continuingly important invention, because while the scroll compelled a linear reading, the codex affords more complex interactions. Hypertext is all well and good, but, with its capacity to hold words and pictures as well as marginalia, and because it affords bookmarking and flipping back and forth, the codex was already a knowledge-sharing technology that facilitated multimedial and multi-authored texts and non-linear reading.

Building on the tradition of pressing papyrus to make a writing surface, innovators in China macerated plant fibres and laid them out to dry sometime around the beginning of the common-era calendar, give or take a century or two – the attribution and date are contested. This invention, paper, was more durable than papyrus but cheaper and more plentiful than parchment. Paper was an important invention, and one that goes hand-in-hand with innovations in communication technologies that were to come. In the middle of the fifteenth century CE, in Mainz, Germany, Johannes Gutenberg invented the printing press. This was an inestimably significant development – but this attribution is incorrect, or at best inadequate in at least two ways. Firstly, woodblock printing had been in use for centuries, so it was less the press itself and more accurately Gutenberg's moveable type that was the crux of his innovation, not to mention the attendant technologies, such as his ink, which is less like ink traditionally understood and more like a varnish — very black and very sticky, liquid enough to handle but tenacious enough to stay on the type long enough to be transferred sharply to the page.[6] Secondly, the attribution of the invention of moveable type to Gutenberg is the Western version of this history, since similar systems had already been in use in China many centuries earlier, with type made from earthenware, porcelain or wood,[7] and the oldest extant book printed using metal moveable type, *Jikji*, had already been printed in Korea in the late fourteenth century CE.[8] The invention of moveable type, however, was markedly

5.   Meggs, *A History of Graphic Design*, 38.
6.   Richard N. Schwab et al., 'Cyclotron Analysis of the Ink in the 42-Line Bible', *The Papers of the Bibliographical Society of America* 77, no. 3 (1983), 285–315.
7.   Kai-Wing Chow, *Publishing, Culture, and Power in Early Modern China* (Stanford, California: Stanford University Press, 2004), 59.
8.   Hak Soo Park and Eui Pak Yoon, 'Early Movable Metal Types Produced by Lost-Wax Casting', *Metals and Materials International* 15, no. 1 (2009), 155–58.

more impactful in Europe than it was in China because the technology is much better suited to languages based on phonetic alphabets, which comprise relatively few discrete marks: it is much easier to make and set type when dealing with roughly twenty-six letters each in upper and lower case, plus some numerals and punctuation, than with the thousands of discrete characters needed to print texts in languages that use ideographic writing systems.[9]

Gutenberg's invention quickly rendered obsolete the scriptoria in monasteries, the principal site of book production hitherto, where texts were reproduced by hand. The mechanisation of writing by the combination of moveable type and the printing press made the reproduction of books faster, easier and therefore cheaper, which ushered in a more widespread literacy and the dissemination of bodies of knowledge previously inaccessible to the masses.

Jumping forward a few centuries, things really start to get interesting. Early in the nineteenth century, in Britain and in western Europe, the Industrial Revolution was picking up steam, literally. In the first decade of the century, the earliest steam-powered version of a Gutenberg-style press was patented.[10] On 29 November 1814, *The Times* newspaper in London was printed with steam-powered presses for the first time, using machines capable of printing 1,100 impressions per hour.[11] In 1846, in the United States, Richard M. Hoe invented the rotary lithographic press, which could print millions of impressions in a year.[12] Amidst this climate of rapid change, new publishing models and new enterprises emerged. Founded in 1837 in Leipzig, Tauchnitz was one of the first and most important high-volume paperback publishers: in the Tauchnitz Editions series, launched in 1841, nearly 5,500 titles were published, and approximately 60 million copies sold, before the company's demise in 1937 in the face of a hostile environment as the Nazi Party consolidated its power.[13] In its role as purveyor of affordable literature to the European masses, Tauchnitz was succeeded by Paris-based publisher Albatross,

9.   Marshall McLuhan, *The Gutenberg Galaxy: The Making of Typographic Man* (Toronto: University of Toronto Press, 2011), 40.
10.   Meggs, *A History of Graphic Design*, 139.
11.   Ibid.
12.   Ibid., 156.
13.   Alistair McCleery, 'Tauchnitz and Albatross: a "Community of Interests" in English-Language Paperback Publishing, 1934–51', *The Library* 7, no. 3 (2006), 297–316; Karl H. Pressler, 'The Tauchnitz Edition: Beginning and End of a Famous Series', *Publishing History* 6 (1979), 63–78; William Burton Todd and Ann Bowden, *Tauchnitz International Editions in English, 1841–1955: A Bibliographical History* (New York: Bibliographical Society of America, 1988).

founded in 1932 under the leadership of a former Tauchnitz employee.[14] It was in the UK, however, where the model of the mass-market paperback found its most famous incarnation, when, in 1935, Allen Lane and his brothers founded the Penguin imprint.

According to the foundational myth of Penguin, Lane conceived the imprint while waiting for a train at Exeter station, but the story of the connection between rail travel and the paperback is not Penguin's alone. It could be said that the paperback is a product of the locomotive: the paperback is the codex adapted to the modern, mobile lifestyle, as attested to by its names in other languages: the term 'pocket book' is not only the North American synonym for 'paperback' but also a literal translation of the German *Taschenbuch* and the French *livre de poche*. Light and small enough to fit into a coat pocket or bag, the paperback rendered literature portable, and its affordability encouraged the circulation of knowledge in way that older and more rarefied book formats did not.

Zen and Love for Sale

When I was sixteen years old, or thereabouts, my father gave me his copy of a small paperback, *Zen and the Art of Motorcycle Maintenance*, by American writer Robert Pirsig.[15] Published in 1974, *Zen* is both a work of popular philosophy and a semi-fictionalised autobiography. It tells the story of the narrator's motorcycle journey with his young son, his journey through philosophy and, ever present, his battle with mental illness.[16]

At one point in *Zen*, Pirsig describes the difference between Euclidean and Lobachevskian geometries.[17] The ancient Greek mathematician Euclid, in his 13-volume mathematical treatise *Elements* (c. 300 BCE), describes the geometries of two-dimensional planes and three-dimensional solids. Euclidean geometry is the geometry you learn in school, and it will serve you very well if you want to design a box, a truck or even a building, but its scalability thereafter soon becomes limited, and so too its utility, since the world, as we now know, is not flat. For greater

14.   Ibid., 301–2.
15.   Robert Pirsig, *Zen and the Art of Motorcycle Maintenance* (New York: Bantam Books, 1974).
16.   The author's note at the front of the book sardonically states: 'What follows is based on actual circumstances. Although much has been changed for rhetorical purposes, it must be regarded in its essence as fact. However, it should in no way be associated with that great body of factual information relating to orthodox Zen Buddhist practice. It's not very factual on motorcycles either.' Ibid., vii.
17.   Ibid., 255.

ambitions, the geometry proposed by Nikolai Lobachevsky becomes necessary, as do other non-Euclidean geometries. Lobachevskian geometry, so Pirsig taught me, is distinguished from Euclidean geometry by a single move. Presuming a straight line and a point that is not on the line, the fifth postulate in Euclid's *Elements* entails that only one line can pass through the point and never intersect the original line. This new line would be parallel to the first, hence Euclid's fifth postulate is also known as the 'parallel postulate'. In Lobachevskian geometry, by contrast, *two* lines can pass through the point and never meet the original line.

Lobachevskian geometry, aka hyperbolic geometry, would be very useful if the earth were shaped like a giant Pringle. Since it isn't, spherical geometry and other non-Euclidean geometries become necessary – but this is a story for another time. Following the lead of the French mathematician and philosopher of science Jules Henri Poincaré, Pirsig evoked this pivotal moment in the history of mathematics in order to point to the roots of the crisis of scientific reason: the existence of internally consistent but otherwise incompatible geometries shook the foundations of modern science. It was not Lobachevsky's challenge to Euclid's geometry *per se* that captured my sixteen-year-old imagination, but rather the unexpected fact that Euclid's other postulates still cohere in spite of Lobachevsky's intervention at the fifth. This geometric anecdote in Pirsig's book instilled in me an enduring fascination with things that reside at or beyond the edge of the phenomenal, and their effects: seemingly illogical or indeed impossible or imaginary things that facilitate new kinds of operations, or which haunt a system. Examples include, but are not limited to: *i*, the imaginary number that is the square root of -1; the aesthetic category of the sublime, which evades representation and therefore problematises all representation; the Lacanian Real; and other noumenal objects and extralinguistic categories in philosophy and psychoanalysis.

Rejecting consequentialist and deontological traditions in moral philosophy, the French philosopher Alain Badiou proffers a view of ethics that prioritises *events*.[18] A revolution in the realms of art, science or politics, or the experience of falling in love, can, Badiou proposes, reorient an individual's worldview and set her or him on a new trajectory. Ethical conduct, on Badiou's view, is characterised by a commitment to the truth procedures that arise from events that in this way disrupt the state of a situation.

18.   Alain Badiou, *Ethics: An Essay on the Understanding of Evil* (London & New York: Verso, 2002).

What I want to propose is that the ethical subject may come to certain evental moments by way of books, and not only through lived experience. In other words, many profound revolutions are mediated across time and space by books. (Importantly, this is true not only of books. Visual art, music and other cultural forms share this evental potential, but I am focusing here on the book because it has such a long and interesting history as a technology for the distribution of knowledge.)

Around the same time that I read *Zen*, one of my high-school art teachers introduced me to the work of Barbara Kruger. I had no access to the work itself, so I pored through Kruger's oeuvre in the book *Love for Sale*.[19] Ranging from the expressly polemical to the vexingly poetic, Kruger's words and pictures and combinations thereof call out masculist and capitalist operations of power that masquerade as common sense. Her work had a resounding effect on me. Provocations such as 'we don't need another hero', 'you make history when you do business' and 'when I hear the word culture, I take out my checkbook' crystallised my teenage discontent into an enduring imperative to question power structures of all types. Carried from 1980s California to 1990s regional Australia via a 96-page, large-format, full-colour paperback, Kruger's messages and formal strategies cemented in me a curiosity regarding the politics of culture and the means by which culture might be put to political ends.

Certain moments of reading are so momentous they have an evental quality; they entail an ethical commitment. Something new becomes known, something that shakes one's worldview. This new knowledge is so significant to the reader that it becomes thereafter impossible to forget or ignore. These evental moments shape and reshape the reader as an ethical subject.

Two Distributions

The book is a technology for the dissemination of knowledge held in common. The practical question of the systems and techniques by which books are circulated is therefore also a political question. Indeed, the problem of politics itself might be nothing other than a question of distribution. Under the rubric of the 'distribution of the sensible', Jacques Rancière recognises that an aesthetic discrimination precedes political

19.   Kate Linker, *Love for Sale: The Words and Pictures of Barbara Kruger* (New York: Harry N. Abrams, 1990).

participation.[20] What is allowed to be known and, concomitantly, who is allowed to know what? Or, more precisely: what is held in common in a community, and how are roles and responsibilities for its government apportioned? Rancière gives the Platonic example of the poet whose work, in ancient times, demanded his undivided attention and therefore precluded him from participating in the governing of common goods.[21] But the aesthetic operations by which a political formation is circumscribed and divided are perhaps more easily discerned in twentieth-century examples, whereby certain rights – to own land, to work, to vote or to hold office, for example – have been conspicuously granted, withheld or contested along the lines of race, class or gender: the suffragettes, Rosa Parks and the Zapatistas, to name but a few, have in common a concern for the redistribution of the sensible.

The irrevocable entanglement of the distribution of books and the distribution of the sensible is well demonstrated by the historical rapport between the book and the church. From Gutenberg's 42-line bible to the Gideon Bible ubiquitous in hotel rooms worldwide, books have long been mobilised as an instrument of religion. Technologies that permit affordability and accessibility have been central to this ideological arms race, as Voltaire well knew:

I should like to know what harm could come from a book which costs 100 écus. A work in twenty folio volumes will never make a revolution; it's the little books costing 30 sous which are to be feared. If the New Testament had cost 1,200 sesterces, the Christian religion would never have been established.[22]

An abridged version of this passage from Voltaire graced the back cover of a recent survey of contemporary independent publishing, and for good reason.[23] Because books can be not only an instrument of control but also one of resistance, many titles have historically been suppressed, across the political spectrum:

20.   Jacques Rancière, 'The Distribution of the Sensible,' in *The Politics of Aesthetics* (London & New York: Continuum, 2006).
21.   Ibid., 12.
22.   Voltaire, in Ian Davidson, *Voltaire: A Life* (London: Profile Books, 2010), 496.
23.   Robert Klanten, Adeline Mollard and Matthias Hübner, eds., *Behind the Zines: Self-Publishing Culture* (Berlin: Gestalten, 2011).

Demotic regimes demand that we forget, and therefore they brand books as superfluous luxuries; totalitarian regimes demand that we not think, and therefore they ban and threaten and censor; both, by and large, require that we become stupid and that we accept our degradation meekly, and therefore they encourage the consumption of pap. In such circumstances, readers cannot but be subversive.[24]

As Alberto Manguel notes in this passage, the power of books lies not only with authors and publishers but also with readers. Disruptive or alternative publishing models, production and distribution technologies, dissemination practices and juridical interventions arise when a prevailing situation does not meet readers' needs. Examples include paperbacks, zines, samizdat, campaigns for open access to the fruits of state-funded academic labour, distributed libraries and copyleft.[25]

A diversity of publishing and reading practices, i.e., 'biblio-diversity',[26] is essential to democracy. Broadly speaking, democracy entails the participation of all citizens in matters of government. Traditional conceptions of democracy assume that its processes tend toward consensus. An agonistic conception of democracy, however, as articulated by Belgian political theorist Chantal Mouffe, recognises that there will always be political contestants with radically irreconcilable worldviews, so any moments of consensus are necessarily contingent, never absolute. On the agonistic view, the immanent antagonistic dimension of politics is constitutive of democracy and not emblematic of a failing of the model or its implementation: 'the ever present possibility of the friend/enemy distinction and the conflictual nature of politics constitutes the necessary starting point for envisaging the aims of democratic politics'.[27] Yet, in order for me to view my enemy as a political combatant within an agonistic framework, and not as an abominable Other that threatens

24.   Alberto Manguel, *A History of Reading*, 2nd ed. (New York: Penguin, 2014), 21–22.
25.   Mass-market paperbacks and their role in the circulation of knowledge have notably been associated with the social uprisings in Europe in 1968: Ben Mercer, 'The Paperback Revolution: Mass-Circulation Books and the Cultural Origins of 1968 in Western Europe,' *Journal of the History of Ideas* 72, no. 4 (2011), 613–36. On samizdat, see: George Saunders, *Samizdat: Voices of the Soviet Opposition* (New York: Monad Press, 1974). On distributed libraries, see Sean Dockray and Benjamin Forster's chapter elsewhere in this volume.
26.   Susan Hawthorne, *Bibliodiversity: A Manifesto for Independent Publishing* (Melbourne: Spinifex Press, 2014). See also Hawthorne's chapter elsewhere in this volume.
27.   Chantal Mouffe, *On the Political* (London and New York: Routledge, 2005), 13 14.

my existence in a way that warrants their eradication, I must have some empathy for their position, however strongly I might disagree with it. This is where the question of distribution comes into play.

Books are a technology for the distribution of knowledge. They can foster evental moments that reshape us as political subjects. Bibliodiversity makes public a variety of worldviews and types of knowledge that are essential to healthy democracy because we might in this way come to recognise the validity of others' positions even when we don't agree with them. Publishing, facilitated by low-friction distribution, is therefore a critical pedagogic practice[28] – a practice of mass education that supports 'political hygiene'.[29] These practices of epistemic pluralism help to shape not only the texture of a democratic social formation (the definition of what is understood to be held in common), but also its contours and the possibility of their redefinition (the question of who is permitted to speak). In summary: the political problem of the distribution of the sensible is entwined with the logistical problem of the distribution of knowledge. And this is an interminable entanglement, on account of the ineradicable antagonism of the social – a concept that I first discovered in the writings of Chantal Mouffe and Ernesto Laclau, having followed the concept of the Lacanian Real into political theory via Slavoj Žizek, driven by a curiosity first instilled in me by the mention of Lobachevskian geometry in a small paperback that my father casually handed to me all those years ago.[30]

28.   The canonical text on critical pedagogy is: Paulo Freire, *Pedagogy of the Oppressed* (New York & London: Continuum, 2000). For a discussion of the role of education in relation to the ideas of Mouffe and Rancière in particular, see: Gert Biesta, 'The Ignorant Citizen: Mouffe, Rancière, and the Subject of Democratic Education', *Studies in Philosophy and Education* 30, no. 2 (2011), 141–53.
29.   Jennifer Daryl Slack and M. Mehdi Semati, 'Intellectual and Political Hygiene: The "Sokal Affair"', *Critical Studies in Mass Communication* 14, no. 3 (1997): 201–27.
30.   Ernesto Laclau and Chantal Mouffe, *Hegemony and Socialist Strategy: Towards a Radical Democratic Politics*, trans. Winston Moore and Paul Cammack, 2nd ed. (London & New York: Verso, 2001); Slavoj Žizek, *The Sublime Object of Ideology* (London & New York: Verso, 1989).

SITTING WITH DIFFERENCE

Martine Syms & Pip Wallis

PIP WALLIS   I would like to start by asking about your practice within publishing and beyond publishing, and about how you think about dissemination across various platforms. Is there a hierarchy, or is it a matter of the appropriateness of a particular channel to given purposes and audiences?

MARTINE SYMS   I came into publishing from independent music. I was involved very heavily in the scene around The Smell, a punk/experimental all-ages venue in Los Angeles. I played music, but I was more interested in having a label and writing about what people were doing, so that was how I initially got involved in publishing. I had a fanzine called *Anger Thermometer*, which I started when I took a class on youth culture at the Armory in Pasadena. We made zines in the class, and I had a natural affinity for it – I got really into the Xerox machine. I was writing stories, and also writing about my involvement with the music scene. It was through that class that I learned about Miranda July's 'Joanie 4 Jackie' project. And there was a video magazine that my brother got me into, called *411*, which was named after what used to be the number you called for information in the States.

So my interest in undertaking media projects and video projects alongside publishing projects goes back to high school. It has always been fluid for me, in terms of their hierarchy. I was going to shows and I had the zine, which I would submit to *Maximum Rock and Roll*, and it would get written up. I got a really bad review in there one time when I was fourteen years old. I remember thinking about the fact that the reviewer didn't know that I was fourteen, and that's what was cool about it. You know, they just reviewed it like it was a legitimate thing.

It became a way for me to meet people. I would get free records and stuff, or free shirts, just because of the way that I could communicate with bands and artists and filmmakers and other people I was interested in. It was amazing: because of the copy shop, I had access to all of those worlds.

That was what initially made me excited about publishing. Then, when I was a freshman in college, I worked at Ooga Booga when they first opened, and I was a fan of Wendy Yao's bands. I had written about her bands in my zines, so when she opened the space I became really excited about other ways that you could make art and share art.

PW   Thinking about the connections between your publishing practice and your art practice, the processes of creating, receiving and disseminating seem to be intertwined. Specifically, you have spoken of being an 'active reader' in your ongoing web project *Reading Trayvon Martin*, in which you collect articles, essays and documents relating to the fatal shooting of Martin that you have read and bookmarked.[1] How do you see the acts of producing and receiving as connected in your work?

MS   I think about my own practice very much as a reader first, making meaning out of pop-cultural texts. A lot of my early work involved found footage and sound material. I had images, videos, et cetera, and I started editing them together. What excited me about that process was how I negotiated or rethought the material, and how other viewers would be doing that as well.

Because we are inundated with information and communication, we are inadvertently prolific producers. As I've been editing recently, I started thinking about this more. On iPhones, for example, you have the details tab of a text message thread. It's a series of photos and screenshots and videos, and if you were to edit together all the exchanges that you had in a day, it would have a narrative to it. I'm interested in that as a way of creating a character, or talking about a time and place.

PW   It's empowering to be an active reader or an active recipient. But online economies position us as the customer/reader and concurrently as the producer/product; the lines between receiver, producer, consumer and consumable are dissolved. Do you think there is a danger in us, as readers online, becoming the product?

MS   Absolutely. I'm working from an African diasporic position. The question of the post-commodity is part of the historical trauma and framework that I'm coming from, on account of black Americans having literally been a product. And so, for me, the reuse of contemporary media artefacts can definitely help us to think through economic and social histories.

1.   *Reading Trayvon Martin*, http://readingtrayvonmartin.com.

I am interested in how the self is shaped, particularly in the medium of TV. With the Trayvon Martin project, I was thinking about how that news story travelled. It wasn't a mainstream story until it was picked up by a wide audience through Twitter, and then it became a national news story. I was the target audience in many ways, and so I was tracing the way the story wound its way into more mainstream channels.

PW   You said recently that you see an opportunity to be vague about blackness. How do you think about the politics of subjectivity – both the power and the paradoxical pitfalls of claiming such a framework?

MS   There is a great essay by Gordon Hall that talks about refusing to identify with or abide by the terms that have been established for you. I'm interested in the ways we claim blackness all the time. I have no issue with that, but, when I'm making something, there are no parameters for me, and I don't find that it needs to be recognisable or that it needs to fit what is expected by markets.

To me, the danger in having your subjectivity shaped by commercial entities or markets is that if you don't fit into a category that is determined to be valuable, then you can lose access to all kinds of resources. And so there is this pressure to be recognisable or identifiable or marketable – whatever term you want to use – and I find it incredibly boring. Most of the stories that we see about blacks are so unimaginative. They're still fitting into the space of the recognisable, acknowledged role of blacks.

My mission statement for Dominica, my publishing project, has always been something of an inside joke between me and people I work with. The statement says that the imprint is 'dedicated to exploring blackness as a topic, reference, marker and audience in visual culture'. What it would mean to represent blackness? Essentially, we are just making whatever projects we want to make, but giving them a kind of agency and framework.

PW   You link on the Dominica website to Kevin Young's book *The Grey Album: on the Blackness of Blackness*. He explores the tradition of fibbing or improvising as a way to reimagine language. Some of my recent research looks at the ways that women of different generations have adapted language as a means of subversion, whether it's radical appropriation, as in the work of Nancy Spero, for example, or net abbreviation by early coders, who employ the materiality of language as a tool for resistance.

MS   In *The Grey Album*, Young outlines how black culture is always described as both unknown and unknowable. It goes through an intense obfuscation, a break, and it's like there is no tradition. When I did an artist talk recently, at some point during the Q&A somebody said something to the effect of 'when I was in grad school in the eighties, there were no black artists, so how did you know that it was something you could do?' This lack of an institutionalised history is obviously a direct result of oppression, and it is very systematic, so I'm interested in creating continuities. And I am thinking about where fiction fits into this. Sometimes the continuity can be imagined, and this is really exciting to me. It can be a really productive way of making work.

The continuity doesn't always have to be factual, there's another kind of truth to get at. I was part of a group show at the ICA in Philadelphia called *Speech/Acts*, which was about how language can be used as a tool of oppression but also about how that creates potential, specifically looking at poetry and black art. A lot of artists are also looking to feminism to think about how language can be a material.

PW   This raises the question of sci-fi as a discipline of imagining, as a means of creating a world that doesn't exist yet, and that being a possibility for emancipation. I know that you've worked with sci-fi writers, but also you've written the *Mundane Afrofuturist Manifesto*, which is about imagining something that doesn't yet exist.

I'm also aware that as well as imagining futures, there is a recognition in your work of the significance of archives. There is a duality between recognising the importance of historical narratives that need to be remembered and the act of creating anew – as you mentioned earlier, the act of future-creating.

MS   Absolutely. I feel like that's a part of creating a tradition. I have been interested in republishing texts that I feel are emblematic of my interests, but also finding and publishing new voices, like Hannah Black, whose collective writing I'm excited by.

The most recent book I published was by an artist named Sara Knox Hunter, who has been running a sci-fi book club in New York. She has this job where she produces very technical writing and she watches old sci-fi movies as she does it. She was really getting into a community of women film reviewers. At the same time, she was going through an intense personal experience of meeting her biological family for the first time. She was bridging these film reviews with this personal timeline that had gaps; there was a lot of her family history that she didn't know. She was calling the texts 'sci-fi poems', and using speculation as a way to fill in those gaps. As you say, I'm interested in experimenting with thinking about things that don't exist: what things can we imagine, and what would happen if they existed?

The publishing press that I run is really small scale and I'm interested in keeping it that way, because of the flexibility it offers me and the kind of urgency it allows. It's important for me to be able to work really urgently and with immediacy.

PW   You've written a little about an idea of blackness in relation to absence. Similarly, there is a discourse around women embracing the void as a position of power. Thinking about absence and the void being sources of agency, how might that relate to publishing, which is conversely a practice of production and dissemination? I wonder if there is a case for anti-dissemination or protecting interiority?

MS   Definitely, I think any kind of absence creates a space. There is a kind of positive that is created by it.

At the last book fair that I did, someone who was looking at the table pointed out that all the covers of Dominica publications are basically blank. They have black-on-black print, or are embossed, and there are no cover images. It had just been happening over time, and I never really noticed until someone pointed it out to me. They were like, why are all the covers blank?

Everybody I work with is interested in this particular idea of resistance, or this realm of unknowability. I think it's definitely a part of a black American experience. But really, also, it's just a human experience, there's so much that we can never know. And the more comfortable you are with that, the more interesting things become, in my opinion. It is about a resistance to being immediately recognisable. And asking for a different engagement of your time.

Why make a book right now? Why publish a book? It's actually to do with what you just said: preserving an interiority. If I wanted more people to see something, I wouldn't publish it as a printed book, because they are finite. The kind of public that gets created around a printed text, whether it's my own work or that of others, is pretty exclusive. I don't reprint books. They're not supposed to be rarefied, but I do think it's about preservation, or, as Project Lampo, a music organisation in Chicago, says, 'it's for anyone, but it's not for everyone'.

PW   You're looking for an active reader.

MS   Exactly.

PW   You made reference to the design of the books, and something that people often mention when talking to you is the colour purple. The multiple references embodied by that colour point to many different black and feminist histories. But, rather than speak about the colour purple, I am interested in how those histories weigh on your mind when you're producing something that will become, in a sense, a future archive. Do those histories influence you?

MS   They do in a way, they do. But I try not to think too much about any kind of legacy or archive when I'm making something, just because it makes it hard for me to make it work. Instead, I try to focus more on what I'm interested in at that moment.

Also, I'm often asked about my interest in business. I think it's kind of funny because, well, if I don't have any money, I can't make anything. It's about a self-sufficiency, and the sustainability of my projects and my work. So that's something that I am thinking about in terms of legacy: how I can keep doing it? In a really practical way, but also in a larger way: I do want there to be an accumulation of these artists' work and these ideas.

PW   I'm reminded of the strong history of collectivity when it comes to socio-politically motivated publishing. I'm thinking of important feminist presses like Sheba, which published black and

queer women's work in the UK and emerged out of the context
of community organising in the 1980s.

Such communities have been instrumentalised as markets
under late capitalism. The model of working as a cohesively
identifying group is therefore complex today and, as you point out,
can be reductive.

At the same time, late capitalism destructively encourages
us to identify as individual subjects rather than collectively.

How do you think collectivity can be re-engaged positively
in today's publishing and arts landscape, as a supportive and
productive method of creating, and in a way that embraces
multivalent experiences?

MS   I frequently go back to this quote from 'Coalition Politics',
an essay by Bernice Johnson Reagon:

'Coalition work is not work done in your home. Coalition
work has to be done in the streets. And it is some of the most
dangerous work you can do. And you shouldn't look for comfort.
Some people will come to a coalition and they rate the success of
the coalition on whether or not they feel good when they get there.
They're not looking for a coalition; they're looking for a home!'[2]

I got a home and it ain't contemporary art. I'm inspired by activism
but my publishing is not socio-politically motivated. I'm only
interested in working with artists. I like to read artists' writing.
I'm excited by the texts that are used to generate or think through
visual material, and I'm very specific about the book object, as well
as other formal decisions that have their own significance. I don't
expect any kind of collectivity from art. I used to, when I was
younger, because I was a part of a community, but as the art world
becomes industrialised and professionalised I think it's naive to
expect that relationship with others. I'm more interested in sitting
with difference.

2.   Bernice Johnson Reagon, 'Coalition Politics', in *Home Girls: A Black Feminist
Anthology*, ed. Barbara Smith (New York: Kitchen Table: Women of Color Press,
1983), 356-368.

PARIS TO TOKYO: AN UNEXPECTED JOURNEY

Jake Tilson

It's 24 June 1980, a hot summer day on the Left Bank in Paris. I'm standing in La Hune (1944–2015), on the boulevard Saint-Germain, an exceptional bookshop somewhat like a larger version of Compendium Books in London (1968–2000). Emile Solo, the shop's manager, is casually looking at a pile of books and magazines that I'm trying to sell to him. It's a cold call, so we're standing next to the cash register as he works. Shoppers keep trying to get his attention by putting other books on top of mine, but one customer is eavesdropping on my awkward sales pitch and attempts to butt in. I presume he's just an annoyed Parisian, queuing to buy a Borges translation or the latest *bande dessinée*. This large bespectacled man with shoulder-length, sleek black hair and a long coat begins speaking to the manager in French at length – heatedly, almost argumentatively. Turning to me, he protests that they'd be crazy not to buy my books. 'They should take them all', he says. Eventually, they do. My new friend then suggests we go for a coffee to celebrate our strange collaborative sales pitch success. His name is Marc Dachy. Apparently there's an exhibition in the parallel street we must see…

Why would any publisher want to distribute books directly themselves? What could possibly be gained from exposing yourself to rejection, shop after shop? Anyone who has experienced social anxiety should probably avoid the embarrassment of trying to be a sales rep for their own work. As a publisher, looking into the hallway of my house, which is full of boxes of books, I can say with some confidence that it is the cause of countless visits to the osteopath! Lugging stock to and from bookshops and the post office certainly takes its toll. But one reason to do it personally is that no one else will do it better than you. There are other reasons too.

Making and distributing have always been part of the same process for me. I was 'dealing' my own publications before I even knew the meaning of the word. At the age of nine, in my primary school playground in London, I sold hand-drawn comics to friends. Sadly, I was unaware of printing techniques at this stage and so I started my publishing career in pre-Gutenberg mode, drawing every copy by hand. My mother was publishing and mailing out an artists' trade directory called *Catalyst* (1968–71) at the same time. A strong memory from childhood was of being brought up surrounded by 'stock'. In the late sixties, the underground press offered an alternative method of communication by producing magazines, newspapers, posters and badges in opposition to the mainstream media. The art world was also attempting to embrace the idea of art multiples as a way of making and distributing objects more democratically. Eight years later, as a teenager, I began selling rubber-stamped share certificates to friends on the school bus to help finance an alternative magazine called *Juice* (1976), for which I was suspended from school. In the sixth form, I discovered the joys of Gestetner printing, a paper-plate stencil system for producing cheap foolscap pages that could be stapled together to form a publication. I hand-lettered the artwork, adding body text composed on a typewriter, all pasted onto boards. Distribution at this point was still one-to-one.

The 1960s 'do-it-yourself' ethos hibernated for a few years before resurfacing in the cut-up, DayGlo, fluorescent glory of Punk. You couldn't move far in the Punk era without finding zines, badges, albums and posters in independent bookshops and at gigs. Studying painting in London, at Chelsea School of Art, which was then on Manresa Road, I felt at the very centre of the scene. At that time, the first colour Xerox 6500 photocopiers were introduced in the UK, in the Learning Resource Centre at London College of Printing. These early copiers literally burnt toner directly onto paper to create thick, shiny images. In particular, I noticed that Xeroxing a collage helped to merge disparate elements together onto one surface – rather like screen-printing. As photocopiers became more sophisticated and 'accurate', this wonderful effect was lost. The real joy of these machines was making multiple copies! Publishing at the push of a button. To explore this new technology, I helped start up a Xerox magazine dedicated to the spirit of Dada, called *LAZA7* (1978), with four art-school friends. Our printing bill was partially paid for by advertising from a local record shop. As we mainly sold *LAZA7* to friends, distribution was still carried out personally.

At art school I had started writing fiction, inspired by the novels of J.G. Ballard and William Burroughs, and in 1979 won the Vogue Talent Contest for writing. Although I submitted short stories to magazines such as *Ambit* and *Bananas*, I found the established world of literary magazine publishing impenetrable to an outsider. My response to a bulging file of rejection slips was to take control and set up a new magazine where I could publish my work alongside writing and artwork by other people. This was co-edited by my college friend Stephen Whitaker. Everything we'd learnt from producing *LAZA7* was taken forward to create a literary/ arts magazine called *Cipher* (1979–91, The Woolley Dale Press). To be more effective as a communication tool it really needed a wider audience. In part, this was helped by a powerful new idea to us: a mailing list. Today, in 2017, there are still people on my mailing list from 1979. Another key element of expansion was the emergence of independent bookshops. Fortunately London was packed with them. Travel opened up other territories to extend our distribution to like-minded shops in Paris, Barcelona, New York and all around the UK. My world map of bookshops and their staff was slowly expanding. As with La Hune, whoever was behind the till was often the owner, so the doorstepping method was most effective. Only once did a salesperson actively challenge me, saying, 'Sell it to me then!' I left in horror, wishing Marc Dachy had been there to negotiate for me. I preferred to sell to people such as the legendary book dealer Martin Stone at The Forgotten Shelf in Islington. If he liked it, he bought it, acting entirely on instinct. Luckily, just showing books to most owners was enough. If I published regularly enough, the staff remained the same from visit to visit. If someone moved on to a rival shop, they would still take my work. Sadly, many bookshops have gone out of business since that time.

Most people would think of visiting shops and hand-delivering stock as an uncreative and unimportant aspect of making books. For me, this engagement with the commercial world became a crucial part of the overall process. Over the years, I got to know the sales staff and owners, and their feedback really mattered to me. Distribution had finally evolved from 'one to one' to 'one to many'.

After leaving the Royal College of Art, I began to exhibit my work at the Nigel Greenwood Gallery, a conventional 'white cube' space. It was its remarkable bookshop, run by Ann Gallagher, that originally drew me to the gallery, with its international selection of artists' books and magazines, all carefully selected and beautifully displayed. The bookshop even had its own gallery space, where I had my first solo exhibition in London, *Excavator-Barcelona-Excavador* (1986). I showed collages, dioramas and an artist's book. However, some ideas I had were solely suited to magazines. Magazines operate in a different way to books; they can sneak art into people's homes without them noticing. *Cipher* by this time had run its course, so Stephen Whitaker and I started a new arts magazine called *Atlas* (1985–93, The Woolley Dale Press). To add an air of authority to the project, I set up numerous side businesses, including a fake distribution company called Invisible Exports, whose strapline was 'Distributed Art'.

Socially, the magazine connected me with artists, musicians, writers, journalists and bookshops. I also began to correspond with the readers through the mailing list of six hundred subscribers that had built up over four issues. Some were invited to contribute to the magazine; I made many lifelong friends in the process. It shouldn't have been a surprise to find so many like-minded people out there because, in hindsight, it was like opening an Instagram account a decade before the invention of computers. During the pre-Internet age, language was another stumbling block to communicating to a wide audience, so *Atlas* was trilingual from the start. The final issue was published in English, Spanish and Japanese, as by this stage the magazine had begun to sell in Japan and Spain. The print run was 2500 copies, eventually selling in thirty countries. Orders ranged from two hundred copies sent to a distributor in Australia – in the same shipping container as *The Face* – to a delivery of five copies posted to a small art bookshop in Colombia.

Sharing became another important aspect of distribution: I began to give work away freely as mail-outs, inspired by a mixture of Dada, Punk and Fluxus. One example was the *Jake's Chilli Shop* mailings. On a visit to the Los Angeles Grand Central Market, I bought large quantities of three chilli powder varieties to re-package as mail art. Each pack contained the chilli samples and a decorative printed recipe card. These were posted out to two hundred friends. Perhaps this could be considered as redistribution?

Atlas eventually managed to nudge its way into a wider cultural consciousness, beyond its immediate readers. It became 'known'. This happened thanks to a mixture of international sales and editorial press coverage, as well as exhibitions, multiple mail-outs and a personal network of contributors, subscribers, journalists and bookshop staff. Distribution had become discussion.

Realising the importance of everything that is peripheral to a publication came into play again thirteen years later, but on a much bigger scale. What was originally intended as a seasonal website about food gradually morphed into a nine-year-long project that culminated in two cookbooks, an exhibition about eels and a BBC Radio 4 Food Programme episode about sustainable fishing. The books were *A Tale of 12 Kitchens*[1] and *In at the Deep End: Cooking Fish Venice to Tokyo*.[2] Rather than self-publish these works, I switched to the commercial mainstream.

1.   Jake Tilson, *A Tale of 12 Kitchens* (London: Weidenfeld and Nicholson; Artisan Books, 2006).
2.   Jake Tilson, *In at the Deep End: Cooking Fish Venice to Tokyo* (London: Quadrille, 2011).

My reason for taking this decision was to see the books published in high volume and distributed worldwide. Having come through the age of pasted-up artwork, negative film and cheap two-colour printing, at this point I was now deeply immersed in the digital world and had accidentally become a website pioneer in 1994 with *TheCooker* (1994–2001).[3] For these commercial books, destined for high-street chain stores, I managed to maintain creative control by being both designer and author, taking all of the photography and designing the five typefaces used in each of them. Another steep learning curve was producing complicated five-colour artwork for *In at the Deep End*, a requirement for foreign language co-editions. Having another publisher actually pay for the printing, marketing, promotion and distribution was a dream come true. Printing my own magazines and books usually only took me to grey industrial estates in south-east London. Nowadays, I more regularly find myself examining proofs on a Heidelberg press in Northern Italy, with a glorious view of the Dolomites. Not distributing these books in person does mean that I've lost the random joy of meeting booksellers, or selling directly through a mailing list, so I'll have to look elsewhere to expand the conversations that making a book can start.

All elements that accompany a book or magazine should reflect the spirit and content of the project – be it an advertising rate card or a book launch invitation. For each cookbook, I constructed extensive websites, PDF posters and elaborate mail-outs containing postcards, herb and spice samplers, squid ink sachets, menu cards and tote bags. For *In at the Deep End* I adapted a fortune telling fish that suggested how you should cook your fish supper, instead of telling you if you were 'in love' or 'jealous'. A free iPhone app version of Fortune Telling Fish was developed in collaboration with Turned On Digital after they read a review of the mail-out in *Creative Review*. Rather than produce an audio version of the book in a conventional way, I produced a podcast of each chapter, in which I acted as a guide to the imagery. Alongside the descriptions were snatches of audio from the actual locations being discussed, such as the church bells of the Carmini church ringing in Venice, or the chanting of tuna auctioneers in the Tsukiji fish market in Tokyo. To my great surprise, the books won awards, and I gained acceptance in the cookery world. I've even appeared on Saturday morning TV and radio shows here in the

---

3.   TheCooker, http://www.thecooker.com

UK, as well as in the US, Canada and Australia. And so the conversation started by a book continues...

Forty-eight years since my first publication, I find myself in Ueno, Tokyo. I am sitting on a tatami mat floor in a cheap *ryokan*, while outside in the park cherry blossom from sakura trees has covered the city in a delicate pink blanket. By email I receive the tragic news that my dear friend Marc Dachy in Paris has died. True friends can be counted on the fingers of one hand. Fortunately, Marc lived his life in the spirit of his lifelong passion, Dada – uncompromising to the end. The exhibition that Marc took me to on the Left Bank in Paris in 1980 was of William Burroughs' collaged sketchbooks. They had strong echoes of my book *Exposure* – the book that Marc and I had succeeded in selling to La Hune.

Distribution is about sharing, friendship and people.

Postscript

An incomplete roll call of bookshops and staff during the 1970s–90s: Marc Dachy, Luna Park, Transedition / Ann Gallagher, Nigel Greenwood Books / Simon Cutts, Coracle Press / Lucy Lippard, Nancy Linn, John Goodwin, Max Schumann, Printed Matter Books, NYC / Nick Kimberley, Duck Soup / Martin Stone, The Forgotten Shelf, Islington / Richard Adams, Open Head Press / Jim Pennington, Aloes Books / Academy Books / Mike Hart, Compendium Books, Camden High Street / Bernard Stone, Floral Street / Nicola Jacobs Gallery, Cork Street / Arts Bibliographic, Great Russell Street / George Snow, Bananas / Battersea Arts Centre, Lavender Hill / Basilisk Press, England's Lane / George Lawson, Bertram Rota, Long Acre / Rob Hadrill, Jane Rolo, Book Works, Borough Market / Andrew Lord, Arts Council Bookshop / Dillons University Bookshop, Malet Street / Dark They Were and Golden Eyed, St Anne's Court / John Eggeling, Phantasmagoria Books, Colwell Rd / Forbidden Planet, Denmark Street / The Other Bookshop, Upper Street / Riverside Studios Bookshop, Hammersmith / Stephen Bury, Clive Phillpot, Chelsea School of Art library / Cathy Courtney, Art Monthly / Su Small, Pluto Press / Matthew Tyson, Spot Press / David Blamey, Open Editions / Geoffrey Soar, Little Magazines, UCL / Village Books, Streatham / Savoy Books, Michael Butterworth, Manchester / Ceolfrith Bookshop, Sunderland / Third Eye Centre, Glasgow / Will Copeland, Orwell Books, Ipswich / Tom and Laurie Clark, Moschatel Press / Jaap Rietman, Spring Street / Tuli Kupferberg, Vanity Press / Guy Bleus, W.A.A, Wellen, Belgium / Emile Solo, La Hune, boulevard Saint-Germain / Shakespeare & Co / Stan Barets, Temps Futurs, rue Dante / Artcurial, rue Jean Mermoz / SITES, New York / Judith Hoffberg, Umbrella / Galignani, rue de Rivoli, Paris / Rabascall, Paris / Actualités, rue Dauphine, Paris / Arnolfini Bookshop, Bristol / Public House Bookshop, Brighton / ICA Bookshop, London.

TECHNOLOGY IS THE ANSWER, BUT WHAT WAS THE QUESTION?

Jens Maier-Rothe & Markus Miessen

JMR   In our first meeting for this conversation, we planned to talk about the architecture of reading rooms and libraries in relation to the distribution of ideas. We made a serious detour and ended up talking about the architecture of books, nomadic archives and digital search engines instead. The more we tried to enter concrete, physical spaces, the more we deviated into less physical realms. Sometimes it is good to get lost. Maybe it is even necessary and reasonable, given your work as an architect spans a wide range combining applied architectural practice with an active engagement in critical theory. What brought you to work at the intersection between architecture and the dissemination of knowledge?

MM   I guess, firstly, I am a person interested in reading, writing, publishing and thinking about forms and formats of ongoing conversations. At the same time, it happens to be the case that my professional background spans architecture and theory, so I'd say it is only natural that I have tried to explore those subjects also in space, both physical and virtual. As an architect, I have been working since 2007 on projects with an interest in the interrogation and development of spaces for social encounters and discourse. Beyond my spatial interest in this subject, which I like to refer to as 'Cultures of Assembly', I have in parallel been working on different sets of investigations in different geographical and institutional contexts, mostly commissioned but sometimes self-initiated, such as the setting up of the Winter School Middle East in the Gulf region. Cultures of Assembly is also the title of a long-term and ongoing research activity of mine, which deliberately blurs the boundary between observation and proposition.

JMR   You collaborate with many artists and art institutions, sometimes co-authoring artworks, sometimes designing artists' studios or revamping museum spaces. You have been teaching for many years, and you also write and publish extensively on the notion of critical spatial practice. What is critical spatial practice for you and what makes it so relevant for our present political situation?

MM   For me, architecture – if approached in a critical rather than business-oriented or service-provisional understanding of the term and practice – is or should be concerned with the production of space in a broad-reaching sense. The moment that one opens up the discussion in this direction, one is facing a complex set of questions that span far beyond the traditional horizon of the profession and its usual-suspect companions, such as urban planning or spatial design, into neighbouring as well as alien fields of knowledge production, which in sum are concerned with an understanding and analysis of – and propositions toward – alternative spatial realities. Those neighbouring fields are of course nothing new to those who have been involved in debates regarding spatial production over the last fifty years, however I am interested in how these debates can be moved out of the academy and into less hermetic contexts, and be tested against reality through physical case studies rather than remaining in the stable and controlled environment of academic publishing. Keywords in this regard would be terms such as 'the production of space', 'post-occupancy', 'use over form', 'critical retrofitting', 'inhabitation, social gathering & assembly' and 'inclusion versus exclusion'.

For many years now, we have been given opportunities – sometimes commissioned, sometimes self-initiated – to use the art world as a testing ground and backdrop for those ideas. And yes, to contextualise this in a more self-critical way, I would say that of course the art world is a bubble, but it helped us, at the studio, to think through and develop certain models of practice, which are now ready to be implemented in other contexts. Although I would love to work on an institution from scratch, i.e., developing its content framework, work methodology, architectural envelope and interior architecture, down to the scale of the workbench, I would also be very interested to take some of our findings and experience and apply these to the contexts of NGOs, cultural institutions and organisations outside of the visual arts, or to formal political organisations or parties.

JMR   That sounds like a good idea. As co-founder of the art initiative and institutional pilot Beirut in Cairo (2012–2015), I found it very useful to learn from other local organisational forms when thinking about how we want to build institutions and how we want them to behave. In Cairo at the time, questions around assembly and public space were, of course, constant undercurrents whenever and wherever collective discourse took place. Going out on the streets and inhabiting public space with resistant bodies was the dominant form of expressing political ideas for most of the population. Those questions were shared by local art and cultural institutions and became the ground for a vital exchange between various types of seemingly unrelated organisations. Having a political voice not only meant being present in public, it also meant exploring and reclaiming forms of organising voices and practices in the public realm. What role and responsibility do art and cultural institutions have in this regard? How can they learn from each other? I still consider this institutional exchange one of the most productive and generous things that happened back then. It made it possible to talk about very concrete things while addressing rather abstract questions. For instance: how are we to articulate and mobilise a collective desire to own the political future in such an exceptional moment of transition? How might we control the past and how it is written every day in order to claim the future? Naturally, there were a lot of initiatives concerned with the collection and distribution of information, to offer alternative views to the state and corporate media apparatus. The independent journalism platform Mada Masr and the collective Mosireen are two examples. Now, seven years later, the question arises: what should we do with all of this collected information, what sort of archives should be built to make use of it? Mosireen recently launched an online archive called *858*, the largest collection dedicated to vernacular videos on the Egyptian uprising.[1] This marks a critical point in the recent history of Egypt and it will show what enduring importance still rests in that material.

You recently co-edited a comprehensive reader titled *The Archive as a Productive Space of Conflict*.[2] In your opening dialogue with co-editor Yann Chateigné, you mention the transformative function of archives, and a few pages later you wonder about 'collective memory and the potential simulation of memory through archives'.[3] Perhaps the Mosireen archive may be able to slowly develop this effect over time and eventually create and sustain a collective memory shared by a growing number of people, who continue to write a different history that will prevent other forms of state violence and oppression from taking place in other parts of the world.

1.   This archive is named after the 858 hours of video footage it contained when launched. It can be accessed online at: https://858.ma
2.   Markus Miessen and Yann Chateigné, eds., *The Archive as a Productive Space of Conflict* (Berlin: Sternberg Press, 2016).
3.   Ibid., 19.

MM   The research endeavour *The Archive as a Productive Space of Conflict*, which was later turned into a much larger reservoir of experiments, works and research, initially grew out of a project that I was working on with Hans Ulrich Obrist in Switzerland between 2007 and 2010. We were spending a lot of time either talking about his archive or being at one of his archives, the main storage space in Berlin. The archive consists of several sub-archives and decentralised libraries, which we attempted to unite in a single location in order for it to generate new content and knowledge. The overall archive at the time consisted of approximately 2,000 hours of MiniDV video recordings (dialogues with artists, scientists and architects; trialogues; public Marathon interviews; etc.), the collection of all exhibitions that Hans Ulrich ever curated in book form, the archive of unrealised projects, the archive of formulas, the archive of futures, the archive of maps, the archive of manifestos, his laptop and hard-drives and of course his private library of over 30,000 books. We were also planning to include the archive of Joseph Grigely, who, since the mid 1990s, has been working on an art project about an archive of Hans Ulrich's exhibitions.

First, the idea was that we needed to define a geography, region and site – or in fact a series of sites. At the same time, we were thinking that the archive could go on a journey. There were three potential models for realising this project: (a) developing a curatorial research institute within an existing university; (b) for it to become the foundation of a new school; or (c) for the archive to turn spatial, i.e., for it to become a building itself. The third option was the model that we finally decided to work on. After ten months of scouting sites in Switzerland, we identified the village of Tschlin as a potential site. Tschlin is a small Alpine village in the Lower Engadine. On the one hand, the project was about finding a controlled, public and accessible mode of representation. On the other, it was about creating a remote place for concentrated research, a contemporary and highly interlinked version of archival production models such as Sitterwerk in St. Gallen or the Fabbrica Rosa, the Harald Szeemann archive – spaces I later visited with my students. The archive combined other programs as well: a summer academy, a small exhibition space, lodging, a residency program and a radio station, which could transmit material from the digital archive, such as the recorded interviews. The central idea was to establish one specific place dedicated to the archive that could contain satellite projects and be nomadic and sent around the globe. So, there are two aspects, one physical and one virtual, each of which could potentially travel.

The project was then extended as a research endeavour. I introduced it into my teaching environments at the time, in Geneva and Karlsruhe. The fact that I was simultaneously based at two institutions also meant that I could experiment with how a set of ideas produces different repercussions in different educational environments. We used the project as an opportunity to expand on the subject and to think about different forms and formats of knowledge and content production by juxtaposing different types of archival material. This was attempted institutionally, spatially, in regard to mechanisms of order and disorder, and by interrogating and bastardising the ways in which interacting with an archive can have effects and affects on the production of new relationships and, ultimately, content.

JMR   Conflict is understood here along the lines of Chantal Mouffe's idea of agonistic pluralism. It is both a precondition of and a productive means for a desired approach towards archives. In the book's introduction, you describe the conflictual archive as an open framework that transforms itself, that is able to apply its own versatility to become a productive stage of dispute and struggle. What activates this versatile and auto-transformative agency? You also mention how important it is to access archives without knowing what one is looking for or trying to appropriate, that 'archives should be the results of conscious mistakes and collisions'.[4] Why is not-knowing so crucial for the conflictual archive to be productive?

MM   One mode of activation is connected to the question of order, ordering mechanisms and the possibility of non-order as a potential trigger for new links and relationships. In this regard, the Sitterwerk represented a very interesting format for us, since it employs a physical and slightly old-school and techno-aficionado version of contemporary online and algorithm-generated links, which I would more generally like to refer to as a 'culture of suggestion'.

4.   Ibid., 23.

In other words: how is it possible to make visible the links between different users and their different approaches to knowledge, knowledge formats and the way in which they interact with those? For me, an interesting library or archive does not have to have it all – it needs to suggest to me what kinds of cross-pollination could be fertile, both in the sense of cultures of knowledge and arguments that nestle around one's own interests, but also, and more importantly, the outliers that circulate around those perspectives that are either not on my horizon or are in conflict with my own work. This does not by default necessitate a huge physical repository of printed matter. It could, for example, be based around reports of research approaches, bibliographies, notes, conversations and the margins and leftovers of academic knowledge production. Finally, the questions are: how can we get those documents to talk to each other, and how can we create a space in which one can work in a different way? This was really what the archive project was about. To answer your question as to whether 'not-knowing' should become a pre-condition of such a model: surely in particular instances not-knowing and a certain naivety can be understood as productive. I have previously worked around this notion in a more general sense to describe the qualities and potential benefits of the role I called 'the uninvited outsider'. However, this role and approach of course has its limits. To summarise: yes, one can often detect links, uncover realities and so forth that people deeply involved with a given subject matter may no longer be able to identify, perhaps because of tunnel vision. The entire economy of consulting essentially rotates around this notion of the outsider. In the context of the conflictual archive, I would say that not-knowing can, at times, be helpful, but it is essential that the setting up of the framework be carefully managed by an individual or group who has a deep insight into the subject(s) that the archive is dealing with.

JMR   In your most recent book, *Crossbenching*, not-knowing appears again as a key driver for your idea of a critical spatial practice: 'Knowledge is often produced at the edges or in the gaps of not-knowing'.[5] Simultaneously, the discrete spaces and grey zones in which intimacy can exist, and which do not give everything away in total

<hr>

5.   Markus Miessen, *Crossbenching* (Leipzig: Merve Verlag, 2016), 69.

transparency, are needed for developing spatial scopes of action for democratic discourse. *Crossbenching* does both: it embraces complexity and meddles with it. To understand space, as you wrote, we have to think beyond the normative bounds of territorial space. Not-knowing can be productive when accessing archives, just as the non-disciplinary alternative to everyone being an expert becomes key for a new 'spatial culture' and a critical practice that understands spatial conditions as situations. Along these lines, your 'crossbencher' follows Bruno Latour's motto that 'The critic is not the one who debunks, but the one who assembles'.[6]

MM   Assembly in this context is indeed key. How does one produce the necessary setting in and through which certain situations and modes of acting can be mobilised? The notion of assembling — which Latour has written much about — plays an important role, both in the concept of crossbenching and in my work in general. In this regard, Cultures of Assembly, as an ongoing research project, explores and exploits the pockets and nooks of everyday spatio-political practices, transferring them into the sphere of spatial design — focusing on the question of how conflictual modes of participation can become a driving force for the production of somewhat awkward and friction-ridden social situations. *Crossbenching*, as a concept, has been borrowed from the English House of Lords, and then bastardised and developed further into a notion of party-free affiliation based on one's own judgement about a wide array of issues. In architecture, too, only an external observer to a particular situation — without any self-interest — can implement new spatial practices, applying them on different scales, ranging from object-scale, to the architectural, urban and geopolitical. Or, as Eyal Weizman has phrased it, in a response to *Crossbenching*, it is:

'a simple and profound proposition: to 'do' architecture is to immerse oneself in a conflictual process of material production — participation is not a productive encounter of multiple practitioners and stakeholders, but a set of conflicts, negotiations, maneuvers, and swindles between and within a multiplicity of agents, human and

6.   Bruno Latour, "Why Has Critique Run out of Steam? From Matters of Fact to Matters of Concern," *Critical Inquiry* 30, no. 2 (2004): 246.

nonhuman alike — equally including architects, clients, financiers, and builders, say, but also silicon, plastic, concrete, each with its conflicting aims and different material means to achieve them. Every building is thus the materialization of such encounter. So, despite the hubris of the field, none of the parties to such an encounter can ultimately control that the result — architecture (unlike real estate), according to Miessen, belongs to no one but affects and is affected by everyone — and this proposition asks that we reframe questions of ethics and politics. They can no longer be the property of an individual but a collective set of interrelations — it is through such profound departure from the terms of architecture that *Crossbenching* demands nothing less than to reimagine how we might finally become citizens.'

JMR   It also says in your book that crossbenching creates an archipelago of knowledge clusters coming in from the outside to permeate given situations and contexts. Do we have to imagine this in practical terms of applied politics, so that the citizen as crossbencher is an external observer who interferes at the same time? Should we think and act more in temporary structures, following Cedric Price's idea of architecture as collaborative and collective action?

MM   Exactly. On the one hand, it is a very collaborative and collective spirit that needs to be fostered, both in terms of civil society and what in German we call 'Zivilcourage'. On the other hand, and more importantly for me, it is about the rethinking of the term 'participation'. I do not want to go into this too much here, but maybe I can shortly introduce my thinking around the terms and what has driven my 'participation project' over the last ten years. I am mostly interested in thinking participation through the individual rather than the collective. What I have found difficult since the late 1990s — and what I find increasingly difficult now — is a growing and unquestioned belief in participation as a saviour from all evil, in politics and beyond. At the end of the day, the participatory structures that we have been conditioned to believe in are simply systemic rhetoric. Those narratives are based not on the spirit of the individual, but the notion of the 'generous gesture', whereby an institutional structure opens itself up and invites us, the general public, in, either to become part of a decision-making process or otherwise. The problem is that the ground in this case has already been sorted, meaning that the problem or issue has most often already been named and described, so the 'participant' essentially becomes a puppet. At the same time, participation has become a means to outsource responsibility, especially by politicians, who are no longer willing to assume their roles as elected and empowered individuals in a representative democracy. What I am referring to in this context, of course, is mainly focusing on the already luxurious situation of a mostly Western model of representative democracy. What I have tried to argue for is that, rather than replacing such a model, i.e., the idea of the roundtable, which invites us to contribute, there needs to be a parallel effort, which would be that of self-mobilisation. In other words, participation, for me, needs to come from the individual — it should be understood as a first-person singular practice of the individual forcing her- or himself into a context or discourse that one was not invited to 'participate' in. This model has been the starting point for a conversation with Chantal Mouffe that spanned a five-year period and ended up in the small book *The Space of Agonism*,[7] which was published as part of the book series 'Critical Spatial Practice' that I have been co-editing with Nikolaus Hirsch since 2011.

JMR   If crossbenching asks that we reframe questions of ethics and politics, as Weizman says, how does the concept affect design politics and the spaces inhabited and transformed by it? It is obviously important to think beyond the normative bounds of territorial space. Nevertheless, I wonder how crossbenching as a practice might influence a public library or a local record store near my home. In other words, how might crossbenching intervene in three-dimensional space as much as it might intervene in virtual spaces designed for consumption, distribution and encounters in everyday life?

MM   Crossbenching, in the context of the everyday, should be understood as a twofold concept: on the one hand, it offers an entry point to a conversation around questions of collaboration, access, self-empowerment and the process of assuming responsibility. On

7.   Markus Miessen and Chantal Mouffe, *The Space of Agonism*, ed. Nikolaus Hirsch and Markus Miessen, Critical Spatial Practice (Berlin: Sternberg Press, 2012).

the other hand, and more concretely addressing the issue of spatial reality, it asks questions concerning how spatial objects talk to one another and what, ultimately, this 'conversation' of 'physical things' can generate. Architecture, at the end of the day, produces very specific and precise conditions that the individual and the collective have to deal with. It both generates a physical envelope and a situational reality. Here, we are again entering Cedric Price territory: 'technology is the answer, but what was the question?'

DEAR SUBSCRIBER

Stuart Bertolotti-Bailey

Dear Subscriber,

Taking a cue from the last issue of *Bulletins of The Serving Library*, on 'Perspective', we, the editors, have been taking stock of our present situation and have resolved to make a few changes. Since launching the journal's forerunner, *Dot Dot Dot*, almost eighteen years ago, we have tried to remain alert to the shifting sands of publishing and alter our path accordingly. Here follows a whistle-stop history of the direction to date, ending with our new incarnation as *The Serving Library Annual*.

Please note that dates and most other bits of information are approximate at best.

2000

The pilot issue of biannual left-field arts magazine *Dot Dot Dot* is produced and published by four graphic designers with literary leanings: Stuart Bailey, Peter Bil'ak, Tom Unverzagt and Jürgen X Albrecht. The cover declares itself to be 'A magazine in flux / ready to adjust itself to content'. Production is heavily subsidised by a friendly Dutch printing house, along with two Dutch art schools, allowing the price to be kept to a student-friendly €10. The print run is perhaps 2,000 copies. We are initially distributed by Idea Books in Amsterdam until they discover we've been offloading our own copies to a local bookstore run by friends. We end up working instead with Central Books in London for the UK market and Bruijl & Van der Staaij in Amsterdam for the rest of Europe, supplemented by a Dutch subscriptions service as well as sales via our own rudimentary website. We run out of copies three years later.

2002

On discovering that many stores are charging more than our RRP, we write 'Pay no more than 10 Euros' on the spine (an idea stolen from old Billy Bragg records), but they continue to literally stick their inflated prices on top of ours. The German half of the editorial team retires, leaving Stuart and Peter to run the enterprise out of Amsterdam and Den Haag. We successfully apply for a (now defunct) Dutch arts grant and so are finally able to pay contributors, yielding an immediate increase in quality and quantity. The magazine is described by one bystander as 'not necessarily about graphic design, but distinctly FROM it'. It's not easy to parse what this means, but we understand.

2005

The apex of our reputation and sales: we are regularly printing 2,500–3,000 copies of each issue that take about a decade to sell out (this is relatively quick, say publishing cognoscenti). At the same time, a brief op-ed, headed 'Elementary Mathematics', on the back cover of #9 describes an oxymoron of independent publishing: although on paper the journal is now financially self-sufficient, we are forced to remain dependent on the subsidy because we can't afford a lawyer to extract the money due. The piece then proceeds to list outstanding debtors and their respective debts in red ink, which totals some €14,000, as well as the typical budget required to produce a single issue, which turns out to be precisely the same amount and so inadvertently proves the point. Although such naming and shaming was never really intended to provoke payment, about half the accused distributors, bookstores and advertisers actually cough up. Unfortunately, this doesn't include the blacklist's biggest crooks, Actar of Barcelona, who owed €7,000 back then. Taking inflation and interest into account, this must have at least doubled by now. Later the same year, #10 is a 'best-of' of the previous nine issues – partly conceived as an 'ideal' collection assembled from the trial and error so far, and partly to buy some fiscal breathing space after the grant evaporates. As part of a project in Tallinn, Estonia, we print the issue there at significantly lower cost than in the Netherlands, then subsequently try a printing house in Vilnius, Lithuania, which is cheaper still. Tallinn also sees the inaugural exhibition of a collection of objects including prints, paintings, Polaroids, record covers, LCD blotter art and a Ouija board, all of which have appeared as illustrations in the journal at some point. The collection grows as it moves from place to place, setting off a whole other parallel logistics of circulation.

2006

Stuart moves to New York, where regular contributor David Reinfurt gradually supplants Peter as co-editor. Then a stroke of luck: Princeton Architectural Press agrees to distribute the journal, boosting US circulation for a couple of years before the relationship starts to wane. Around 150 boxes of journals (about 35 per box = 5,250 back issues) are shipped from Den Haag to Dexter Sinister, a basement space in New York's Lower East Side that Stuart and David have just established as 'a just-in-time workshop and occasional bookstore'. Riding a modest wave of local media attention, the shop proves successful enough to accommodate a range of other publications, which seems perverse at a time when most other small and medium-size bookstores are being forced out of business by the bigger chains' monopoly and the proliferation of online retail. Within another couple of years, Amazon will have largely decimated those bigger chains too.

2008

While profits from the Saturday shop begin to cover its rent, they don't stretch to the cost of the journal. After a couple of years of surviving on sales and irregular advertising we are broke again, and the absence of any public funding for the arts in the United States equivalent to that in Europe becomes fully apparent. However, out of nowhere, we start to be invited to participate in large-scale contemporary art exhibitions, usually city biennials or themed group shows in museums. Our reflex proposal is to produce an upcoming issue of the journal in line with the invitation's premise – and, around this time, production frequently is the premise. The first is #15, made from scratch at the Centre d'Art Contemporain Genève as part of a Swiss-funded group exhibition on so-called speculative art and design. We secure control of a significant lump sum from the exhibition budget and use it to bring a group of international contributors to work in the gallery over three weeks, and transplant an unusually sophisticated Risograph printing setup from a community centre known to us back in the Netherlands. Another advantage: by tapping into the institution's circulation channels, we have access to a whole other audience. We initially plan to make a series of charts or diagrams that register how the Centre's money is spent, then slowly realise we're inhabiting our own de facto infographic: as two monumental stacks of virgin paper gradually diminish, smaller piles of printed pages pop up around us to form a living image of input/output. Equally performative setups are contrived for #17, with material first programmed and disseminated live over three nights at Somerset House in London, then written up into a documentary issue; and #19, first released as six editions of a newspaper that reported on the beleaguered state of the news industry for Performa, a performance art festival in New York, then compressed into *Dot Dot Dot*'s usual B5 format.

2010

Although the journal's reputation and influence on a certain strain of art publishing continues, actual sales and subsequent print runs decline, falling to 1,500 by the end of the decade. From what little information we can extract from our third-party distributors, it is becoming increasingly difficult to get ailing bookshops to stock the journal. We are reportedly 'difficult to place', both in terms of category (book or periodical?) and subject matter (art or design or literature?). The malaise dovetails with a desire to dismantle certain aspects of what the journal has become, namely self-referential, obscure and somewhat predictable. Stuart moves to Los Angeles. Something has to give.

2011

A busy year. David writes *A Short Account of the Library*, in which former 'archiving' and 'circulating' paradigms of information dispersion are contrasted with a contemporary 'distributing' model. It points out that when documents are made available to retrieve on a digital network, they are no longer merely consulted or borrowed, but instead duplicated – automatically leaving a trace of the duplicator in the process. This precipitates a wholesale recalibration of the *Dot Dot Dot* setup into a reversible publishing/archiving platform called The Serving Library, which involves a number of moving parts: (1) a new editorial team, with writer and artist Angie Keefer brought in to broaden the journal's subject matter, temperament and gender balance; (2) a new publishing mechanism based on an 'engine room' website of freely downloadable PDF contributions, or 'bulletins', that are then collected into a printed publication, *Bulletins of The Serving Library*, continuing the format and trajectory of its predecessor; (3) the dismissal of our existing printers and distributors, replaced by separate operations in Europe and the United States to avoid the increasing headache of the export/import procedures – the former via Sternberg Press in Berlin, the latter via a cheap journal printer in Pennsylvania to be disseminated ourselves; (4) the amalgamation of the collection of objects and an attendant pedagogical programme under the same 'Serving Library' umbrella; (5) an application to become a 501(c)3 not-for-profit public institution in the United States, the key contractual text of which is subsequently included as an 'Article of Incorporation' at the back of each new print edition; and (6) a successful crowdfunding campaign that raises $10k to fund it all. The new dual digital/printed format is conspicuously vanilla, designed primarily to be read on a phone, tablet or screen and only secondarily poured into a printed page – each of which includes a time stamp in the bottom left corner that marks the moment it was last saved as a Portable Document Format. An equivalent digital 'stamp' in the corner of the website links to a live inventory of every download (= copy), including the downloader's server address, which to our amazement is soon recording two to three hundred downloads per day. To emphasise the digital bias and otherwise cut costs, the printed publication is based on the astringent aesthetic of the academic art journal *October*, and against the markedly heterogeneous grain of *Dot Dot Dot* we begin to loosely theme each issue, starting with 'Time' and 'Education'. The new website offers two types of subscription, two or twelve years (i.e., four or twenty-four issues), aimed at individuals and institutions respectively. The price of a single issue by now has risen to €15. Five years after opening, it is necessary to terminate the shop's regular Saturday schedule: Dexter Sinister becomes 'open by appointment' instead.

2012

The crowdfunds have run dry so we return to the strategy of binding each issue to an art-institutional request: *Bulletins of The Serving Library* #3 doubles as a pseudo-catalogue, on 'Typography', for a language-based group exhibition at MoMA; #4 is conceived as part of a residency project, on 'Psychedelia', at Charlottenborg in Copenhagen; German-themed #5 is assembled around a programme called 'The End(s) of the Library' at the Goethe-Institut in New York – and so on. This blunt opportunism continues to work surprisingly well and often, though we often find ourselves fielding institutional requests or demands that dilute our intentions, and so resolve to reduce our dependence on such relationships.

2015

We make #8, on 'Mediums', in view of a major exhibition at Tate Liverpool showcasing The Serving Library's ever-expanding collection of objects. Stuart has recently relocated to the city, and is on the lookout for a permanent physical home for the archive, inventory and pedagogical aspirations after attempts to find a space in the United States have so far fallen short. We file a successful application for a UK Arts Council grant, just as Sternberg announces they are no longer willing to pick up the printing tab, though are willing to carry on distributing the journal if we cover the production costs.

2016

Stuart's wife Francesca joins the editorial team to propel a new set of ambitions. Through her efforts, we find a space in a remarkable building in Liverpool's old mercantile district and finally open The Serving Library's first physical space in July. With a nod back to *Dot Dot Dot*, *Bulletins of The Serving Library* #10 samples the best of the previous nine publications. As before, it is partly a means of avoiding one issue's contributor costs while generally recalibrating. Mindful of bookstores still claiming they don't know where to place the publication, it shrinks to half its former format, thinking this might suggest we're more book than periodical and make it easier for them to decide on a shelf. Naturally, this also reduces printing, storage and shipping costs. To compensate, we go full-colour and make 'Colour' itself the next theme. Remaining copies of any given back issue are still running out about a decade after publication. Ten years after opening, the Dexter Sinister shop closes for good and its website inventory becomes an archive. We ship half the current stockpile from New York to Liverpool (a hundred boxes: approximately 3,500 copies) and plan to start distributing all non-American orders from there.

2017

Having been kicked out of the first space after only nine months by the UK tax office, which is appropriating the entire block, The Serving Library's physical incarnation moves to the gallery of Exhibition Research Lab, an academic initiative within the John Lennon Art and Design Building at Liverpool John Moores University. It opens on April Fool's Day, continuing where the former space left off with a monthly programme of *Bulletins*-related public events. Following a third issue of the reduced-scale edition, and tired of still finding the journal conspicuous by its absence in even the most obvious of bookshops across the world, we decide to terminate the relationship with Sternberg for good and contrive another fresh start. This brings us full circle, back to Amsterdam, where we strike a deal with Roma Publications – and, by proxy, back to their regular distributors Idea Books – who are eager to instigate new energy by once more changing the format and re-asserting its designerly 'object quality' after years of austerity. And so we settle on making the journal half as frequent but twice as large, duly changing the name to *The Serving Library Annual* and the format to a sturdy 200 pages of A4. Each issue from now on effectively amounts to two of the previous ones, i.e., the same labour and content is now fed into a single publication released each autumn. A two-year subscription therefore now amounts to two issues, and its twelve-year sibling to twelve. Meanwhile, the website continues to operate as before, with each *Annual*'s component *Bulletins* immediately uploaded as and when they are complete.

All of which brings us bang up to date. Thanks for bearing with us,

Eds.

DARWENISM

Alex Coles, Neil Arthur & Jonathan Lindley

ALEX COLES   Both of you grew up in the northern UK town of Darwen in very different eras. Jonathan stayed and put together Sunbird Records, an independent label and venue, in the 2010s. But Neil, why did you need to leave to form the New Wave group Blancmange in the late '70s?

NEIL ARTHUR   To answer this I need to start at the beginning: I went to art college – initially a foundation course in Preston, and then London to study illustration. Like many young people, I had a love of music and was fortunate enough to be exactly the right age when punk hit. Even though it didn't last very long, the fireworks and aftershocks that came with punk made it an absolutely brilliant era for people of my age and it impacted on many of us in very different ways. Punk threw everything up in the air, and we had to pick up the pieces and find new means of expression with them. Eventually it became apparent that I was going to do music: I didn't necessarily think I was going to play an instrument, because in fact I couldn't. And that's part of the reason I did it.

ALEX COLES   In '76/'77 music was predominantly accessed through vinyl and live concerts. The platforms available were fewer, and took up more bandwidth. There was also a clearer delineation between mainstream culture and subculture. How did this affect the way in which the music you were drawn to circulated?

NEIL ARTHUR   Unlike today, news travelled relatively slowly. A mate introduced me to Roxy Music and then to Brian Eno and eventually to Krautrock. It was all via word of mouth and *New Musical Express*. In terms of live music there were only a few safe havens away from the mainstream. The Lode Star in Ribchester had Roxy and Bowie nights and these eventually led to it becoming a punk venue. The' other thing was fanzines. *Sniffin' Glue* was gold dust. As you say, most radio and TV stations played mainstream music, but late-night radio was different. First Radio Luxembourg, and then Radio 1 had John Peel, whose show was very eclectic and informative.

ALEX COLES   What's interesting is both the niche nature of that punk and post-punk subculture and the degree of importance assigned to the few platforms it played out on. Against this backdrop, what were the first pieces of music you wrote and recorded, and how were they accessed?

NEIL ARTHUR   Stephen Luscombe and myself had made cassette recordings of noises and semi-structured songs. We wanted to put synthesiser over it but couldn't afford one, so made our conventional instruments sound like synths instead. In 1980 we put out the do-it-yourself EP
Irene & Mavis together and had a thousand copies cut. I designed the
front of the sleeve and Stephen the back, which looked like it was typeset
but in fact was a photograph with the credits written on his bedroom wall
– cheaper than having it typeset and printed. In an afternoon we stuck
all the inner sleeves to the outer sleeves. With this record we started
looking into distribution. Twenty-five press copies were put aside and
fortunately ended up in the hands of significant people who helped us
along. But to sit comfortably within *NME* and the post-punk world we
should have named ourselves The Bleak Industrial Cooling Towers. Of
course we called ourselves Blancmange, and that made it very difficult.

JONATHAN LINDLEY   Three decades later, with Sunbird Records the goal was to
find new tactics for independent artists, as I believed a cartel was restricting
the movement of these self-governing cultural producers. I wanted to stay
in Darwen and design a label capable of critiquing this cartel. In 2016 I
opened a music venue to actively localise the experience of music. One
thing I wanted to ask you, Neil, is whether you think that digital distribution
like streaming services and shared networks act as a barrier today?

NEIL ARTHUR   I'm not sure by what you mean by a barrier. On the one
hand, having music accessible to a potentially larger audience should
be a good thing; on the other, royalty returns from streaming services
are not great. Is it better to have the music out there and for musicians
and producers to fight for a better return, or do we react by rejecting
streaming altogether? I wonder whether our music in the digital domain
has become more of a calling card, a means to build up a profile, and
perhaps that is its use.

JONATHAN LINDLEY   In coming out of punk during the mid-to-late '70s, you were
creating a classic subcultural narrative. But things must have changed quite
radically in the early '80s as that moment receded in your rear-view mirror
and Blancmange became more popular…

NEIL ARTHUR   I would have been quite happy for it to carry on ticking
along at that independent level, but a couple of things happened that

took us elsewhere: Rough Trade accepted a certain amount of our EPs, so by the time we got signed in 1982 Blancmange had built up a live presence by touring with the likes of Grace Jones and Japan. So we were quite happy to embrace this opportunity – to embrace pop – and said, 'Look, let's have a go at this'. Our first London Records single was *God's Kitchen* (1982) and the second single, *Feel Me* (1982), was a dance track. London just let us go with it, which we did. That is, until we decided to stop in 1986.

ALEX COLES   Can you give us a sense of the shift from working with independents, like Rough Trade, to being signed with a major such as London Records, in terms of the platforms you could then access and their impact on the type of music you made and the way it circulated?

NEIL ARTHUR   We didn't have a contractual relationship with Rough Trade: they took a few EPs from us on a sale-or-return basis, so our experiences with the two are not comparable. London Records wasn't going to accept cassette tapes as masters or a twenty-minute piece called 'Leek and Potato Soup' for the first single.

When it came to the artwork for our first album for London Records, *Happy Families* (1982), instead of Stephen and I saying, 'I'll do something for it tonight', and grabbing a picture from *Time Out* or somewhere, we were in discussion with the art department months in advance of the release. When it came to manufacturing the vinyl, instead of thousands it was tens of thousands, and it just moved at a very different rate. Suddenly we were in advertisements in the daily papers and being played on national radio. At this point, the label becomes an investor, 'the bank', and you become a unit for sale. Experiencing marketing as a means of broadening our presence was bizarre, absolutely bizarre. We were playing in Manchester on a sell-out tour to promote our second album, *Mange Tout* (1984), and saw a poster advertising it overlaid with graffiti saying 'Get Stuffed'. Someone in the marketing team obviously thought this was a good idea – and it was, but it signalled our loss of control to the bank's head of marketing.

JONATHAN LINDLEY   Like their counterpart labels, independent and grass-roots venues are currently at risk and adopt neo-tribal tactics like localisation and co-production in order to survive. This is one reason why I wanted to establish a venue alongside the label: to counteract what feels to me like a culture industry regressing towards an environment of absolute compliance whereby producers must use the given access points or be ignored. Do you think the industry and its consumers should be paying more attention to small venues, since they are catalysts for new forms of music?

NEIL ARTHUR   Yes – definitely for some types of music, as the small venues are where many bands get exposure and a chance to test and develop their material beyond the rehearsal room, garage or bedroom. They should be supported irrespective of whether it's an independent or a major label.

ALEX COLES   What you've been a part of with Blancmange is the transition from punk through early New Wave and onto the New Romantics' embracing of mainstream pop stardom. Or is that over-simplifying things?

NEIL ARTHUR   Punk and the DIY attitude was our inspiration. New Wave was happening, but we weren't aware that we were part of it – or anything else going on at the time. Later, having some success in the charts meant that we embraced the pop mainstream, but we never went near embracing the New Romantics. Do I look like someone who would dress up like a pirate?

In reaction to this, I decided I wanted to get off the treadmill and find a new way to do music away from the industry and its '80s-style machine. The chance to compose for film and TV meant I could work in the background more.

ALEX COLES   Blancmange split in 1986?

NEIL ARTHUR   Yes. It happened at the Royal Albert Hall, when I just looked around and didn't recognise what we were doing as Blancmange. We'd become something else and it wasn't what I wanted to do or where I wanted to be. Blancmange became a victim of the machine, and the record companies got a bit carried away with some of their ideas. They were convinced of their own infallibility.

ALEX COLES   Coming full circle – from 1977 to 2017 – do you feel that getting yourself back into a productive place has been partly triggered by becoming independent again?

NEIL ARTHUR   You've hit the nail on the head. What we did with *Blanc Burn* in 2011 (Proper Records) was to revisit our initial formula (even though we thought we never had one). We realised that control – of our music, its packaging and distribution – was crucial. With the help of friends, we set up a website and a method – initially using Fanbridge – to keep in touch with our audience. This was now a different world to the one in which we simply put Stephen's address on the back sleeve of our first EP in case someone wanted to contact us.

The first time around, in the '80s, there was always a sense that the record company would want to interfere with everything. So instead of saying 'I've written this, what do you think?', our new approach was to go to the company and say, 'This is finished, can you put it out?' They are two very different ways of going about the same thing. Even though both use the same amount of paper and words, the recipient has to respond in a completely different way. As we did with our first EP, in 2011 we decided to release something with all its flaws intact by presenting a finished album to a distributor. That attitude was exactly what we started with and tried to maintain in those few years in the '80s when we were signed to a major label – but the machine is really powerful, and sometimes you get dragged and pulled out of shape. I don't think there was an artist who went through that period who wasn't impacted in some way by this force.

JONATHAN LINDLEY   As you stated earlier, we now access information in a much faster way, and consumers appear to want to engage with culture faster, with as little commitment as possible. The larger cultural production lines are capable of responding to these demands more effectively. But do you think the majors still have – or should have – relevance, and are there ways for independent record labels to provide alternatives?

NEIL ARTHUR   I'm sure the major labels would argue that they are still relevant. Until recently I've had few direct dealings with them, save for issues with our back catalogue. The majors, like a huge ship wanting to change course in a small channel, need time and the help of tugs. Independents can shift tack relatively quickly.

ALEX COLES   With the recent 'super deluxe' edition of the Blancmange box set (*The Blancmange Tapes*, Edsel Records, 2017) it's interesting to watch a major record company repackage old content in a gambit for what could be considered the '80s nostalgia business. What keeps things interesting, I think, is the way you treat this as an opportunity to curate your past through the optic of your present music that is being released through more independent platforms.

NEIL ARTHUR   Recently our back catalogue was bought by a very interesting French label, Because Music, which was responsible for signing artists like Daft Punk and AIR. They're looking at sourcing our assets from the '80s, the original masters and the artwork, with a view to releasing them on vinyl in as close to their original state as is possible.

JONATHAN LINDLEY   With becoming independent again, does a greater degree of control allow your audience to access Blancmange more directly?

NEIL ARTHUR   If by that you mean access as contact, then at times yes. It can be beneficial to both sides: giving fans direct contact with us, and from our side the opportunity to build a database for future emails. I and my manager handle the social media and respond to fans' queries. This is undoubtedly a good thing in general, leading to situations that would not have arisen forty years ago.

In the first week that *Living on the Ceiling* (London Records, 1982) was released, I got a phone call to say 65,000 records had been sold in one day. Record sales like that are no longer common. Merchandise is a huge part of the whole experience we offer fans. Our merchandise distributor, Merch Cargo, and our e-commerce company, Townsend Music, are very important in this. Another big difference is that when I go out and do signings you can see it directly affecting the sales. I personally box up and label stuff, it arrives here and then we take it on tour. In this sense, it's very much a return to how we started out.

ALEX COLES   The generational difference partly explains it, but it's interesting to see how you've come full circle over nearly four decades. By contrast, with the label and venue in Darwen, Jonathan has chosen to stay with that initial independent platform and develop a micro-community around it. Where he has stayed north, you went south. What was your rationale for that at the time, especially given the success of labels like Zoo Records in Liverpool and Factory in Manchester?

NEIL ARTHUR   It was really easy for me because I didn't have any intention of making music when I was living up north, and it wasn't until I went to art college that I thought about getting a band together. Blancmange was always a London band.

JONATHAN LINDLEY   I had this vision of investing in my hometown instead of just moving to London, where everything was already exciting. I wanted to create a hotspot for culture in a location that was relatively cold. I've been working on the label for nearly six years, often struggling to convince people that supporting independent culture is worth their time, particularly when compared with the efficiency, scale and spectacle of major-label productions. What makes this even more difficult is the way these companies have well-established networks of consumers who already have a relationship with them. Establishing a unique and tactile relationship with your audience – and distributors – is crucial for the survival of an independent.

FROM VISHNU TO VEGAS

Rathna Ramanathan

It is 1988, the early hours of a September morning. The quiet corridors of the Lady Wellington Nursing Home in Chennai are interrupted by the faint echoes of a baby's cry, followed thirteen minutes later by another. Anxious family members (two sets of grandparents and aunts) stand outside the delivery room, waiting for the father to emerge with news. The nurse comes out cradling two babies, twin girls, one in each arm, bundled up in swathes of soft white cotton. You can only see a part of their faces but it is obvious that each has downy black locks covering their soft heads. The family is jubilant. It does not matter that the babies are not boys; their daughter has given birth to healthy, hungry twin girls. The babies are fair-skinned, with silky, thick, South Indian hair. They are beautiful.

The next morning, a lifelong daily ritual for girls in India begins. The babies' locks are oiled, washed and combed, and nurtured to grow. For South Indian women, long hair is a virtue. It is a sign of traditional beauty. South Indian women take great care of their hair, and learning to do this properly is a rite of passage for young women. It is usually never let loose, except within the privacy of the home. Chemicals are rarely used. It is also common practice in South India for mothers to berate their daughters for not having oiled and combed their hair in the mornings after bathing, as well as in the evenings before prayers are said.

On Sundays, in many South Indian households, it is a ritual for women to take an oil head bath. The ritual of the oil head bath entails soaking your hair and scalp in warmed sesame or coconut oil. After an hour of soaking in, the oil is washed off with a natural soap, usually shikkai, which is made from the fruit of a wattle called acacia concinna. The dark brown powder carries a distinctive smell and is said to both soften and reinforce the hair. The hair is then air-dried with incense smoke, using hot coals and sambrani powder, made from benzoin resin. The entire process is said to reduce hair loss as well as reduce stress, since the combination of warm oil, hot water and scented smoke is deeply relaxing. During the week, Indian women usually wear braids – for neatness, but also to keep away the dust, heat and sweat of the tropics. The hair is oiled for conditioning and a small garland, usually of jasmine, is woven in for scent.

When the twin girls are two years old, the family takes a road trip to the famous Tirumala Tirupati Devasthanams temple in a neighbouring state in Southern India. The temple is 133 kilometres away from Chennai by road, in the temple town of Tirupati, in the Chittor district of Andhra

Pradesh, right by the Tamil Nadu / Andhra Pradesh state border. The area is also known as the Tirumala Hills, which are 2,799 feet above sea level, comprising seven peaks. The temple sits on the top of the seventh peak, Venkatadri.

Tirumala Tirupati Devasthanams is a landmark Hindu temple dedicated to Lord Venkateswara, an incarnation of Vishnu who is believed by Hindus to have appeared in order to save mankind from the age of Kali Yuga. The name 'Venkateshwara' means 'the God who can destroy all sins' in Sanskrit. There are inscriptions on the temple walls that date back to 614 AD. The Alvars, who were religious saints, praise the temple in their accounts of around the fifth century AD. Different ruling kings in Southern India – Krishna Deva Raya and Achyuta Deva Raya, Sadasiva Raya and Tirumala Deva Raya – helped maintain and expand the temple from medieval times until the seventeenth century. The temple, built in the southern Dravidian architectural style, survived invasions from both the Persians and the British. The inscriptions in the temple are in different languages – Sanskrit (the business language of early India) and Tamil, Telugu and Kannada (the languages of the three nearest states). Signs directing visitors to the temple today carry five languages – Hindi, Tamil, Telugu, Kannada and English. It is the most visited holy place in the world, with roughly 40–50 million pilgrims visiting the temple each year, bearing different offerings. There is a myth behind this story. When planning his wedding to the goddess Padmavathi, Vishnu accumulated a large debt to Kubera, the gods' treasurer. This is a loan that Vishnu is still paying off. When pilgrims bring offerings, they believe that they are helping Lord Vishnu to repay his lifelong debt.

The family of the twin two-year-old girls is here to offer their hair to Lord Vishnu. This is an offering of thanks for their good health and well-being. They are not alone. Every day, hundreds of pilgrims shave their heads in an offering to Lord Vishnu. The temple is amongst the largest collectors of human hair in the world, amassing roughly 500 metric tonnes (500,000 kg) a year. Tirumala Tirupati Devasthanams is also the world's top supplier of 'Remy' hair or 'temple' hair, which is also called 'virgin' hair because it is uncoloured and untreated. Remy hair is collected and cut by the temple barbers in such a way as to preserve its strength, feel and lustre. This is the most prized, best quality hair you can buy.

But why offer your hair? The myth is that Lord Venkateshwara was once hit on his head by a shepherd, resulting in a bald spot. This was noticed by the Gandharva princess Neeladevi, who cut a portion of her hair and implanted it on his scalp with healing powers. Lord Venkateshwara is said to have acknowledged her sacrifice – a significant one, because hair is considered an essential part of South Indian beauty – by naming one of the surrounding hills after her. Today, for many South Indian women, giving one's hair to God is also seen as an act of giving up being egotistical about one's physical appearance. To sacrifice one's beauty to the gods is believed to bring good luck, and it is also a way of giving thanks. Eighty-five percent of Indian people, men and women alike, have had their heads tonsured.

It is early in the morning, and yet there is already a large crowd eager to make their offerings. Slippers are removed at the entrance. Barefoot, the crowd inches forward through a series of gates to the temple's cutting area, known as the Kalayana Katta. The concrete floors are cold as one moves nearer to the centre, where the family is greeted by a uniformed temple representative who hands them two paper tokens with two pictures of Lord Venkateshwara. At the next station, another gentleman hands over two clean razor blades enclosed in waxed paper. Further down a staircase, men and women are separated into different rooms. Each person goes into a vast, white-tiled room with long lines of temple barbers sitting along the walls waiting for the devotees.

The twins, one held by each grandmother, are placed in front of the barbers. Next to the twins is a woman with long, thick, black locks that reach down to her waist. The barber gestures to her to unplait it and begins to shave it off. She, like many women around her, is here to make an offering to Lord Vishnu in the hope of overcoming problems in her life that she has been unable to solve herself. For Chellamma, it is a drunken husband who does not work or support the family. When asked about giving up her beautiful black tresses, she says it is about faith. If you believe things will be of help, and if you give with this belief, then it makes you feel better. She says that giving up her hair will bring her some peace of mind. Others are here to give thanks. Rajiamma is shaving her head in gratitude, honouring a vow she took after her father recovered from a critical operation.

The twins' hair is collected in a bucket by a temple worker, and then emptied into one of the tall steel vats that stand in the cutting room. The hair in the vats is collected daily and is auctioned by the temple every Thursday at 1pm. According to the newspaper *The Indian Express*, the temple has a steady revenue of 23 million US dollars a year from hair auctions, though in some years this figure has risen to 46 million US dollars.

Hair is big business in India, and much of this happens in the states of Tamil Nadu, Andhra Pradesh and Karnataka – the three states that surround the Tirumala Tripathi temple. Each year, India exports 540 million US dollars' worth of hair. Seventy percent of the world's hair business is in synthetic hair, and 30 percent is temple and 'comb waste' hair. Indian exports make up 80 percent of the latter category, which is the most expensive and sought after. In May 2017, the newspaper *The Hindu* published an article on the Narikuravars, peripatetic gypsies who live 120 kilometres outside the capital city, Chennai. At 6am every morning, the Narikuravar women and men travel on their mopeds and motorbikes to collect human hair from households. This is comb waste hair, saved by women of the household following their daily combing, or small collected tufts of hair that have fallen from people's heads. Some Narikuravars show an ingenuity in this daily adventure, and travel with a taped message which they broadcast as they drive by. They pay a rupee for every gram of hair. They take any amount, big or small. They take any colour, including grey. There are even dark rumours of hair collection for the black market, whereby women asleep in public spaces or watching films in dark cinemas have their hair cut without permission. The hair is then sold to auctioneers further up the market chain, eventually reaching a hair exporter, at which point the hair is checked for lice, washed and untangled.

Not far from the back streets in which the Narikuravars travel, situated in the T. Nagar shopping area of Chennai, is Raj Hair International, one of the top Indian exporters of hair. Raj Hair International receives 10–15 metric tonnes a month of temple hair from Tirupati. They note that this hair is considered the best in the market for its quality and length. On one of the floors, a big airy sunlit room is filled with women seated on stools at low tables amongst blue plastic packing crates. They wear green shower caps and face masks for hygiene, and sift the mounds of hair between them. In another room, with a shiny white tiled floor, more women are sitting behind weaving looms. This part of Southern India is renowned for its silk looms that create wonderful heavy gold silk saris, called Kanchipuram silks. These looms, however, are divided into sections depending on the kind of hair they are weaving. This is the Steam Curly Section.

Raj Hair International ships hair to 56 countries. The United States is a big market, as is Africa. The number of products offered on the company's website is mind-boggling. There are choices of Remy and non-Remy hair. Hair products include machine hair wefts, hand hair wefts, clip-ons, Keratin-tipped extensions, hair closures and wigs. Further to this is a range of colours for each of the products: virgin colours (black, dark and light brown, dark, medium and light grey); blonde colours of 11 different shades; and 'international' colours of 42 different shades, from every natural colour of hair imaginable to bright greens, yellows, pinks and purples. The company exports about 12 metric tonnes of finished hair products annually; in order to do this, they process double that amount of hair. After processing, the hair sells at $400–700 per kilogram, de-pending on its length; the longer the hair, the greater the demand and the higher the cost. According to an interview in *The Hindu* with Benjamin Cherian, Chairman and Founder of Raj Hair International, Chennai, Michelle Obama's hair extensions are made of Remy hair sourced by Raj Hair International. His extended client list includes Shakira, Queen Latifah, Sofia Vergara and Lady Gaga. He also has a list of US films featuring wigs or extensions supplied by him: *The Hunger Games*, *Pirates of the Caribbean*, *X-Men*, *50 First Dates* and *Planet of the Apes*, amongst others.

Stories of the global hair trade crop up in the international mass media and in local publications. India is not the only source of the raw product: Cambodia, Peru, China and the Ukraine are also big exporters of human hair. There are reports in UK newspapers of women and children being exploited by the hair trade in countries such as Peru: 'Very small amounts of money are being paid for something so personal and which takes a long time to produce, and children who sell their hair often don't have a choice'.[1] In 2012, *The Guardian* carried a story about London salons, such as Great Lengths, whose business is in hair extensions made with Remy hair. The article notes that the company works with an Indian representative to ensure that the raw material is donated willingly, and that the money goes back to the local community.

Just Extensions is a popular hair salon in Los Angeles. They specialise in extensions. The salon website offers several packages, organised in four categories: Just Pretty, Just Beautiful, Just Gorgeous

1.   Tanith Carey and Francesca Cookney, 'The ugly truth behind multi-milion pound hair extensions industry', *The Mirror*, 8 March 2016, https://www.mirror.co.uk/news/world-news/ugly truth-behind-multi-million-7513507.

and Just Amazing. You can 'apply' hair to your own hair in multiple ways – micro-links, keratin tips, braided sew-ins, beaded sew-ins, skin wefts and clip-ins. The hair is attached to your scalp using glue, double-sided tape, clips, wax, or thread. This is not a fancy Hollywood parlour but one that is popular with everyday American women, particularly black women. Those who visit hold a variety of jobs: some are teachers, and some are students, budding lawyers, doctors and actresses. A single bundle of Indian natural-wave hair costs about $140, and the salon's recommendation is to buy at least two or three bundles. But that is just the material cost. In addition, there is the making of the kind of look you want – you are offered a consultation and then an application. In the US, it can cost anything from $1,000 to $3,500 to get your extensions made with real hair. The charge is based on originality, creativity and style; the more bespoke the look, the higher the cost. Black American women refer to their hair with different adjectives — natural, curly, straight, processed, silkener, dreads, good hair, nappy hair. Good hair is straight and 'natural looking' whilst 'nappy hair' is a derogatory term used to refer to Afro-textured hair. It appears that standards of beauty for black American women are led by Asian and Caucasian hair. In India, it is the Caucasian styling and colour of hair that is considered more attractive among middle-class and upper-class women. As Maya Angelou noted, 'hair is a woman's glory'. Nowadays, you have the freedom to change your hair as easily as you change your shoes.

In 2016, BBC News interviewed Benjamin Cherian. He noted in the broadcast that he sees his future in Africa. The Raj showroom in T. Nagar, Chennai, is popular with customers from Africa and with African-American women. Cherian describes the joy that he sees lighting up the faces of women when they walk into his showroom. Is it our place to judge? Sue Walsh, Creative Director at SYPartners and a member of faculty at School of Visual Arts, noted in a recent article: 'Our imaginations are born from our pasts, our presents, our hopes, our desires, our heartbreaks—creating a unique vantage point. Each of us brings this landscape of our lives to how we see and perceive the world. We each see through the lens of the most significant frame: our own identity. To ignore this is to ignore the reality of being human.'[2]

2.   Sue Walsh, 'Between Image and Reality: How We All Perceive the World', *Observer*, 21 December 2016, http://observer.com/2016/12/between-image-and-reality-how-we-all-perceive-the-world/.

When the story of India's hair exporting is shared with Chellamma, she is philosophical. If it benefits God, she has earned peace of mind twice over. Then she comments: 'I have only heard of America and will never have a chance to visit there. At least my hair will have had the opportunity to travel.'

The twins are both adults now, and recently married. In their wedding ceremonies, their special hairstyles were supported by hair that was not their own. These were expensive Remy extensions, which are now becoming all the rage in India. As India modernises, how much of the centuries-old tradition of tonsure will be maintained remains to be seen. As Cherian notes, as long as men and women still want to look beautiful, there will be a business in hair.

THIS IS FOR YOU

David Blamey

The most rewarding work often goes unpaid. Or, to put it more precisely, work's most valuable compensation need not take monetary form. Those who volunteer their services, operate from a position of deeply held belief, with a sense of *karma*, or just for the pleasure of participation and contact with other people, often do so in the hope that their actions might cause an influence that has a positive effect further down the line.

What goes around comes around.

Please Like Me

The passing of Horace Duke in 1995 removed from public life an extraordinary character visible on the West Sussex streets for more than twenty years. Known locally as 'the Mad Major', 'the Duke of Shoreham', 'the Toff' and 'Burlington Bertie', Mr. Duke enjoyed dressing up as a gentleman of class from a bygone era and posing at points of maximum visibility between Worthing and Shoreham-by-Sea. The sole purpose of this endeavour was to incite a response from members of the public as they drove past in their cars. Dressed impeccably in a striped blazer, flannel trousers, straw boater, white gloves and monocle, 'Bertie' was a figure of particular sartorial extravagance dislocated in space and time. To some he was nothing more than an eccentric, but for others 'Bertie' represented something quintessential within the English cultural context.

According to the slim amount of documentary evidence available, it seems that Mr. Duke began his self-image dissemination project some time in the 1960s, when he used a small motorcycle to travel to the various locations that were his favourite places to be seen. In a local 1967 newspaper interview he claimed to have only jettisoned the motor for a pedal cycle when his plus fours caught fire on the hot cylinder while journeying home to Lancing from Arundel one day. A competing account by someone who knew him at the time, however, states that the switch to his better-known sit-up-and-beg bicycle occurred when a new law was introduced in the UK to prohibit riding a motorbike without a helmet. This account seems more plausible, the humour of the news report notwithstanding, given our protagonist's demonstrable commitment to the top hat and boater and the obvious inconvenience of incorporating a crash hat into the range of clothing ensembles that he liked to wear.

I remember seeing 'Bertie' periodically throughout the summers of my teenage years in the 1970s, most commonly outside The Bridge Inn in Shoreham High Street, or at the Saltings roundabout on the A259. His appearance always came as a bit of a shock. It was probably the first time I'd seen a man taking such obvious pleasure from adoring himself, other than the odd Glam rocker who happened to appear on *The Old Grey Whistle Test*. There was actually something a little sinister about him, irrespective of the hilarity and camp posturing. He could strike a pose that embodied the kind of darkness sometimes attributed to clowns. One commentator, posting on the *Brighton & Hove Albion North Stand Chat* forum, recalls: 'That guy gave me the creeps. I remember being stuck in traffic on the roundabout once and I looked at him and he looked back at me in a way that made my blood run cold...' Another report says: 'He could be an obnoxious piece of work at times. I remember him yelling abuse at motorists on Grove Lodge more than once'. There are certainly plenty of testaments to the breadth of his vocabulary when it came to swearing, but apparently he knew that there was a line to be drawn between his everyday self and the character that he adopted and put on display. A local postman who delivered mail to the Marylebone Optical Company in Worthing, where Mr. Duke was employed for most his career, has a thought on this: 'He was great to talk to but warned me never to speak to him when he was dressed up, as he is a completely different person then'. To most people, though, the arrival of 'Burlington Bertie' at the roundabout in Shoreham seemed to signal the end of winter each year. Wider opinion on his antics was overwhelmingly supportive. A writer notes, on the online *Kent Sussex Hants History Forum*: 'In reality he was just a humble cleaner living in a bedsit without much of a social circle. His main contact with people was dressing up [...] He was a lovely bloke whose death left the world a less colourful place.'

One wonders what the impulse was that compelled Mr. Duke to make such an intriguing public statement in this way? To suggest that brightening up the lives of other people or enjoying dressing up were valid reasons seems a little frivolous to me. Couldn't this over-the-top visual statement be a cry for help that no one heeded, rather than the narcissistic frolics of a fool? It was hard to tell. With his bicycle typically propped up against the kerb by a pedal, 'Bertie' seemed to us an exotic stripy creature from a faraway place. His acts of preening, marking territory, and displaying his worth were reminiscent of the Australian bowerbird's enticement behaviour. Could all this drama have been a futile courtship ritual in which the male dressed up like a dandy and stood at a busy roadside in a doomed attempt to attract a passing mate?

The isolating conditions that make us yearn for deeper interconnectedness in today's commodity culture certainly resonates in Mr. Duke's 'Burlington Bertie' manifestation. His alter-ego image may have been given away without any apparent recompense, but it circulated as a talking point around which a kinship was created and reinforced. Echoing social models of unification in tribal societies where goods and actions that have no intrinsic value are exchanged for purely symbolic reasons, Horace Duke's representational offering placed himself at the centre of a community of his own making. His act of goodwill may have confronted recipients with an outrageous image of opulence that was far beyond their reach, but a remarkable effect of this was a boost to his own social standing in a way that wasn't possible in the workplace.

Teenagers used to taunt 'Bertie'. He seemed to enjoy the attention, whether it was favourable or not. My father liked to try to get a bit of a reaction from him by honking the horn of our Austin Princess as we passed by on family days out. 'Bertie' would shudder with pleasure at this – especially if he considered our advances complimentary. There is a short video clip[1] of him online that manages to capture a typical reaction to a positive horn blast. He flinches in theatrical ecstasy before resuming his promenade. It's as if the object of his transient desire has physically touched him, the way that he responds. The transaction that takes place between suitor and subject via the mutual act of recognition is in a strange way, enacted as a kind of 'dominance and submission' exchange of power. It just isn't altogether clear who has control over the other's actions. Another commentator, this time posting on the *Kent Sussex Hants History Forum*, shrewdly observes: 'Isn't that what's now described as performance art?' Well, yes, it could be. But this craving for recognition also relates to the alienation in late twentieth-century life and the burgeoning human need to prove our existence that Jean Baudrillard recognised when he said: 'The need to speak, even if one has nothing to say, becomes more pressing when one has nothing to say, just as the will to live becomes more urgent when life has lost its meaning'.[2] In the parlance of social media, it seems probable that Mr. Duke just wanted to be 'liked'.

1.   www.youtube.com/watch?v=oJi7OtrMC5M – David Harris shot this video footage (c.1989) in North Lancing, close to where Horace Duke lived.
2.   Jean Baudrillard, *The Ecstasy of Communication* (New York: Semiotext(e), 1988).

The Artist Will (No Longer) Be Present

Following a £260m revamp by the Swiss architectural practice Herzog & de Meuron, on 17 June 2016 Tate Modern opened its new Switch House galleries with a permanent collection exhibition on Level 2, titled: 'Between Object and Architecture'. The display thematically gathers together a constellation of works made during the last forty years or so that either looks like architecture, is made with materials associated with construction (such as bricks, breeze blocks, building site detritus, spirit levels, etc.), or is displayed in relation to the new building's architectural features. Tate's press release says that the works in the exhibition are notable for their determination to be brought down from the pedestal – a support structure which has traditionally separated art from the viewer – and placed directly onto the floor, or attached to the wall. The idea behind this presentation, then, is for the spectator to engage more directly with the art by un-inhibiting the conditions under which it would normally be displayed.

This intention was amply embodied by much of the work, but one piece pitted itself against the museum's rhetoric and raised some interesting questions about the power of art institutions, the rules of the art world and artists' complicity in limiting the reach of their own work. Leaning against the back wall of the gallery, next to a floor-to-ceiling window that looks down on the bookshop below, stands a skinny rod of cylindrical wood blocks. About the length of a pilgrim's staff, the individual segments that make up the rod are painted in a scale of recurring colours: red, white, yellow and green. The separate shades have dulled to suggest a bit of age, and any precision in the object's line of trajectory from the floor to the wall that may have been present at the time of its making is gone. The succession of cheerfully coloured components sags ever so gently in the middle, under the weight of gravity and time. Titled *Round Bar of Wood* (1973), the work is by André Cadere, a migrant artist from behind the Iron Curtain who plied his trade in Paris in the 1970s before being taken by cancer at the age of 43.

Cadere was a one-idea artist. He travelled a single path. During his career he made 180 'round bars of wood', each following the same system of colour permutations. The colours employed were always black, white and the six colours of the rainbow: yellow, orange, red, violet, blue and green. The one at Tate Modern is composed of fifty-two segments that account for every combination possible of the four colours chosen, plus a repetition of the first four and a built-in error. The last sequence of colours is always a repeat of the first, reflecting the artist's view that a pole came to its natural conclusion as soon as the first group of colours reappeared. The mistake is introduced to the mathematical system on purpose to create, as Cadere said, a dialectical link between order and error. These 'mistakes' also relax the formality of the chromatic compositions and deprive the eye of an opportunity to detect a pattern. This effect of schematic uncertainty also raises the prospect that there might be some other purpose to this handiwork, some deeper intent.

In fact, the true significance of these poles has very little to do with how they look, but more about *how* and *where* they appeared. Their presence in the art world during the 1970s stems from Cadere's arrival in the West from Communist Romania and his sense of being an outsider – but crucially, one with an unshakable determination to infiltrate the dominant cultural circuit, come what may. The tactic employed to inculcate himself was as opportunistic as it was symbolic: he simply turned up at other people's exhibitions with his wooden poles and installed them temporarily, either by placing them in a suitably visible place or carrying one under his arm as he mingled with the crowd. He said in an interview about his strategy: 'I can go to the Museum of Modern Art or Castelli's and present my work without anyone inviting me'.[3] One can only imagine the sort of reception he might have got from fellow artists, let alone the snobby dealers who controlled the commercial art world at the time. He says of this: 'Obviously, it is not because I go to Castelli's that I am exhibited there. [But] nothing can prevent me from being concretely, materially inside the place. He can throw me out, and it's interesting if he does. This has happened elsewhere, and in other circumstances. When the institution defends itself, it becomes, in no uncertain terms, brutal and aggressive.' And, on the reasons why other artists might feel that he was a louse for gatecrashing the openings of their shows, he cites: 'Jealousy and competition, for the most part'. This was art that must have divided audiences and artists alike, and yet, by persisting and remaining true to his cause, Cadere began to build a network around his interventions. He became a familiar figure on the scene. In due course the Minimal art dealer Yvon Lambert showed an interest and the rods began to sell. He

3.   Sylvère Lotringer, Issue 8, *Schizo-Culture: André Cadere,* (New York: Semiotext(e), 1978).

was eventually invited to exhibit at the ICA, documenta 5 and in many private galleries across Europe and worldwide.

The thing that appeals so much about this venture isn't the folksy irregularity of the wooden bars' minimal colours and proportions, nor the delightfully chippy attitude that Cadere holds against the establishment that he's so keen to impress, but rather the idea that, by cutting out middlemen, the artist will always be present when his work is on display. Holding his own art, instead of just screwing it to the wall and walking away, enabled Cadere to create a mobile condition of engagement in which viewers were forced to consider the work in relation to the art system. In a conversation with Lynda Morris in 1976 he says bluntly: 'My art is the situation of my work in the art world'.[4] This objective was ably achieved by operating in the margin between 'closed' museum and 'open' public space. Whether standing in the crowd at the opening of a show, walking in the street to an exhibition or sitting in a pub near one of the important galleries, his *modus operandi* opened up a conversation about where the 'art world' and the 'real world' begins and ends, and about the art gallery as a structure of power that needs to be challenged.

In his book *The Gift*,[5] Lewis Hyde argues that although art can circulate simultaneously in two economies (market and gift) there exists a conflict of interests for the artist whose source is the gift of creative talent, but whose livelihood is dependent on a commercial context. The reasoning here is that when thought of as a gift, what we get from art beyond selling or owning it is a kind of 'blessing'. The artist shares his gift, Hyde proposes, in a way that 'revives the soul'. A problem with this analysis, as the author openly acknowledges, is the emergence of a state of affairs wherein the twin spheres of 'gift' and 'market' economies become mutually exclusive. If a fundamental difference between gift and commodity exchange is that giving establishes a bond between two people, while selling leaves no meaningful connection, does the art market always taint the purity of the work of art? The example of Cadere's insightful navigation between the separate spheres exposed this predicament, but in so doing generated understanding – and understanding, the avatar of knowledge, is itself a gift.

Today, in the absence of the artist, leaning against the wall of the Tate gallery stands the red, white, yellow and green staff by André Cadere that was purchased in 2006. Much against the wishes of its maker, it has

4.   Lynda Morris, *Documenting Cadere: 1972-1978* (Modern Art Oxford, 2008).
5.   Lewis Hyde, *The Gift: How the Creative Spirit Transforms the World* (Edinburgh: Canongate Books, 2006).

become more beautiful over the years. (Cadere once said in a lecture: 'Tones are rejected because they would automatically make the work harmonic and aesthetic'.) In this formal setting, unaccompanied and framed by the protective cord of a barrier system, we can only admire the work for its use as a prop in a performance that took place many years ago. Where once *Round Bar of Wood* (1973) operated as a modern version of the ancient native talking stick, an instrument of democracy and symbol of the holder's authority to speak in public with whoever came his way, sadly now the conversation has moved on. On this winter Sunday morning most visitors to the gallery are thronging around a peek-a-boo mirror piece by Yayoi Kusama: it offers a more interesting photo-opportunity to people carrying smartphones.

Spread Love

If you were a part of the generation that benefited from that moment in 1980s culture that mixed socially progressive ideals with all the advantages that relative global stability and social mobility provided, you will be familiar with the concept of the 'gap', or 'sabbatical', year. Generally understood as an extended period of time away from your accustomed environment, the 'break' interlude was created to change a person through the experience of contrasting a different system for living with the stagnation and predictability of your own life. A typical manifestation of the idea was for UK teenagers to go to Israel and live in utopian agricultural communities called *kibbutzim*. I seem to remember there was a military association with this option that didn't appeal to everyone; more of a draw in my social circle was the ashram version put forward by The Beatles, who went to India in between albums in the 1960s to expand their consciousness under the guidance of Maharishi Mahesh Yogi, founder of the Transcendental Meditation movement. In both cases, though, there was a suggestion that time out from normality of this kind provided the space to make a journey of moral or spiritual significance, akin to a pilgrimage. Many people in the West made such expeditions during the 1980s and '90s in reaction to the culture of individualism that was developing. Instead of accepting the Gordon Gekko adage that 'greed is good', free-thinking and disillusioned prospectors went out in search of inspiration from other people's way of life.

It was against this cultural backdrop that I first became aware of a female Hindu spiritual leader in India known as Amma, who was gaining a rosy reputation for dispensing doses of unconditional love via a disarmingly simple transference technique: the hug. Something formally reminiscent of Richard Long's 1968 hand-shaking performance – but preceding Marina Abramović's invitation to gaze into her eyes by more than twenty years – here was someone else who seemed to be giving away something personal for free. The difference was that in this case the offer wouldn't end: the hugger will hug all day, every day, for her whole life.

The story goes that as a child 'The Hugging Mother' (Mata Amritanandamayi) demonstrated an unusual empathy with other people's suffering. She often gave her own food to more needy strangers, consoled the sick, spent long hours meditating by the seashore and once even sucked pus out of the contagious wound of a leper to relieve his pain. Years of contemplating the hardship of others led Amma to cultivate a practical notion of *karma*, the Hindu spiritual principle of cause and effect in this life and the next: she simply concluded that inaction was an inappropriate response to another person's distress. She says: 'If it is one man's *karma* to suffer, isn't it our *dharma* (duty) to help ease his suffering and pain?'

Amma is unusual among Indian gurus in that she is a self-made success. Instead of spending years training with an instructor, as would be normal practice in a spiritual quest, she seemingly achieved full enlightenment on her own. Buoyed by a resulting sense of duty 'to lend a helping hand to those less fortunate', as it says on her website, Amma was then able to 'move forward with confidence in her life of service and compassionate care for all beings' through the unique expression of a 'motherly embrace...' Initially setting up shop in a cowshed at home, she began to receive people for *darshan*, a Sanskrit term roughly translated as 'auspicious sight of a holy person'. Audiences responded favourably to her kindness. Her reputation spread. Soon she welcomed visitors from all around the globe. The idea of hugging people took off and over a thirty-year period since its inception she has reputedly embraced more than thirty-three million people.

Many who receive the hug are so profoundly moved by the experience that they donate money to Amma's various charitable causes. It is estimated that three million dollars can be raised in one of her seven-week hugging tours. Accusations have inevitably been made that the love giveaway is cynically planned to make a lot of money by harnessing the concept that experience can be commercialised. From the perspective of behavioural economics we know that people gravitate towards the free offer because, once obtained, it generates a perception that what is being given is immensely more valuable than it really is. But what price can be put on love? Even if the merchandise (branded key rings, dolls, stickers, postcards and cassette tapes, etc.) is a bit tacky, Amma's various health, education, housing and sanitation initiatives are funded partly by its sale. Using divine authority (albeit self-appointed) has enabled her to build an effective administration that is the envy of India's public and commercial sectors. Stories of gold bars being smuggled out of the country under the robes of her *swamis* only serve to increase the mythology surrounding her enterprise. A good way to think about any shady business that might go on would be to weigh it in the balance with the amount of good that comes from her talent for redistributing other people's wealth.

Inspired by these and other accounts from fellow travellers while on a sabbatical of my own in India, I decided to make the journey to Amritapuri ashram on the coast of Kerala one New Year to procure a measure of eternal love for myself. Descriptions of the experience had been inspiring. People spoke of having their problems dissolved, of bursting into tears of joy, and of being overcome by a profound sense of comfort, clarity and calm. Naturally, I was curious to investigate these testimonies and to understand what strategy lay behind the scheme. But I was also fully open to the possibility that something in my life could change.

First impressions of the ashram on arrival mostly related to scale. Indeed, the hugging business had become an enormous undertaking since its humble debut. Behind the entrance gates stood two enormous concrete skyscrapers built to sleep up to 5,000 permanent and semi-permanent residents at a time, a meeting hall where the mass hugging takes place and a couple of canteens that provided everyone's food. The place was swarming with visitors. There were many Western faces in the crowd, some of which were drawn in lines of obsessive devotion. I had seen these signs before: at Osho's ashram in Pune and at the Dhamma Giri Vipassana meditation centre at Igatpuri, where emaciated western inmates slunk around the gardens like zombies in faded Swadeshi robes. After registering my attendance at a busy reception desk I soaked up the harmonious atmosphere for a few hours before proceeding to my dormitory bed, in preparation for an early rise.

The travel alarm went off at 6am. Slipping into a pair of drawstring trousers and a Khadi shop *kurta*, I quickly made my way to the auditorium downstairs where *bhajans* were already in full flow. There were so many pairs of shoes and sandals left on the steps leading up to the hall that I was fearful of missing out on an early place in the queue. Once I was inside, a warden gave me a numbered token and directed me to my seat. Bleary-eyed but excited, I settled down and waited for Amma to arrive. By 9am there were thousands of people in attendance. All of a sudden the 'Hugging Mother' appeared. She joined the final *bhajan* before taking up a position on a cushioned throne, from whence her blessings would be bestowed. Everything was meticulously organised, and yet it was disconcerting to see sudden groups of newcomers pour into the *darshan* line entrance ahead of our group. It was then that I remembered the 'flexible' queuing system at the High Commission of India visa office in London, so I asked one of the wardens if there was a quicker way to proceed. He simply gave me a new token and directed me to a special line for people who were 'short of time'.

With Amma and her heaving entourage within sight now I contemplated the hug that was soon to come my way. The Mother's healing embrace is said to set us on the true path to self-realisation, but as our line draws closer I begin to have doubts. Two Indian boys behind me have brought ballpoint pens with them to be blessed for success in their forthcoming exams. But why am I here? What's to stop me from just walking away? As I reach the edge of the stage where Amma is sitting, the Amritapuri ashramites are pressed so closely together that it would be difficult to turn around now. A rush of emotion rises unexpectedly within me and I have to struggle to keep control. Incense and drum-beats hang heavily in the air. An usher pushes me to my knees and I inch my way towards her chair. She is smiling and holding a man, his head buried in the folds of her white gown. There are attendants translating her words into different languages, and countless followers meditate while devotional songs reach fever pitch from the hall below. Suddenly I'm in her breast with both my arms wrapped around her waist. I'm aware that she's rocking me gently for the briefest of moments and muttering something in my ear, but then I just sink into tranquillity and peace. Like a child I'm consumed by her love. There is simply no way to resist.

LIFE IS GOOD & GOOD FOR YOU IN NEW YORK [1]

Billie Muraben

1.	William Klein, *Life is Good & Good For You in New York: Trance Witness Revels* (London: Photography Magazine,1956).

As Rufus Humphrey prepares for the opening of the latest exhibition at his eponymous gallery, for which no one has RSVP'd, Lily van der Woodsen-Bass – née Rhodes, and formerly Humphrey and Bass – is arranging the final details for her Sotheby's auction, to benefit the Art Production Fund. Scandal ensues.

It's episode six of the sixth season of the US drama *Gossip Girl*, which was broadcast from 2007 to 2012 and produced by Stephanie Savage and Josh Schwartz – of *The OC* – for The CW. The ruling passion is power. It's dry with a dash of satire – knowing and sarcastic, without losing the magic of the unreal. *Gossip Girl* embraced the truth of our never really leaving high school, and festooned it with the perks of adulthood.

The teen drama focused on exactly that: the trials and tribulations of insufferable, privileged teenagers as they navigate addiction, affairs, murder and property empires, and dip in and out of being related to each other. Rampantly jealous and wildly loyal, the central characters – Serena van der Woodsen, Blair Waldorf, Nate Archibald, Chuck Bass and Dan Humphrey – oscillate around each other, twisting and turning between love and hate. The story goes that an anonymous blogger, Gossip Girl, is tracking the every move of the senior class at a prep school on New York's Upper East Side; and the show opens with the mysterious return of former 'Queen Bee' Serena, who disappeared to a Connecticut boarding school after sleeping with the boyfriend of Blair (her BFF), among other dramas.

Gossip Girl may be one of the first programmes to engage so enthusiastically with the inanimate as character. The disembodied voice of Gossip Girl – who turns out to be played by a man – is a woman, who plays what may be considered the central role, and is not 'seen' or 'known' until the final episode. She/he/it lives in the mobile phones and on the screens of the characters, and directs their lives. Arguably, the animated inanimate precedes the animate.

Through the six seasons the characters speed through relationships, surnames, jobs, colleges and principalities, and although the teen amateur oligarchs are certainly busy, the central characters populating *Gossip Girl*'s New York aren't always the teen idols. First there's the aforementioned disembodied narrative voice of Gossip Girl and second the artwork – closely followed by the borderline hysterical product placement.

In 2007, the executive producers behind *Gossip Girl* worked with the Art Production Fund (APF) – a non-profit organisation which produces public art projects – on one of the first instances of a collaboration between a TV series and contemporary artists. In consultation with the *Gossip Girl* team, APF chose works by artists such as Kiki Smith, Marilyn Minter, Ryan McGinley and Richard Phillips, which were hung in the penthouse apartments and hotel suites populated by the key screen families.

The main location was Lily van der Woodsen's apartment, and her 'collection' was unveiled in the fifth episode of Season 2. She enters the apartment already in conversation with her art consultant, Bex, who, on exiting the lift, introduces Lily to her newly adorned surroundings:

BEX Kiki Smith greeting you in the foyer, Elm & Drag pulling you into the main room...

LILY I love that.

BEX And making a statement on the stairwell, Richard Phillips.

LILY ...isn't it just breathtaking?

BEX Any museum would be thrilled.

Richard Phillips' *Spectrum* is the star piece. Hung at the centre of the space, above the glass stairwell, it features not only in conversation but also as a central character. Known by the core gang as 'the rainbow woman', in the final season the painting is embroiled in an elaborate scheme.

The episode's title is 'Where the Vile Things Are', and *Spectrum* is at centre stage. Nate, the local all-American, dead-behind-the-eyes good guy, has a rare brainwave and steals the phone of the financial advisor to Bart Bass (the formerly dead, hotelier father of Chuck, Nate's best friend), in the hope of unearthing the secret of where Bart has hidden a suspicious envelope – the records of an illegal oil deal with a Sudanese sheikh. (Really.)

Nate and Chuck trawl the phone for clues and find one in its calendar: 'Bass, *Traffic*'. It turns out that the advisor records each of his money-saving plots with the name of a film, and in this case it's *Traffic*, a film in which, as Chuck kindly explains, 'the head of the drug cartel stored his illegal account information in the back of a painting'. But Chuck has been banned from his sort-of familial home – his mother may or may not have died soon after giving birth to him, and his father had been long dead before he unceremoniously reappeared in the back room of a brothel in upstate New York, only to commandeer his real estate empire from Chuck who, at 19 and in the midst of grief, had continued his father's legacy – so Nate takes on the responsibility of 'paying them a visit'.

On entering the apartment, Nate realises that 'The rainbow woman is gone!' It is in fact at Lily van der Woodsen's Sotheby's art auction for the APF, where Rufus Humphrey is wreaking havoc with his current spouse, and former step-daughter (scandal), Ivy Dickens. Ivy inherited half of Lily van der Woodsen's mother's estate, having been employed by Lily's sister to impersonate her daughter, with the aim of commandeering her trust fund. She is now masquerading as Rufus's girlfriend, but is actually in cahoots with Lily's ex-husband, William van der Woodsen, to destroy Lily – or so she thinks…

Back at the auction, in an effort to resolve the gallery panic, Ivy has bought every painting, and made a deal with Sotheby's to display the work from Rufus's gallery. Lily panics at the thought of sharing the spotlight with both Ivy and her ex-husband, and so enters *Spectrum* for auction. The painting – behind which Bart Bass has hidden the afore-mentioned microfilm – stars in a live auction, a battle between Lily, Ivy and Chuck, which ends at a crescendo of one million dollars. From here, it's just a hop, skip and a jump through promises of ruin and sex games before the evidence goes up in flames. It's really very straightforward.

'Snobbery is looked down upon.'[1]

The distinction, or lack thereof, between the animate and inanimate in *Gossip Girl* is the only aspect of the series in which the hierarchy is flat, if not non-existent. The characters' clothes speak with more clarity and purpose than the characters can seem to portray; they trade each other as often as they sell stories or hotels (and occasionally for hotels); and the art that surrounds them has a life of its own – in and out of the show.

After the collaboration between *Gossip Girl* and the APF came to fruition, a series of prints went into production, selling at 250 dollars apiece, and APF co-founder Doreen Remen – who also guest-starred in 'Where the Vile Things Are' – waxed lyrical about the impact of displaying work on screen: 'Exhibiting artworks in this context is a way to engage people in their daily lives; a chance to generate a spark of interest that may grow into something thought-provoking and mind-opening'.[2] In the

1.   *Metropolitan*, dir. Whit Stillman (United States: Westerly Films, 1990).

2.   Art Production Fund, 'Gossip Girl', news release, n.d., http://images. artproductionfund.org/www_artproductionfund_org/Gossip_Girl_Press_Release.pdf.

episode, Remen reflected this statement, and Richard Phillips went along with Humphrey's questionable interpretation of art history:

REMEN   I like that your art is reflecting the same socially relevant projects we commission at the Art Production Fund.

HUMPHREY   And I like that you can see the street art influence. I'm not talking about the '80s, but the '40s Dubuffet, Pollock, Ray Johnson.

PHILLIPS   When artists were the stars of New York, instead of celebutantes.

In this star turn, *Gossip Girl* did what it did best, layering references upon references. Phillips' comment makes a joke of the show, and somewhat of himself. By having artworks 'starring' in a network show, and guest-starring in the show himself, he reaches the apex of Pop, and somehow brings *Gossip Girl* into its history. In an interview with *The New York Times*, Phillips said: 'It's so wonderful how my work has been able to reach out, Warhol would never have been able to dream of such a thing'.[3]

Not unlike Andy Warhol's Factory, *Gossip Girl* attracted a wild mix of personalities while it mass-produced images – of artworks, of themselves, of New York – and moving images. The show regularly spliced the realms of fact and fiction, the plausible with the implausible, and was somehow just dry enough to convince established artists and organisations to go along with its high jinks. Politicians, ballet dancers, designers and musicians both star and are referenced, and real-world scandals are accounted for. New York plays itself. Mayor Bloomberg plays himself. Sonic Youth play a special set for Rufus and Lily's wedding.

The inner circle's relationships crossed over in reality and on the show, and gossip about the actors was as popular as gossip about and between the characters. Real-life columnists reviewing *Gossip Girl* appeared as characters, and character arcs appeared in real-world exåpressions. Serena and Dan dated on the New York set while Blake Lively and Penn Badgley, who played the aforementioned characters, dated on the New York streets.

Every episode would reach a crescendo at a high-production gala, auction or masked ball, with the characters walking the red carpet, being

3.   Phillips, in Nelson, Karin, 'Where Soup Cans Never Went', *The New York Times*, 29 November, 2009.

chased by paparazzi and being featured in Page Six. Every week would close with a mirroring reality for *Gossip Girl*'s stars, often in the same elaborate outfits, on the same marble steps. In a conversation with *New York* magazine, Penn Badgley (Dan Humphrey) said: 'Look, the show that we're on, it wants us to be celebrities, it's trying to launch us into the media like a project. You know. Like a social experiment.'[4]

Gossip Girl was distributed internationally and spawned a number of spin-offs, but it was the way that it permeated and was scattered across New York that was most remarkable. In a bizarre, regurgitating food chain, *Gossip Girl* would be consumed by New York, and New York would be consumed by *Gossip Girl*. Like pigs in shit. The show went high and low, far and wide, extolling the virtues of VitaminWater, Windows phones and Chanel make-up with the regularity and fervour of an underfunded lifestyle magazine. In addition to featuring figures such as publisher Jonathan Cape, critic Charles Isherwood, novelist Jay McInerney and journalist Hamish Bowles, the show also coupled up *n+1*'s former editor Keith Gessen with Elizabeth Hurley, when she was moonlighting as a newspaper editor at *The New York Spectator,* sleeping with Nate and pretending to be Chuck's mother.

Elmgreen & Dragset's *Prada Marfa* sign, which holds a prime spot in Lily van der Woodsen's apartment, was made especially for the show – as a precursor to the permanent *Prada Marfa* sculpture in Texas, which was made in partnership with the Art Production Fund. The print, known on APF's site as 'Elmgreen & Dragset - *Prada Marfa Sign* (Prop Art)' can be bought for as little as $149.99 on Art.com. It has also spawned countless imitations, including images of signs pointing to Paris, New York and London, and a variety of 'PRADA' signs in a mix of typefaces, printed in gold, on marble and in millennial pink.

In 1977, Printed Matter was founded in Tribeca, New York, by Sol LeWitt and Lucy Lippard, with the intention of disseminating artists' books. To quote from details of the organisation's history on Printed Matter's website:

Large-edition and economically produced publications allow-ed for experimentation with artworks that were democratically accessible, affordable, collaborative, and could circulate outside of the mainstream

4.   Badgley, in Pressler, Jessica, and Chris Rovzar, 'The Genius of Gossip Girl', *New York*, 21 April, 2008.

gallery system. Printed Matter provided a space that championed artists' books as complex and meaningful artworks, helping bring broader visibility to a medium that was not widely embraced at the time.[5]

Why shouldn't the next logical step be dissemination in the background – and foreground – of teen drama?

There were few – if any – redeeming features of the characters who made up *Gossip Girl*'s New York – and that was their best quality. If anyone had a virtue, it was in their total, uncompromising embrace of viciousness and vacuity. This doomed bourgeoisie, in 'love', addressed culture and politics with the same confident lack of care they inflicted upon each other. If an art of and for the people is what we want and need, here's a playbook. To quote Jean Genet, in *The Thief's Journal*: 'To achieve harmony in bad taste is the height of elegance'.[6]

XOXO, Gossip Girl

5.   www.printedmatter.org/about/mission-history
6.   Jean Genet, *The Thief's Journal*, trans. by Bernard Frechtman (London: Grove Press, 1949), 106.

WIDENING CONCENTRIC CIRCLES

Gareth Long

Roman Circles

It is easily and often assumed that little is known regarding how literary texts circulated in the Roman world, as only scant details about the Roman book trade have come to light over the centuries. Surprisingly, however, a great deal is known about Roman book circulation, even though little about the book trade is known.[1]

Romans circulated literary texts in a series of widening concentric circles,[2] determined primarily by friendship, which were probably influenced not only by literary interests but also by the forces of social status that regulated friendships. Bookshops and public libraries, which made a text available to individuals personally unknown to the author and his friends, were comparatively late developments.

When a work had reached draft form, authors routinely sent a copy to those very close to them for comments and criticism. This copy was made at the author's own expense, in his home, and completed by his slaves. He tacitly assumed that his friend would not show the draft to anyone else. Cicero often sought feedback from Atticus. Brutus, in turn, asked Cicero for advice on a speech he was re-working into written form.[3] Pliny often asked his friends for advice on his compositions: he wrote notably about his reciprocal exchange of works (and feedback) with Tacitus.[4]

Although these (and other authors) sought honest and constructive criticism, they did not seek impersonal criticism. The ancient sources do not preserve a single case of an author requesting comments from a stranger. Rhetoricians, for example, did not ask for the opinions of other experts, unless they were friends. The restricted sphere in which comments

1. For information on the Roman book trade I am drawing heavily from three main sources: Raymond J. Starr, 'The Circulation of Literary Texts in the Roman World', *The Classical Quarterly*, New Series, 37, no. 1 (1987): 213-223; Edward J. Kenney, 'Books and Readers in the Roman World', in *The Cambridge History of Classical Literature*, Vol. II: Latin Literature, ed. E. J. Kenney (Cambridge: Cambridge University Press, 1982), 3-32; and Kenneth Quinn, 'The Poet and His Audience in the Augustan Age', *ANRW* 30, no. 1 (1982), 75-180.
2. Ancient Latin literature is commonly divided into four periods: early writers, to 70 BC; Golden Age, 70 BC–18 AD; Silver Age, 18-133 AD; and later writers. Here I am looking mostly to everything before the 'later writers', when public libraries started to become more prevalent and the book trade in general widened significantly. I'm using 'his' for this discussion, as we have a dearth of records of women authors in Roman antiquity: those we do have include Sulpicia I (who some have argued was a man), Theophila, Sulpicia II, Claudia Severa, Hypatia, Aelia Eudocia (Eudocia is one of the figures represented in Judy Chicago's 1979 installation *The Dinner Party*). I haven't detailed their processes that pertain to this discussion.
3. Starr, 'The Circulation of Literary Texts in the Roman World', 213.
4. See Pliny the Younger's Letter to Tacitus, 7.20, for an example.

were sought and given encouraged insularity, since the author's friends shared his background, and therefore his attitudes toward such things as what was appropriate, and the standards by which a work of literature should be judged.

Once the author had received his confidants' comments and initially revised the draft, he slightly widened the circle to which his work was accessible. This could be done by sending draft copies, again made in his home by his slaves, at his expense, to several more friends. Often he would also invite a few close relations to his home and read or recite the text to them in order to elicit their comments and reactions. Such private sessions were always small, since too large a gathering would obstruct the free flow of give and take between the author and his friends.

The small audiences at these 'test flights' were made up of the author's friends or, in a more general sense, people with whom he was already in social contact, including patrons and clients. Just as an author did not send his first draft to a stranger, so he did not invite strangers to an experimental reading of a work in progress.

When the text was ready, polished and in its final form, the author sent copies to a wider group of friends, and this was the point at which the written form of a text attained some significance in its circulation. There was no impersonal, commercial copying at this stage: the copies were still made in the author's home by his slaves or in the home of a friend. Authors presented gift copies only to their closest allies. We do not hear of a single author who sent a gift copy to a complete stranger. The first recipients were the dedicatee of the work and other friends intimately connected with it. Cicero assumed that Atticus had a copy of Tyrannio's study of Homeric prosody, because the book was dedicated to him.[5]

Slightly widening the circle, once the author had sent copies to these individuals, he sent copies to other, less close, friends. Ausonius, for instance, thanks Pontius Paulinus for sending him a copy of his condensed version of Suetonius' three books on kings.[6] Martial refers to this custom when he asks, 'Why don't I send you my little books, Pontilianus? For fear you might send me yours, Pontilianus.'[7] Sending Pontilianus a gift copy would be admitting him to a closer friendship than the epigrammatist would like.

5.   Letters to Atticus 12.6. Translated by Shackleton Bailey.
6.   Starr, 'The Circulation of Literary Texts in the Roman World', 215.
7.   Martial, Epigrams, 7.3, *Oxford Anthology of Roman Literature*, ed. Peter E. Knox and J.C. McKeown, 447.

A Ghost Reading an Empty Book [8]

Hi Gareth,

I have been dismally sick again with bronchitis. Not sure if it is a new bout or the same one that just submerged for awhile. Very debilitating and annoying... but I am out of bed now at least.

This is probably not what you are thinking but if you want to see a model of successful distribution driven by friendship, it is Nieves, out of Zurich, who primarily publish and distribute zines, about one zine every month. It began as just publishing his friends and as life goes on and he meets more people the number of zines grow. Most of the zines are in editions of only 100 and most sell out within a few months. The distribution is mostly to friends as well, for example Printed Matter. The friends who carry his zines mostly go for a standing order for all the zines, because otherwise they are gone before you know it. And his maximum for any one venue used to be 5 copies, not sure what it is now but most likely the same. So he gives ten copies to the artist, most likely keeps 10 for himself, puts 10 copies in his own little shop, and then distributes five copies each to 14 venues worldwide and he is sold out... it is a remarkably simple formula. Everyone waits eagerly to see what the new titles will be and Printed Matter, for example, has four or five customers who take one of every zine, again, usually friends. It's a kind of international conversation. A network of friends.

Of course Amazon would not consider that to be successful distribution, but I very much do.

But ultimately it is based on his editorial eye and the quality of friends and friends of friends with whom he mixes buying and selling (because everyone who is published also becomes a faithful customer).

x aa [9]

8.   The Nieves logo is a ghost-like figure reading an empty book.
9.   Email, AA Bronson to author, 16 October 2017, Subject: Re: Wallpaper!

Using Nieves as an exemplar of artists' publishing, there is a measurable series of ever-widening concentric circles of friendships that determine distribution and circulation. These circles in the world of artists' books and zines are an uncanny analogue to those found centuries earlier in the Roman literary world. It might be quickly assumed that there is not much common ground between the ancient Roman literary trade and our own. The books at that time,[10] after all, were produced in a pre-Gutenberg world; all reading material was laboriously copied out by hand. Instead of a Risograph or photocopier, digital offset printer or 'print on demand', the equivalent to all of these production methods was a battery of slaves, whose job it was to transcribe as many copies of Virgil, for example, as the Roman market would buy.

In my experience, not only as a maker of artists' books, but also as someone who has had close relationships with institutions such as Printed Matter, Art Metropole and the New York and London Art Book Fairs, I have witnessed and actively participated in this very kind of distribution through friendships. Often an equal – if not greater – number of copies of a work are gifted and/or traded amongst friends, peers and like-minded makers than are sold. My personal collection of artists' books, ephemera, multiples, prints, etc., have mostly been acquired as gifts from friends. Many of my friends have also received books and editions of mine as gifts.

Artists' book fairs are sites of another unique phenomenon. Before the fair is open to the public, while many vendors and publishers are still setting up their booths and displays, there is a flurry of activity. In this moment the sellers exchange amongst themselves. Trades are arranged. Zines are gifted. Friendly bartering for an Ed Ruscha can sound just like haggling for a better price for tomatoes at the market. These publishers have all been to these fairs before. They have, through their similar practices, established professional relationships and camaraderie. It is often through these moments at book fairs ('in the trenches'), though, that these relationships develop into friendships. There is a palpable sense of conviviality in the air. And then, the following year, at the fair again, these publishers make sure they bring some extra material to trade/gift/exchange with their new friends.

10.   Scrolls, mostly, though there were some instances where a codex was used.

HC

In printmaking traditions – particularly those that came to promi-nence in the nineteenth century – the artist (and printmaker if they are not one and the same) designates a certain number of prints to be made from a plate to comprise the edition. These are limited to a small number, and marked 1/30, for example. Alongside these prints, some are desig-nated as 'artist's proofs', and marked AP or P/A or sometimes EA or Ed'A (*épreuve d'artiste*). In some instances, however, another set of prints would be pulled from the run and marked 'HC', for *hors de commerce*. These prints were usually of a quality equal to the impressions pulled for the regular edition and APs, but were never intended to be sold; they were outside of commerce, literally. These prints, then, were given a distinct life and distribution. Rather than being sold, these were prints the artist would keep and give as gifts to their friends. HCs were those in the run of an edition that were expressly intended for a gift economy.

Printmaking was often looked to as a way to increase an artist's public, to provide a method that would allow their work to be seen by a greater number of people.

Sadly, it's now common to find prints marked HC popping up at auction. They have been abducted from the realm of generosity and have been subsumed into the gaping maw of the market.

First Glass Loving Cups

In 2012, I had one of those years where everyone around me was suddenly getting married. I found myself looking at plane tickets, new suits and wedding gift registries. I had a number of conversations with other artists about what was expected of us in terms of wedding gifts. Depending on the wedding, of course, I knew some of my friends would much prefer it if I gave them a work of mine rather than a blender (but other friends certainly preferred a blender). As all these weddings were approaching, I considered making a new artwork that was to be a 'wedding edition': a work that was specifically made to be given as a wedding present to friends, and never to be sold. As with many of my ideas, I never got around to actualising it.

It wasn't too long after this that I heard that Josiah McElheny had already created such an edition: *The First Glass Loving Cups*. Given only as wedding presents to the artist's close friends, the cups – like a specialised HC – operate outside the art market's commercial modes of circulation. Instead, these cups embody this other kind of distribution I've been writing about.

The First Glass Loving Cups comprise two glass goblets that are held together with a glass chain. This seven-ringed chain loops through a torus (or, more poetically, a ring) that interrupts the stem of the goblet. Within both the chain and the torus are infinitely repeating patterns, a white line that resembles a Möbius strip. These chains, though symbolically here relating to the bonds of marriage, can be seen as analogous to Marcel Mauss's concept that the gift responds to a societal 'need to forge links between individuals'.[11] The chain-links, here, give the unity of wedlock a visual representation and are produced by Josiah for his friends, performing the links (as friendship) between those individuals linked (as spouses). The artwork, its ideas and all it espouses has moved between friends.

The First Glass Loving Cups

This set of linked goblets was made by a late 16th or early 17th-century glassblower on the island of Murano, Venice. He made them during his lunch hour to celebrate a wedding in his own family. The links are made out of glass to remind one of the delicacy of relationships and the care which must be taken with them. The two offset rings in the stem represent the wedding bands and the endlessly intertwining white canes within them symbolize the permanence of union. The First Glass Loving Cups are well known on Murano for the fine lampworked joinery of the chain, and therefore the poignant delicacy with which they must be used. Two people can drink from them at the same time only if they hold the cups in a certain manner. The goblets may have been used in a wedding ceremony or privately by the couple.

A loving cup is a traditional vessel in metal, ceramic or glass used to celebrate a wedding or marriage. It can be a large communal cup or a pair of cups used in the wedding ceremony, shared either by the couple only or by all those present. Loving cups were also made as commemo-

11.   Marcel Mauss, *The Gift: The Form and Reason for Exchange in Archaic Societies*, trans. W.D. Halls (New York: W.W. Norton, 2000), 67.

rations, decorated with portrait of the couple, the date of the wedding, a pair of joined initials, or depictions of allegorical wedding scenes. While individually similar to other Venetian empire goblets, the glass chain that permanently connects this pair is unique in the history of loving cups.

Made by Josiah McElheny for

_______________________________________ *AND* _______________________________________

SIGNED _______________________________________ *DATE* _______________________________ (12)

How I Got Here

David Blamey asked me to write a text for this book. I became friends with him after we were both in an exhibition together and ate large amounts of Chinese food at Congee Village in New York. This exhibition had been organised by Dave Beech and Paul O'Neill – who would also go on to be a very close friend. Paul knew of me and my work through (my now wife) Frances Loeffler, who had mentioned me, but also who showed him an exhibition catalogue of mine that had essays by Paul's close friends Liam Gillick and AA Bronson. It was indirectly through AA Bronson that I met Frances. I had met Liam and AA while studying at Yale University. Liam and I became friends partly because of his relationship with the curator Emelie Chhangur, who was a friend of mine from Toronto (and who had helped with an exhibition Liam had had at the Power Plant). She and I had been emailing about Liam ahead of his first visit to my studio. She was also emailing him saying to look out for me. This paved an easier way for us to forge what would become a very productive friendship. Emelie had been part of a group of friends during my under-graduate study in art at the University of Toronto. I had ended up in the art programme inadvertently because of taking a class on a whim in first year. In this class, it so happened, was Lisa Harrison. Lisa and I became aware that we had had a common friend – Steven Dale. It was because of this common friend that Lisa and I would become friends, I would meet her friends (like Shanan Kurtz, who was certainly paramount in helping me find my way in an art programme), and continue on in the art department,

12.   From the certificate that accompanies the artwork.

ultimately to become an artist. Steven Dale and I had gone to high school together and collaborated on a number of theatre productions.

This text itself was shared, tested, debated, and discussed with Ameen Ahmed, David Blamey, AA Bronson, Nicholas Brown, Kari Cywnar, Jacob Gallagher-Ross, Liam Gillick, Frances Loeffler, Jayne Long, Josiah McElheny, Zach Seely, Danielle St. Amour, Charles Stankievech…

This list of names and connections, from my own circles and of those named throughout this text, is a diagram of what got me to this text, and to these ideas. This is a map of distribution via an ever-widening series of concentric circles of friendship. Some have labelled the way the art world works as nepotistic. There are elements of truth to this. But there are also deep and profound friendships that lead to other friendships, which lead to productive collaborations, and to beautiful and generative discussions and debates.

Similarly, in *Six Years: The Dematerialization of the Art Object*, Lucy Lippard activates friendships as part of her methodology. She wants relationships to shape her work. The text is peppered with quotations from artist-friends, and she includes in the book a collaboration between herself and Douglas Huebler. She revised the book's introduction in the mid-1990s, foregrounding her personal position more explicitly. She notes that she was married to Robert Ryman, a process-oriented Minimalist, when her interest in Conceptualism began. Her close friends included Sol LeWitt, Eva Hesse, Sylvia and Robert Mangold; her larger circle included Dan Graham, Robert Smithson and Joseph Kosuth. These friendships, along with her staunchly left-leaning politics, informed her belief in Conceptualism as a potential *tabula rasa* that could separate art from the 'system' or 'establishment'. She optimistically hopes that the 'most exciting "art" might still be buried in social energies not yet recognized as art'.[13] In detailing her own relationships so thoroughly, she attempts an honest picture of how much she wanted from the work her friends were making.

All of this – and the series of names and associations dotted throughout this discussion – leads to a question. I'm unsure of its relevance to this text, but I feel it would be remiss of me not to raise it. The question is about the limitations of these circles that I've outlined above, and the places in which these productive collaborations and debates possibly

---

13.   Lucy Lippard, *Six Years: The Dematerialization of the Art Object from 1966 to 1972* (Berkeley and Los Angeles, CA: University of California Press, 1997), xxii.

fall short. This list of names is appallingly homogeneous. Though I value these friendships immensely, I also recognise that there is much room to open up these exchanges along ever-widening lines of class and race. What good is an HC if it is only ever exchanged amongst those from the same backgrounds, speaking the same language, who have roughly the same education and who, generally, are of the same political bent? Are these fruitful exchanges actually bearing fruit of any gravity when they are only being bandied about in rather hermetic confines? Or, are these ever-widening concentric circles of friendship only ever-widening so far? Could these circles be otherwise known as echo chambers? As similar concentric circles – with similar limitations – can be found in most communities, what can be done to ensure that we find opportunities to make them overlap?

HELP! DAVID CAMERON LIKES MY ART.

Eva Weinmayr

My Work Received Approval From the Wrong Audience

They saw the work on a gallery website. Looking for another artist's work, they stumbled across the *Today's Question* series that I had exhibited in a group show in the same gallery. They expressed an interest in acquiring the works for the UK Government Art Collection. This collection, they explained, purchases works of art for display in British government buildings around the world to promote British art and culture. However, they said the price I was asking was too high. But I was reluctant to let them strike a cheap deal and the board eventually decided to acquire only two works from the seven-piece series. The choice, it was later argued, reflected not just the limited budget, but also the fact that some pieces in the series were not really appropriate for the Government collection. Apparently the content was considered politically controversial and raised eyebrows in some quarters.

The works they selected read: 'How should we fight foot and mouth? – Kill or Vaccinate – Please tick' and '31mph – A Crime? Yes or No. Please tick'. The large text works were based on questionnaires that had been jamming my fax machine for many months in the early 2000s. The faxes had been sent out by a company pretending to poll opinion on different subjects: it was claimed the poll results would be presented to important politicians and institutions, in order to influence their decision-making. However, what purported to be a way to enact direct democracy was actually just shoddy business practice, if not fraud. The company charged people for faxing back the poll slips with the 'Yes' or 'No' boxes ticked, and so a handsome profit was made by getting people to react and send in their vote. The costs for faxing back the response included a £5.00 connection charge, the very small print stated.

The works the Government Art Collection did not like, or which were above their budget, asked:

Scrap all speed bumps? *Yes or No.* Should we close St Bartholomew's Hospital? *Keep it open or Close it.* 24 hours drinking. Should pubs be able to open 24hrs? *Yes or No.* Should we stay in Europe? *Stay in or Get out.* Should the government return 11,000 illegal immigrants back to France? *Yes or No.*

I was both fascinated and appalled by these faxes. It was their audacity – their use of reductionist and propagandist language as a strategy to make money, while pretending that participants contributed to democracy – that disgusted me. These questions were worded to strike at people's hearts, and the raw 'yes/no' binary choice they offered felt violent and irresponsible to me. Even if I had just binned the faxes, their sheer presence would have been aggressive enough. I resolved to do something with them.

So I enlarged the text and the basic layout of the questionnaires and sprayed them in different colours with automotive lacquer on large aluminium panels. For this toxic spraying and baking process, I worked in a spray shop near Munich, where the car manufacturer BMW once produced its Art Car series with famous artists. The guys in the spray shop proudly showed me snapshots of Andy Warhol, with masking tape in hand, standing next to the Art Car he decorated for BMW in 1979. The spraying process itself is pretty fancy. It happens in a high-tech, temperature-controlled spray booth, where an extraction system sucks out any floating particles such as dust, hair or any other microscopic material that could cause even the slightest blemish on the pristine lacquer surface. We sprayed multiple layers of paint and clear coat. Using this method, the text eventually stood slightly in relief over the surrounding area. The layering also resulted in a beautiful, vitreous depth of colour, which in my view stood strikingly for the political complexity that was reduced on the original questionnaire to a banal 'Yes' or 'No' dichotomy.

I fully understand why the Government Art Collection was attracted to these works. Their surface was so shiny and seductive. They do look kind of cool. On one occasion, I was invited to a private view of their display with other works in the collection at the British Embassy in Paris. I had assumed that this was to be the permanent place for their display. Years later, I still pictured the works residing on that elegant wall in Paris, until an unexpected email dropped into my inbox:

Hi Eva,

I'm a journalist with the Sunday Mirror newspaper in London. I was intrigued to know what you think of the Tory PM David Cameron choosing your work (31mph a crime? and How Should We Fight Foot and Mouth?) from the Government art collection to hang in his office? I was interested to know if you have met Mr Cameron or his wife Samantha or if you know how they came to know of your work. I'd also be interested to know what you think of Mr Cameron's policies, including of course the decision by his Government to slash funding for the Arts!

Regards, Gary.

I was confused. I was just on my way to the dentist, trying to get rid of a throbbing toothache. As soon as I got back home, I rang the number of the Government Art Collection. Nobody was available to give me any information, but two days later I received a letter from the collection's director:

Works of Art on Display in 10 Downing Street

Further to our telephone conversation, I am writing to let you know that there is a very strong possibility that your paintings 31mph a Crime?, and How should we fight foot and mouth?, will shortly be installed in a room in 10 Downing Street. We wanted to let you know in advance of our plans, as sometimes displays at 10 Downing Street attract publicity, as you know already.

With good wishes
Penny Johnson, Director

I tried to gather more information. Was it only 'a very strong possibility' that the works would be displayed in Downing Street, or were they already there? They were already there. Who selected the work? It was Samantha Cameron. Where exactly were they displayed? In the Camerons' private residence at 11 Downing Street. Why? No answer. I then sat down and wrote a letter to the Prime Minister and his wife, stating politely that I was flattered – I kind of was – and asking what they liked about my work and why they had selected it. No answer.

I felt compelled to find other sources of information to answer my questions. I searched online for anything I could find about David and Samantha's apartment in Downing Street. An image of Michelle Obama and Samantha Cameron came up, in which the two women were sitting on a mustard-yellow sofa in the Camerons' open-plan kitchen at Downing Street. At the time the exaggerated costs of remodelling their kitchen diner was being discussed in the news. What troubled me was the particular yellow shade of the sofa: it matched too perfectly the yellow shade of my *Kill or Vaccinate* piece. Was it really just the nice colour they liked my work for?

Some time later, at a private view at the Whitechapel Gallery in London, selected works from the Government Art Collection were on view – including one of mine. There I was introduced to the Facilities Manager at Downing Street. We had a lively conversation at the bar. He said he was a big fan of my work and that, if I wished, I could come round to Downing Street for a guided tour. Wow. I was excited to do that. In the emails that followed, he clarified that of course the tour would exclude the private residence, but that he could show me around the rest of the building one evening. Still wow. In further email exchanges, he started to back down, stating that because of workload it might be tricky to find a date soon. The summer came. Then complete silence.

Meanwhile, sources close to the art collection told me that one MP proposed a question for a Prime Minister's Questions. The MP wanted to ask: is the artist Eva Weinmayr British enough to be collected by the UK Government Art Collection? The request, fitting the current political climate, apparently did not make it through to PMQ at that time.

Eventually my moment of opportunity came. During the re-election campaign, David Cameron's private residence was opened to a film crew from *The Sun* newspaper. They produced a ten-minute clip, 'A day in the life of David Cameron', which showed the Prime Minister preparing breakfast in the kitchen at home. In the film, the camera sweeps over shelves with glasses and tumblers. It catches a glimpse inside the fridge, and then follows Mr. Cameron to the central dining table, which stands in an open-plan living space. The camera's gaze rests on the table, which is crammed with books, papers, a Weetabix box and a jar holding pencils and a toothbrush, before pulling back to a wide shot of the prime minister sitting at the table with a steaming coffee mug. Leafing through a disorganised stack of papers, he sits in front of my picture, which is given pride of place on the central wall. The prime minister of Great Britain relaxes at home under the unmistakable motif *Kill or Vaccinate?*

Version A

Start from Dave's [Cameron] entrance. Eva [W] and Samantha [C] are sitting in the drawing room having tea. DC comes in. Ah, PM, hello I am E. Good to have you here, etc., replies DC. More shallow banter occurs and E starts to filter in her political messages: that she finds his cultural policy abhorrent, that he should remove the plan for wide-ranging cuts for everything art. She goes on to detail her point while SC sits still and is remarkably quiet. Then comes the moment.

Eva produces a huge fire axe and puts the spike into DC's head. He immediately falls to the floor and dies. SC, still calm, says: OK now let's put him into the credenza. The V&A people will be here any moment [to collect it] and this is a good way to get rid of this man who is good for nothing? You are so right to raise your voice for the arts.

This new evidence of the work's conspicuous location in the Camerons' living room was too much for me. Before this revelation, I had a hazy imagination of my works being installed somewhere else – a corridor perhaps, or among other pieces jam-packed across a wall, or even behind a door. But it was not to be. The prominent and solitary position on the prime minister's living room wall and its proximity to the goings-on in the room were a cause of growing anxiety for me. What instances, private moments and very private moments had my picture been forced to witness? A silent companion held hostage, being forced to dwell with a man who stands for the most ignorant cultural budget cuts, education bills and housing politics proposed in a long while. It was precisely this – the imposed companionship – which infuriated me. Johnny Marr, guitarist with The Smiths, was similarly frustrated about David Cameron back in 2010 when the prime minister publicly declared himself a fan. Marr tweeted: DAVID CAMERON, STOP SAYING THAT YOU LIKE THE SMITHS, NO YOU DON'T. I FORBID YOU TO LIKE IT.

'I forbid you to like it.' That is wonderful. I am not naïve. For the last ten years, I have been working on the complexities of circulation – deeply convinced that once a work is out it is out. Whether published, sold or broadcast, you relinquish control and let the work go to have a social life of its own. It can inspire, comfort, alert or make people think in many different ways. But, fuck, why is it so wrong on this occasion? Maybe I need to examine my own reaction more closely?

Version B

Eva does not show up. Nothing happens for ages. Samantha is just sitting in the sitting room doing nothing. Eventually Dave comes in and asks her what she's doing. I'm waiting for Eva Weinmayr, the artist. Dave replies, 'Ah' and sits down. Nothing happens for a while longer. Then he says, 'When... when is she supposed to arrive'? Samantha replies, 'She is a little late.... She might be stuck on the tube. Do you think she'll be here soon'? I imagine so. But you don't know? No. Can't you text her? I haven't got her number. And she hasn't texted you? No. She hasn't got mine. Another long pause. It's just that I'm expecting the Ambassador of Belugistan, Dave blurts out. Samantha shrugs.

Let me explain my agony. The work in the prime minister's living room points towards the implicit violence of 'Yes or No', a judgment without nuance, arguments, discussion, negotiation or room for compromise. In that sense, the work is a critique of propagandist language. Has he missed that? Has he simply interpreted the works as celebratory cenotaphs of direct democracy? Has he even, perhaps, been attracted to the vicious polarisation that the fake opinion pollsters prompted? Seen the need to translate the questionnaire one-to-one into real-life politics? I am asking because throughout Cameron's life, he and his country have never been friends of direct democracy. Britain's strictly representative parliamentarism, after all, is nine hundred years old. However, contemplating the bland words 'please tick' on his wall, he might have suddenly felt urgently that the British people must have their say...

Version C

Eva shows up and has a polite conversation. Eva sits in the sitting room having tea with Samantha. They exchange pleasantries. DC comes through the door and further politeness ensues. Everybody is bored by this. The actors are reading from prepared A4 sheets and fail to fall into any kind of dramaturgy. In this style the scene rumbles on with an embarrassing cheesiness. It gets so boring that the Uzbek ambassador, who is a side character here, dozes off. Things start flying in the direction of the stage: a tomato, a Diet Coke can, various fruit.

Welcome To Your New Home

David Cameron had to leave Downing Street in a rush after resigning, following the failed Brexit 'Remain' campaign. There was not even time to clear the table of empty coffee mugs the morning he learned that the referendum was lost, or so I have been told. Imagine the moment Theresa May stepped into the deserted kitchen dining room with the oversized questionnaire offering two boxes to be ticked: *Kill or Vaccinate*. I see Theresa May clearing Cameron's dirty mugs in uncomfortable awe. I hear the jangling sound of teaspoons on porcelain and I see her staring at my work and finding it utterly perplexing. After all, she has just swept into Downing Street as the newly elected Conservative leader after a similarly simple-minded, divisive question was put to the British people. Thirty million Brits had put their cross either behind 'Remain a member of the European Union' or 'Leave the European Union' – with a slim majority picking the latter option. The political nature of my work made her shudder while she tried to move the mugs onto a tray, and eventually she had to put them down again on the table, perhaps struck by a coughing fit.

Has Theresa May kept the artworks up on the wall? Her taste and style is certainly very different from that of the Camerons. She apparently modified the sleek, industrial-style modernist kitchen into something more floral and colourful. Her thing is seemingly all about patterns. But what about the art? Again, I wrote a letter:

London, 12 July 2016

Dear Theresa May,

First of all, congratulations on what must be a very exciting new appointment for you. I wish you every success.

As you arrive in Downing St, you'll probably notice some images on the walls of your new flat that have a decidedly referendum-esque feel about them. These are artworks and, as their author, I thought I ought to write to you to introduce them.

They are part of a larger series Today's Question *(2005), which are based on fake opinion polls, unsolicited faxes sent to UK households. I was so interested in the strategic and emotional rhetoric in these documents that I enlarged them and sprayed them with car paint and lacquer on aluminium boards.*

As it happens, by sheer serendipitous coincidence, there are two other works in the series that are particularly relevant to the present situation. These are: Should we return 11,000 illegal immigrants to France?, *and the even more prescient* Should we stay in Europe? Stay in/Get out.

Wouldn't it be amazing if this work was in Downing Street now? Perhaps I don't have to evoke the impact these could have on visitors during some of the more 'informal' negotiations you're likely to be involved in over the coming months or even, dare I say it, years. Imagine, for instance, Angela Merkel arriving for a cup of tea and seeing Should We Stay in Europe? *in pride of place above the mantelpiece! What could better impress upon her that the question is constantly uppermost in your mind? Not least because these works are authored by a (mainland) European artist.*

Unfortunately the Government Art Collection has never acquired this freshly resonant work. However, now that it has certainly gained a different weight at this specific moment in time and most likely in British history, perhaps you might find a way to secure it in perpetuity for Downing Street? I would love to be able to meet with you to discuss this or the works.

Yours faithfully,
E

This time around I received a response:

9 September 2016
From the Direct Communications Department

Dear Ms Weinmayr,

The Prime Minister has asked me to thank you for your correspondence from 12 July, requesting a meeting with her. I apologise for the delay in replying.

The Prime Minister appreciates you taking time to write to her. However, owing to the tremendous pressures on her diary, I regret that it will not be possible to arrange a meeting. Thank you, once again, for writing.

Yours sincerely
Correspondence Officer

What a shame. No word about the artwork swap. Later, I learned from news reports that she had replaced most of the artwork at Downing Street with enlarged quotes from her own speeches. Apropos speeches, remember the Frida Kahlo bracelet Theresa May wore during the most important speech of her political life at the 2017 Conservative Party Conference in Manchester? The bracelet showed miniature self-portraits of the Mexican painter, a lifetime Communist Party activist concerned with the plight of the impoverished and imagining that one day we could live in a classless society. Art again slipping into unintended contexts? Would Frida have tweeted 'I forbid you to like my art'? I have my doubts – but only because Twitter was not available back then.

Watch 'A Day in the Life of David Cameron' on *The Sun*'s YouTube channel: www.youtube.com/watch?v=z9hqE5HVVQk

The theatrical inserts are taken from *Downing Street* (Los Angeles: New Documents, 2015), a play I co-wrote with writer John Moseley and journalist Titus Kroder in order to have the conversation I had been denied.

The script imagines Samantha and David inviting Eva for a visit. The audience, which is scripted as a character in the play, comes up with scenarios suggesting how Eva should solve the dilemma of her art being appropriated as 'radical chic'.

PHYSICALITY AND FACSIMILE: TRACE CONNECTIONS AND EARLY DIGITAL COMMUNICATIONS AT THE ROYAL MAIL

Robert Hetherington

Throughout history, postal services have profited from the constraints of physical communication, built on the simple fact that to correspond with those outside of the immediate vicinity messages had to be mediated – formed as objects, put down in ink on paper. Etymologically speaking, a message, and the action of its sending, derive from a common Latin root – *mittere*; *missus*[1] – and, as such, you can't have one without the other. But as transient thoughts become tangible things, the laws of their material properties fix them to one place, and one time, and they certainly aren't going to move themselves.

To reach its recipient, therefore, a letter must be carried between two points. In the early days of the Royal Mail, when it served only the King,[2] each dispatch was assigned to a single individual: a messenger who would act as representative, delivering news and orders. These messengers travelled across the country at a gallop: three horses were required to be stabled in each town, so that information would not be delayed by the inevitable inconvenience of exhausted muscles. A quick pit stop, a change of steed and the rider could continue unhindered. So was established an extensive system of 'posts' – as these points of exchange came to be known, after the sturdy pieces of timber to which the horses were tethered. During the intervening five hundred or so years, the popular understanding of the term has expanded to become both noun and verb, describing at once an aspect of the infrastructure, 'a post', the object which moves through it, 'the post', and the act of distribution itself, 'to post'.

In time, regal dictation inevitably gave way to popular communication: the service was opened up to the public in 1635. With the establishment of a General Post Office in 1660, the linear routes from a single, central hub diversified and became entwined, creating a complex and interrelated network.

Over the centuries, organisational structures naturally shifted and the service steadily adapted to an ever-developing world – industrialised, mechanised and at points even automated. But, whilst technological advancements made the service increasingly efficient, they also gave rise to alternative means of transmission (telegraphy, telephony, etc.) that

1.   *Missus*, 'message', being the past participle of *mittere* 'to send' – see: *Oxford Dictionary of English* (Oxford: Oxford University Press, 2016).
2.   The first Master of the Posts, Brian Tuke, was knighted by Henry VIII in 1516, and given authority to establish a formal system of delivery.

threatened to challenge the established order and traditional methods of communication.

The message of Samuel Morse's inaugural telegraph was sent, for example, with no shortage of spectacle, from Washington DC on 24 May 1844. At Capitol Hill, in the Old Supreme Court Chamber, Morse, along with members of Congress, waited in anticipation as his assistant, Albert Vail – stationed at a Baltimore railway depot, some 40 miles away – tapped out the ceremonial communiqué. Pulsing down the line, it arrived almost instantaneously, coded in the combination of dots and dashes that was soon to become familiar, a quotation from The Old Testament Book of Numbers (23:23): 'What hath God wrought?' Whether this was an expression of wonder and awe at the march of progress or an ominous anticipation of what might come as a result, however you look at it, the significance of the shift represented in this moment was clearly not lost on the men who ushered it in.

Whereas to post something emphasises and objectifies the content communicated, to send information telegraphically it must be deconstructed in order to travel through a fundamentally physical network. Carried by wires stretching out across the landscape, metaphorical lines of communication became tangible. 'Connection' was literal and direct. In positioning the infrastructure, the network, the route by which information travels as the central object, messages themselves could be liberated from the baggage of their previous necessarily physical form. And with language compressed into little more than a binary of impulses, clarified into a linear construction of currents, words were no longer bound by the maximum speed of the messenger charged to convey them. Seemingly dematerialised, information could now move freely and unrestricted, transferred across ever-increasing distances – at first between cities, soon across continents and later even under oceans – all at apparently miraculous speeds. The world, it seemed, had begun to shrink – in terms of communication, at least.

But, whilst a significant shift had undoubtedly occurred, the introduction of the telegram did not spell the immediate end of the postal era. For speed isn't everything, and hard copy offered a versatility that was not easily matched. Messages could be longer, were less likely to be intercepted and could contain a wider range of information, both visual and verbal (not to mention the opportunity to send packages...). But even beyond the practical differences, as a singular article the letter conveys more than just the signs and symbols inscribed on the page: it offers a palpable connection between sender and recipient, which dots and dashes and disembodied voices simply cannot replicate. The sense of holding a message penned by the hand of a loved one, maybe with the hint of a familiar scent embedded into the pores of the paper... these tangible traces, sometimes barely perceptible, are significant. Retained naturally within the material, they are lost when information is compressed to the point of almost total detachment.

Although on one level telegraphy may have offered connection in the strictest sense of the word, ultimately the result was abstracted too far, feeling cold in its stripped-back utility. To put it simply, the letter remained a substantial thing to send and receive, as opposed to other, more ephemeral, options. Because of this, the postal service had never needed to consider significant innovation, and as a result the fundamental activity of sending and receiving ultimately remained unchanged.

We are, however, well aware of the fact that in recent years the Internet and the advent of digital communications have rapidly encroached on the traditional postal service – in a way that the telegram never quite managed in over a century of competition. Online, the written word has been completely dissociated from its material form, existing in time much more than it does in space. It is now perhaps closer to speech than it is to print. Information appears only to exist in discernible form when we choose to access it. Our screens work as lenses through which malleable pages are made anew each time. Data storage has therefore become the new delivery, as nothing is ever truly sent but simply uploaded – to hover mysteriously, held in suspended animation, within an apparently immaterial cloud. The reality, of course, is that it all resides on immense and unseen servers, humming away in some high-security desert compound.

Both the paper post and the telegram required an obvious intermediary: someone employed to direct specific pieces of information through costly infrastructures that would otherwise be inaccessible. The easy interface of the Internet, however, has concealed this from view. The acts of writing a message and of its distribution have blurred to become a single gesture and our sense of individual autonomy and control over communication has shifted. While we must still go through all manner of hosts and providers, the overriding sense is that our access to one another is possible without intervention – essentially, it is immediate.

In its contemporary omnipresence, the Internet has prompted a reconsideration of our relationship to information generally. With our homes (and mobile devices) connected and constantly supplied, the

Internet has come to be regarded as an essential utility – we think of the network in the same way as drinking water, gas, electricity, or perhaps (depending on your perspective) the sewer.

But as email heralded the potential demise of our need to objectify in order to communicate, and thus an apparent death knell for the postal service, an unexpected saviour was found in the form of e-commerce and online shopping, and the rapid reduction in letter traffic was offset by a steady increase in the demand for package delivery. Even in a networked world, there are certain things that still need to be transported, and with online sales continuing to increase[3] a balancing of the books appeared attainable.

However, somewhere along the way, a tipping point was reached. Amazon, the golden goose of the market, began to take matters into its own hands. Circumventing traditional models, it moved to establish an in-house distribution network, Amazon Logistics, staffed largely by self-employed delivery drivers working long hours for low wages. It looked very much like a tactical attempt to destabilise the old order, the first step towards an expanded monopoly not only of the retail market, but also of the supply chain. However, in outlining its rationale, Amazon's CEO, Jeff Bezos, offered a much more mundane explanation: simply put, Royal Mail 'ran out of capacity at peak'.[4] In the digital age, competing with 'gig economy' models in which even physical distribution can be decentralised, those centuries of near monopoly seem very much a thing of the past.

Royal Mail's archives are currently housed a stone's throw from the Mount Pleasant Sorting Office (now Mount Pleasant Mail Centre) in Clerkenwell, which, as the capital's central postal hub since 1889, has played a significant role in enabling the flow of post around the United Kingdom. Today the physical qualities that once ensured effective communication and a profitable business characterise a varied and extensive collection in which ephemera from five centuries of postal distribution are carefully catalogued – from ancient-looking ledgers, recording the wages and responsibilities of delivery boys in centuries past, to piles of promotional material for some short-lived service. Other items include:

3. Up 15% year on year – see: UK Office for National Statistics, *Retail sales, Great Britain: July 2017*, accessed 31 October 2017, www.ons.gov.uk/businessindustryandtrade/retailindustry/bulletins/retailsales/july2017.

4. Patrick Sawyer, 'Royal Mail can't cope with our demand, claims Amazon boss', *Daily Telegraph*, 3 June, 2016, www.telegraph.co.uk/news/2016/06/03/royal-mail-cant-cope-with-demand-claims-amazon-boss/.

proposals for unused stamps, roughly sketched by giants of British graphic design; training manuals, explaining in detail the functions of some long-obsolete machine; and private internal communications, sent in the strictest of confidence but since opened to the public eye. All the ephemera that has surrounded the postal service over the years finds a home here. Regardless of the age or historical value of their contents, documents requisitioned for study emerge in uniform manila folders of varied thickness and density – those bulging with material are tied shut with white cotton tape.

In one particularly thin file, classified as Post 104/34, a bizarre correspondence can be found. A pair of somewhat saccharine poems, on two thin sheets, sent between senior figures in the organisation – perhaps with too much time on their hands? At first glance, these jaunty verses appear insignificant, incongruous to their surroundings and the dry formalities of day-to-day operations. But on closer inspection it becomes clear why they have been preserved. Buried in the archive and barely re-membered, they mark an important moment in the technical history of communication, as we tentatively adjusted to a fledgling digital age.

The first is a telegram sent on 1 October 1982, the final day of a service that had, in the United Kingdom, been in constant commercial operation since its introduction by the Post Office in 1870.[5] Written in rhyming couplets by a Mr M. D. Orbell (a suitable name for the Director of Postal Administration on the island of Jersey), it is addressed to Ron Dearing, then Chairman of the Post Office. Steeped in nostalgia, his message laments the passing of the telegraph:

> ...And now the wire is cut at last
> Greetings and timely grief are past
> Yesterday's speed becomes at most
> Tomorrow evening morning post...[6]

As we have seen, the wire serves as a direct signifier of physical con-nection, a tangible thread linking one location to another. The suggestion of its severance therefore anticipates the apparently imminent disman-tling of the infrastructure.

5.   Telegrams would, however, remain in use elsewhere – the final functioning service, operating in India, ceased in 2013.

6.   M.D. Orbell and Ron Dearing, 'Telegram Sent on the Final Day of Broadcast' (Post 104/34), 1982, The Postal Museum.

'The grams', he informs us, had been 'laid to rest; at British Telecom's behest'.[7] Having been rebranded as Telemessage, the telegram had steadily been phased out, as attention was focused on new and progressive technologies in which more complex information could be handled by machines with substantially more power to process larger quantities of data. Amidst these developments a new service had been established, one which seemed to suggest an exciting direction in which the Royal Mail could progress towards the end of the century. 'Intelpost' was, according to Orbell (playing on the boss's name), 'far more en Dearing'.[8]

Intelpost was in essence a commercial application of 'fax' technology – available privately but not yet widespread – in which a document is scanned at the point of origin, then formed as a copy (a facsimile) upon arrival at its intended destination. And whilst this was essentially nothing new – experiments into the potential of 'pictures by wire' predated even Morse[9] – within the Royal Mail, Intelpost was seen to represent a significant shift. Utilising satellite technology, it enabled the transmission of documents at speeds at least equal to telegraphy whilst retaining the formal appearance of hard-copy communication (more or less). An apparently ideal hybrid, it provided 'a relatively close substitute to the letter post',[10] whilst matching the pace of electronic communication.

A reply to Orbell's telegram was sent three days later, in the form of a traditionally posted letter, from a Jonathan Evans, Personal Assistant to the Chairman. 'Mr Dearing' was, it seems, 'away where skies are blue' ('hence this reply from me to you'),[11] so it was left to Evans to thank Orbell for his cheering note before enthusiastically affirming the virtues of the new service:

Words of Joy Words of sorrow
All here today and there tomorrow. [...]
With Intelpost there's no delay –
It's here today and there today![12]

7.   Ibid.
8.   Ibid.
9.   Scottish inventor Alexander Bain received a patent for his 'Electric Printing Telegraph' as early as 1843.
10.   G.T. Edwards, 'Initial Report on the Future Environment of the Postal Business' (Post 72/1164), 1973, The Postal Museum.
11.   Orbell and Dearing, 1982.
12.   Ibid.

Much like the telegraph, information would be dismantled, broken down into code, but technological capabilities had progressed sufficiently for this fragmentary form to be reconstructed at the other end into an exact replica of that which had been input (if a little blurrily). But already, in this sense of being both here and there at once, we can see an important distinction from the models that had come before. If the paper post objectified information, and telegraphy had codified it in the linear combination of abstract units, then the facsimile, or fax, offered something different again: a model in which the page is essentially treated as an image. As it is scanned into the system, it is split in two – the original document stays put whilst it is translated into data, beamed in the binary distinction of white and black, before its likeness is reconfigured and reproduced at the other end. And so, when Evans speaks of 'it' – the thing that appears miraculously to be both here and there at once – what exactly does he mean?

In and of itself, the document does not move anywhere, certainly not in any literal sense of the word: it has simply been doubled – the pages at points A and B are totally distinct, the same in appearance only. Logically, therefore, it becomes clear that it does not reference an object but rather the information, which of course is not bound by physical form and naturally can exist in multiple locations. It is thus evident that with Intelpost and the adoption of the fax we took a significant step towards the dematerialised communication landscape in which we now exist.

On 17 June 1980, Dearing launched the service with a communication sent from a terminal at the London Stock Exchange to Toronto. In his ceremonial opening transmission, he addressed the Canadian Postmaster General and 'the people of Canada', heralding the arrival of 'the world's first electronic mail service'.[13] He concludes with great enthusiasm for the future, stating prophetically, but with more than a hint of irony, given what we have seen transpire in the years since the event: 'We, on our side, look to this service as the first step towards a major international network'.[14] He could not have been closer to the truth.

In contrast to centuries of steady demand and little need for renovation, in the early 1970s something had clearly shifted in the mindset of the organisation. An enquiry into the postal strike of 1971 had highlighted

13.   Ron Dearing, Publicity leaflets relating to Intelpost (later known as Faxmail) (Post 28/92), 1980, The Postal Museum.
14.   Ibid.

a culture in which the willing acceptance of the status quo had finally begun to catch up with the Royal Mail. A particularly damning passage in the resulting report openly addresses the fact that 'low expectations of the rate of innovation and change in the postal business' had, it seemed, 'become self-fulfilling'.[15] Within months an independent unit had been established at the heart of the organisation, the Long-Term Planning Unit (LTPU), the stated aim of which was to 'consider the socio-economic, commercial and technological environment in which the postal business will exist up to the end of the century',[16] with the purpose of developing a greater understanding with which the Royal Mail might weather any oncoming changes whilst still retaining its identity. Confidential early memoranda produced by the unit show a willing embrace of the opportunity for reform. One particular report, 'The Management of Change in the Postal Business', for example, opens with a quote from Machiavelli:

There is nothing more difficult to carry out, nor more doubtful of success, nor more dangerous to handle, than to initiate a new order of things.[17]

Their vision for the future of the postal service was certainly ambitious, although (it must be said) conclusions were often speculative.

Now open to the public record, these documents offer a fascinating insight into the attitudes and ethos of the company at this crucial juncture. The postal service is examined in great detail in the wider context of contemporary communication technologies and – with some trepidation – suggestions for progressive next steps begin to be spelled out. But these early attempts to harness digital technologies have not been well remembered. Even the archivists only nod in vague recognition upon hearing the names of services such as Postfax, Datapost or the prophetically titled 'Electronic Mail'. No one has written nostalgic verses marking the passing of Intelpost, as Mr. Orbell did for the telegram. Submerged deep within the archive are countless documents relating to a range of experimental services that were introduced following the

15.   *Hardman Report* (London: HMSO, 1971). As referred to in Memorandum No. 5: 'The Management of Change in the Postal Business' (Post 72/1164), 1973, The Postal Museum.
16.   Papers relating to the setting up of the Long-Term Planning Unit (POST 72/1136), 1972, The Postal Museum.
17.   Machiavelli, *The Prince*, 21.

establishment of the LTPU. They attest to a determination to reorient a company that was clearly not ready to accept its obsolescence.

Viewed from today's perspective, however, the unconscious rhetoric found in documents from this period appears shocking in its naivety. With each example the assessment of the changing landscape proves to be correct in the general sense, but fundamental, essential aspects epitomised by the shift in technology are consistently underestimated, or completely misjudged. When, for example, Dearing speaks of the establishment of an international network, his vision is of one in which the Royal Mail is still required to act as mediator, in the way that it always had done. But, crucially, his sense of scale is inaccurate. In hindsight, it is clear that, even beyond its ability to reproduce the appearance of hard copy at telegraphic speed, the significance of the fax lay in the fact that it offered a means for the individual to employ the network without assistance or further facilitation: it allowed users to circumvent the old, centralised institutions and, for the first time, take ownership of, and responsibility for, the distribution of their messages.

To examine these records today is to watch a curious sort of death drive unfolding. Despite the emphasis on long-term vision, each of these services served only to hasten the Royal Mail towards the uncertain position in which it now exists, working, in each case, to popularise technologies that would ultimately lead to its own undoing.

In documents sent back and forth between Post Office executives and advertising companies during the lead-up to the introduction of Intelpost in 1980, a series of potential campaigns for print, radio and television are sketched out. They highlight the exciting potential of seemingly space-age communication – 'Royal Mail by satellite'[18] – evoking images of gleaming, orbiting objects, reflecting our documents through the atmosphere. Circumventing the winding, wiggling inefficiencies of earthly infrastructures, these hyper-modern messages would soar beyond the grubby realities of the world below.

With the primary market for the service anticipated in a corporate context, most of these adverts were aimed at businesses and professionals, focusing on the stress of impending deadlines or the long, frustrating wait for a response. In a draft script for a radio advert, the scene is set around a telephone conversation:

18.   Intelpost – Launch Campaign 1980 (Post 154/78) 1980, The Postal Museum.

VOICE 1	… but… but there's no courier service in the world that would get them to Toronto by then.
SFX	Irate muffled voice jabbering down the telephone.
VOICE 1	Yes, I understand but…
SFX	Receiver being slammed down. Phone goes dead.
VOICE 1	(into internal phone) Miss Jones, could you come in, please?
MISS J	Yes, Sir.
SFX	Door opening/closing.
VOICE 1	Look, Miss Jones, the customer wants those sales graphs in Toronto for tomorrow morning… he's going to close his account with us unless… unless… Miss Jones, can you fly over to Toronto and give them to him?
MISS J	But there's no need, I'll send them by Intelpost.
VOICE 1	Intel what?
MISS J	Intelpost, it's the Royal Mail Facsimile transmission service It means you can send A4 copies of those sales graphs to Toronto in a matter of hours.
VOICE 1	Well I'll be…
MISS J	Thinking about giving me a pay rise…
V.O.	Send your graphs, designs, documents and plans by Intelpost. The Royal Mail direct Facsimile service by satellite from London to Toronto.[19]

All that we have discussed has revolved, in one sense or another, around the economies of scale and efficiency that are fundamentally involved in the transfer and distribution of information. When the boss uncomfortably asks his assistant to fly across the Atlantic, to carry the sales graphs to their client, he is balancing the cost, speed and reliability of sending a complex document a vast distance in a short period of time. The resulting action may appear insanely inefficient – not so far removed from that of the King's messenger heading out into the country – but nonetheless in 1980 it seemed to be the only viable option. With a little more time in hand he could have used the postal service, which could perform the same task for a low cost, by the nature of its ability to balance micro and macro scales. The individual letter will ultimately reach a highly specific destination, but in order to get there it must be combined with other, separate things that happen to be heading in the same general direction – moved

19.   Ibid.

en masse. The sorting process makes physical communication viable, cost effective for the sender and practicable for the company itself. But, even when automated, it is a laboriously slow operation – in the grand scheme of things, at least.

The telegram was fast, that's for sure, but limited in its capacity. Information could move great distances in short amounts of time, but only by means of a drastic compression of its content – a deconstruction of previously complex forms. It leaves behind all but that which is deemed to be essential.

With its ability to cope with greater quantities of coded information and pull it back together again, the fax therefore seemed to offer the best of both worlds – it was fast, cheap, and (just about) complete. Later, email would go even further, as increasingly complex data could be recalled and reconfigured into instantly accessible manifestations. Audio, video, text, image – all made up of immense, unseen encryptions.

But everything is relative, and today, as we become increasingly dependent on this seemingly intangible network, demand has once again begun to outstrip the capacity of the infrastructure through which information moves. As offices become completely paperless, and entire industries proliferate within an ever-expanding digital space, the data required to run the world has become so massive that in many instances we have already exhausted the potential of even the most efficient of fibre-optic cables.

In November 2016, at the Amazon Web Services (AWS) conference in Las Vegas, the company launched a new initiative. In an age defined largely by the constant novelty of every ultra-high-tech announcement, it seemed somewhat surreal. Amongst the audience, mostly filming on their phones, a ripple of applause and laughter burst out as an 18-wheeler truck – 45 feet long – rolled slowly onto the stage.[20] It carried a shipping container, filled with huge hard drives capable of holding up to 100 petabytes of data. The purpose of this vehicle – the AWS Snowmobile – is to be driven to a company's HQ or data centre and, using the fastest connections available, collect their entire digital archives and freight them, over land, to be uploaded to the cloud: 'A complete […] migration'.[21] Although it may at first seem backward,

20.   'Move Exabyte-Scale Data Sets with AWS Snowmobile', Amazon Web Services [YouTube video], accessed 31 October 2017, www.youtube.com/watch?v=8vQmTZTq7nw.
21.   'AWS Snowmobile', Amazon Web Services', accessed 31 October 2017, https://aws.amazon.com/snowmobile/.

this physical transportation of digital information is weirdly logical, if you consider the fact that to upload such vast amounts of data at standard network speeds would take not just hours, days or weeks, but years.

Amazon's Snowmobile operates as a natural extension of the concept of the 'sneakernet'[22] – when interns (in trainers) are sent with USB sticks filled with files between the departments or offices of large businesses – or of cycle couriers, who are employed to take hard drives across the city, able to outpace the tedious transfer of those same documents online. Whilst digital space may be hugely efficient in its ability to store our data, it seems that moving it is another matter altogether.

Previously (in the 'space-age' of Intelpost, perhaps) it had seemed so simple. Bulky physical things were slow and cumbersome to move through the world, but by becoming dematerialised the information contained within them would be unbounded, free to whizz through both the network and the ether. But as this data swells and becomes too big for the system that led to its creation, it in turn starts to slow down, highlighting once again the fact that in both the old and the new order, in one way or another, communication will always be defined to some extent by an awkward but essential correspondence between information and material objects.

22.   'Sneakernet', *Wikipedia*, accessed 31 October 2017, https://en.wikipedia.org/wiki/Sneakernet.

BIBLIODIVERSITY: THE POLITICS OF KNOWLEDGE AND THE DISTRIBUTION OF IDEAS

Susan Hawthorne

Publishing has been undergoing massive structural changes in the last decade or so, particularly in areas such as digital publishing and marketing, but also in the ways in which books are chosen for publication. It operates in a context of 'the free market gone mad' and is increasingly affected by monopolistic and corporatised behaviour on the part of mega-publishers. Independent publishing is an important counterpoint to this. It reflects in many ways the feminist response to capitalist patriarchy. Just as feminists have had to be on our toes, forever dancing between overarching issues such as violence and exploitation, independent publishers have had to seek ways to survive while simultaneously producing books in which social justice, peace and environmental concerns take priority over profit. This essay is a personal response to the shifting sands of patriarchal publishing and an exploration of the concept of bibliodiversity, which is central to the resistance of independent publishers around the world.

The Politics of Knowledge

It is impossible to be a feminist and not notice that knowledge is political: how we know what we know and whether our take on the world is noticed or not.

I grew up in a multiple knowledge system.[1] The accident of my birth in the Southern Hemisphere was the first knowledge dislocation I noticed. Later, with political activism around feminism, lesbian culture, Aboriginal culture and disability, I noticed other systems. But my first understanding of the dual system – Northern Hemisphere/mainstream, Southern Hemisphere/margins – occurred on a daily basis throughout my childhood. Christmas cards filled with snow and reindeer accompanied blistering hot days, withering grass and ice creams. My grandmother told us stories of innocuous rabbits such as Peter Rabbit, while my father went out on shooting expeditions to rid the land of the introduced pest: the European rabbit. At school the textbooks were filled with images of oaks and elms, God and the church; only in Nature Study classes did anyone mention the *eucalyptus* and *callitris*; no one mentioned the dreamings of the Indigenous owners of the land. The history we learnt had more to do with the British empire than the 70,000 years (and more) of continuous

---

1.   I wrote this paragraph for my 2002 book *Wild Politics*, but reproduce it here because this story of the background of my practice remains current. See: Susan Hawthorne, *Wild Politics: Feminism, Globalisation, Bio/diversity* (Melbourne: Spinifex Press, 2002), 87–88.

Aboriginal culture, or even the mere 200 years of white habitation. What was conveyed to us was that knowledge of Britain or Europe was more important. It represented 'truth'. What we learnt in Nature Study, or by living on the land, was incidental, only of interest to us, and not the sort of knowledge that would carry you through your life. This was the 1950s in rural New South Wales. We knew we were a long way from where the real and important events of the world occurred. Nevertheless, the first twelve years of my life gave me a rootedness in the local, in the land, and a real sense of my place. It is the background against which my thinking and imagining takes place.

In addition to the above experience, I have worked with Arabic women learning English, with unemployed young people, with Aboriginal students at secondary and tertiary level, with students of writing in India and a host of other knowledge-expanding locations. What I value is the chance to see the world through a different lens. I have carried these lenses into my practice in the publishing industry, in which I began work in 1987.

As an editor, and later commissioning senior editor, at Penguin Books I set out to get as many diverse voices published as I could. As Valerie Solanas suggested, subversive feminists should 'become members of the unwork force'.[2] In that role I succeeded in contributing to a diversity of writers being published, among them Aboriginal women and men, lesbians, immigrants and writers with disabilities. Fortunately, I was supported in my first year by the forward-thinking publishers Brian Johns and Jackie Yowell, and success builds success, so my ability to pick some winners worked in my favour over the following three years. But then came the 1990 recession in Australia. The opportunities for publishing outsiders fell away. In early 1991, I left Penguin to co-found, with Renate Klein, Spinifex Press, an independent radical feminist press based in Australia. In the 26 years since then, Spinifex has published a wide range of authors, both local and international, from every continent. The Spinifex mission statement is 'To publish controversial and innovative radical feminist books with an optimistic edge', and our name, 'Spinifex', is after an Australian desert grass that holds the earth together. In this essay, I am drawing on books published in that period and our philosophical approach to publishing.

2.   Solanas, Valerie, *SCUM Manifesto* (New York: Olympia Press, 1967), 42.

Bibliodiversity

Bibliodiversity is a term first used by independent publishers in Chile in 2001.[3] It is a term that brings to mind ideas around ecology and biodiversity linked to a love of fine books and important ideas. My definition of bibliodiversity grows out of earlier work I did on biodiversity and multiversity:

> Biodiversity is the complex self-sustaining system of an ecological niche in a very particular locale. It includes diversity in genetics, within species and within ecosystems. It includes plants, animals and micro-organisms.[4]

> The idea of multiversity is that knowledge is born out of experience as well as through research and study. That is, it is located in a particular cultural milieu that is not necessarily the dominant culture. It arises out of respect for other ways of knowing.

> Multiversity is an epistemological approach that takes account of the location and context of the knower. It values local knowledge. It does not attempt to straitjacket those who bring the most original ideas, ideas that resist the mainstream with its global supports of religion, capital, libertarian consumerism, and militarism.[5]

> Bibliodiversity is the idea of multiversity applied to the publishing industry. Like biodiverse ecology, a thriving publishing culture is one in which bestsellers and formulaic genre titles do not dominate the culture. Instead, voices from the margins are given breathing space. Human culture, like ecological systems, can become monocultural. A lack of diversity in publishing diminishes the richness of our reading experiences and is, like an agricultural monoculture, unhealthy.

> Bibliodiversity is a complex self-sustaining system of story-telling, writing, publishing and other kinds of production of orature and literature. The writers and producers are comparable to the inhabitants of

3.   'Bibliodiversity', International Alliance of Independent Publishers, accessed 25 November 2017, https://www.alliance-editeurs.org/bibliodiversity?lang=en.
4.   Hawthorne, *Wild Politics*, 382.
5.   Susan Hawthorne, *Bibliodiversity: A Manifesto for Independent Publishing* (Melbourne: Spinifex Press, 2014).

an ecosystem. Bibliodiversity contributes to a thriving life of culture and a healthy eco-social system.[6]

The problem of the politics of knowledge in a globalised world is exacerbated by a 'not seeing', a kind of perceptual *terra nullius*. It is basic to colonisation because the colonisers create a vacuum, an invisibility, where previously there had been a people, language, culture and traditions around all kinds of social activities. If they are not invisibilised, they are exoticised,[7] cultural forms appropriated, distorted and sold back to the 'natives' at a profit. Even the most 'domesticated' of social groups – women – have been exoticised by the sexualisation industries of pornography and prostitution through which they are then sold back to the society in which they live.[8] These and other forms of exoticisation dispossess the oppressed of their dignity and humanity, reducing both to commodities to be bought and sold. In the world of literature, precisely the same thing can happen when an author considered 'other' is lionised but then, when the fashion changes, is dropped without a second thought. The author is used to fill a consumerist gap, possibly a spiritual gap or a sense of meaninglessness encapsulated by sentences like 'Thirty years of shopping, and I still have nothing to wear'.[9] In our technological and global world, knowledge has become 'capital, a commodity, and a means for exclusive market control'.[10] The final outcome of the neoliberal consumerist process is 'that the mind becomes a corporate monopoly'.[11]

6.　　Hawthorne, *Bibliodiversity: A Manifesto for Independent Publishing*, 2. Examples of orature include Homer's *The Odyssey* and *The Iliad*; the Indian epic the *Mahabharata*; Australian Aboriginal song cycles, such as *Djanggawul*, and a vast array of spoken literature from around the world. It also includes a wide range of traditional songs, poems and stories, as well as recipes for food and medicines. In the trade and craft context it includes particular instructions for making objects, such as musical instruments, and more.

7.　　Susan Hawthorne, 'The Politics of the Exotic: the Paradox of Cultural Voyeurism', *Meanjin* 48, no. 2 (1989); also published in *NWSA Journal*, 1, no. 4 (Summer 1989).

8.　　For more on this process, see Caroline Norma and Melinda Tankard Reist (eds.), *Prostitution Narratives: Stories of Survival in the Sex Trade* (Melbourne: Spinifex Press, 2016).

9.　　Hawthorne, *Wild Politics*, 99.

10.　　Vandana Shiva, *Protect or Plunder? Understanding Intellectual Property Rights* (London: Zed Books, 2001).

11.　　Shiva, *Protect or Plunder?*, 113.

Distribution of Ideas

Whatever is unnamed, undepicted in images, whatever is omitted from biography, censored in collections of letters, whatever is misnamed as something else, made difficult-to-come-by, whatever is buried in the memory by the collapse of meaning under an inadequate or lying language – this will become, not merely unspoken, but unspeakable.[12]

Adrienne Rich is writing about the gaps and distortions in writing about and by lesbians, but her words apply also to any person or group or being that is marginalised or despised, for whatever reason. In the last few years, the mainstream publishing industry has picked up on the idea of diversity, but the trend is for a consumerist version of diversity: one blue, two green, one purple person within the larger group that is mainly white, male and mobile.

The distribution of this idea of diversity has risen from grassroots publishers (note that Adrienne Rich wrote this in 1977), up through the middle publishing range and now to the six multinational global English-language publishers. Small and independent publishers have been engaged in this for decades. I will take as examples the practices of Renate Klein and myself prior to setting up Spinifex Press. More than half a decade before we came together to establish the press, we were each already writing and practising diverse approaches. In 1985, in London, Klein edited 'Rethinking Sisterhood: Unity in Diversity' as a special issue of *Women's Studies International Forum*. Klein puts forward a passionate plea for feminists to 'validate and learn from each other',[13] even when we disagree, and 'to deal with differences, conflicts, anxieties, hurts and pains between women and within ourselves'.[14] On the other side of the world, in Melbourne, Australia, in 1985, I organised a nine-day women writers' festival called 'The Language of Difference'. In the introduction to the anthology published to mark the festival, I wrote that its purpose was 'to create a community of women to speak across the differences that separate us and to begin to recognise the distortions that result from

12.   Adrienne Rich, 'It is the Lesbian in us ...'. *Sinister Wisdom* 3, (Spring 1977), 6.
13.   Renate Klein, 'Editorial', *Rethinking Sisterhood: Unity in Diversity. Women's Studies International Forum* 8, no. 1 (1985), 1–3.
14.   Klein, 'Editorial', 3.

difference being viewed as a source of weakness, rather than a source of strength'.[15]

Renate Klein and I had not met, and our publishing house, Spinifex Press, was still six years in the future. The ideas we both drew on were being very effectively distributed internationally through books, articles, conferences and poems some thirty years before the mainstream publishing industry began to pick up on just a few of them. In the decade between 1984 and 1994, there were six International Feminist Book Fairs, held in London (1984), Oslo (1986), Montréal (1988), Barcelona (1990), Amsterdam (1992) and Melbourne (1994). These events resulted in feminist publishers and feminists working inside mainstream or independent publishing houses to come together, share information and ideas and buy and sell rights. Numerous books were co-published and translated during this period. It also provided feminist authors with an opportunity to have their work heard by interested audiences.

I mention this because, half a decade on, in the middle of the anti-globalisation movement, with social forums being held in different cities around the world, the word 'bibliodiversity' came into use, and it has been at the core of policy for the International Alliance of Independent Publishers ever since. The Alliance describes itself as an 'international network of 400 publishers in the world in favor of bibliodiversity'.

Like the International Feminist Book Fairs, this organisation assists in the networking of independent publishers and brings together publishing houses from every continent, operating in languages such as Arabic, English, French, German, Persian, Portuguese and Spanish, as well as a number of publishers working in languages such as Turkish, Italian, Bulgarian and Armenian. As a distributor of knowledge, the Alliance is very effective in helping to establish links for co-publication and translation.[16] Publishers are working across the South/North and East/West divides, which remains something of a rarity in the publishing industry.

The Feminist Book Fairs and the Alliance have also engaged in opportunities for training, though inevitably the Feminist Book Fairs had

15.   Susan Hawthorne, *Difference: Writings by Women* (Sydney: Waterloo Press, 1985)

16.   An example is my own book, *Bibliodiversity: A Manifesto for Independent Publishing* (2014). It has been published in the following languages and territories: English (Australia, USA, NZ, UK, 2014, and Canada, 2015); Arabic (Syria, Egypt, Tunisia and Lebanon, 2016); French (France, Switzerland, Mali, Benin, Cameroun, 2016); German (Germany, 2017); Spanish (Chile, Argentina, Mexico, Bolivia, Uruguay, Colombia, 2017).

far fewer resources, since funding for feminist actions is never viewed as a priority.[17] The Alliance has run workshops in developing countries, covering topics such as distribution and digital publishing.

Diversity has become a buzzword in publishing in the last few years, but the mainstream still does not approach the richness or the international and linguistic variety that is currently seen in the indie publishing scene. Nor do I expect it to ever do so, because publishing is a 'fashion-led' industry, and the idea of diversity will soon fade.

Free Speech

Speaking freely, as linguist and philosopher Julia Penelope terms it, is critical inside the 'Patriarchal Universe of Discourse'. Indeed, it is particularly so for feminists and lesbians, for whom that discourse is often threatening. Penelope's book *Speaking Freely: Unlearning the Lies of the Fathers' Tongues* concludes with a call to 'learn to speak freely, imagining ourselves into an age when oppression is obsolete'.[18] But in our global neoliberal world, speaking freely is not the same as 'free speech'. In contrast to Penelope's imagined future, one of the biggest proponents of free speech is an organisation called the Free Speech Coalition. It is the mouthpiece of the pornography and prostitution industries in the United States. It was founded in 1991 to protect these industries from having their 'free speech' curtailed. Penelope would recognise this as a distortion perpetrated by the Patriarchal Universe of Discourse, because while the Coalition uses the language of rights and civil liberty, their intent is to allow the speech of the powerful while curtailing the speech (and the lives) of the powerless.

Betty McLellan, in her book *Unspeakable: A Feminist Ethic of Speech*, draws a connection between free speech and free trade. As so many movements for social change have noted, including the anti-

17.   The International Feminist Book Fairs each had funding from a variety of sources, such as governmental, commercial and philanthropic. What distinguishes them from the Alliance's activity is that each group had to find its own funding and there was no continuing funding from city to city. Two years is not long to raise funds, employ staff, develop programmes and run a five-day fair that has to work as a political, artistic and commercial venture.
18.   Julia Penelope, *Speaking Freely: Unlearning the Lies of the Fathers' Tongues*, The Athene Series (New York: Pergamon Press, 1990), 236.

globalisation movement of the 1990s,[19] free trade does not benefit the poor, the dispossessed and the marginalised (the vast majority of whom are women). Rather, free trade makes the wealthy capitalist and corporatist richer and more powerful.

As a long-term critic of free trade agreements, I have critiqued not only the impact of trade on the oppressed, but also the language used in the treaties:

> The language of 'free trade' and 'free choice' … misrepresents the idea of 'freedom' as one that is closely intertwined with responsibility. Within the realm of neo-classical economics, globalisation and free-trade mantras of transnational companies, freedom has no association with responsibility at all. In the world of international trade, transnational companies, the US government and institutions such as the World Trade Organization are playing a free and irresponsible game. As the more powerful players they get to make the rules, tip the playing field so that it is not level, and score the game as well.[20]

Or, as McLellan points out:

–   free trade / free speech favours the powerful
–   free trade / free speech fosters and entrenches inequality
–   free trade / free speech focuses on the individual
–   free trade / free speech ignores quality of life.[21]

The global financial crisis of 2008 has had a cascading effect on free trade and has contributed to a playing field that is even more surely tilted against the dispossessed. In this historical context, 'disaster capitalism' has become normalised.[22] Changes in publishing are a reflection of this. The merger of Penguin Random House is one such outcome; another is

19.   I make a note of the date because the anti-globalisation protests of the 1990s and early 2000s were critiques of capitalism, environmental destruction and social inequity. By contrast, the appropriated Trump-inspired moves against globalisation (and, in Australia, those prompted by right-wing politician Pauline Hanson) are in fact fake critiques used simply to generate votes in the rust belt and other working-class areas of industry from which, had the left anti-globalisation movements been more successful, alternative industries might have been developed.
20.   Susan Hawthorne, 'The Australia-United States Free Trade Agreement', *Arena Magazine* 63 (February–March 2003), 29.
21.   Betty McLellan, *Unspeakable: A Feminist Ethic of Speech* (Townsville: OtherWise Publications, 2010), 52–58.
22.   Naomi Klein, *The Shock Doctrine: The Rise of Disaster Capitalism* (Camberwell, Vic: Penguin Australia, 2007).

the rise of increasingly powerful media gorillas, such as Amazon, Google and Apple, now joined by Facebook and Netflix. Large publishers have made moves to become booksellers. The Italian company Mondadori, a company chaired by Marina Berlusconi, daughter of former Italian president Silvio Berlusconi, is a good example of this. On the other hand, booksellers like Amazon now want to be publishers. But an author signing with Amazon should be aware that the contract with Amazon that she or he signs includes a clause that reserves the right of Amazon to change any part of its contract at any time. Furthermore, Amazon, while often cited as a *monopoly*, given its position as the most powerful *seller* of books, is also a *monopsony*, on account of its distorting power as a *buyer* of books and ebooks from publishers.

Fair Speech

Building upon her critique of free speech, Betty McLellan came up with the idea of 'fair speech'.[23] In doing so, she is challenging the Patriarchal Universe of Discourse exemplified in the destructive power of 'anything goes speech' that allows hate speech – the vilification and subjection of people, especially when directed at others because of race or ethnicity, sex, class or caste, religion, sexual orientation or disability.

An analysis of fair speech must consider the effects of silencing. Censorship is not only the straightforward culling and banning of the words of writers and artists, and the imprisonment, torture or killing of those who utter rebellious words. It also ventures into the realm of social conditioning. In *Pornography and Silence*, Susan Griffin makes the connection between the violence of pornography and women's silence.[24] She argues that the silence is as much internal as external. This is also the case for colonised peoples in general. Judy Atkinson outlines the trauma inflicted on Indigenous people, which is passed on from generation to generation.[25] Those from the working class are familiar with similar kinds of transgenerational trauma, as are people marginalised by hatred (in a Christian-dominant world, Jews and Muslims have suffered this fate).

23.   McLellan, *Unspeakable.*
24.   Susan Griffin, *Pornography and Silence: Culture's Revenge Against Nature* (San Francisco, CA: HarperCollins, 1982).
25.   Judy Atkinson, *Trauma Trails, Recreating Songlines: Transgenerational Trauma in Indigenous Australia* (Melbourne: Spinifex Press, 2002).

While McLellan does not specifically articulate the contrasting axioms regarding free trade and free speech cited above, the consequences of her ideas for fair trade and fair speech are as follows:

–   fair trade / fair speech decentralises power
–   fair trade / fair speech fosters justice and fair treatment
–   fair trade / fair speech focuses on the common good and engagement
–   fair trade / fair speech highlights the importance of life over profit.[26]

The Alliance recognised silence as a form of speech control and thus the need for a policy on fair speech in its International Declaration of Independent Publishers 2014, arising from a meeting of 400 publishers in Cape Town, South Africa:

Thought is not controlled by censorship alone. In an environment of excessive information, media concentration and the standardisation of content, it is essential to be careful that freedom of expression does not only serve the voice of the dominant groups or powers. We, the independent publishers, defend Fair Speech in order to make a multiplicity of voices heard, which in itself secures bibliodiversity.[27]

For a publishing industry to foster bibliodiversity, the above must be taken into account.[28] The upshot of this is that women's voices must be heard, as must the voices of people who have been historically marginalised: the colonised, peasants and workers. As Maria Mies and colleagues so presciently noted in 1988:

The realisation that the women's question is related to the colonial question and that both are related to the dominant, global, capitalist-patriarchal model of accumulation, did not dawn upon us suddenly or in our studies. Our perception of the systematic relationship between these

26.   Hawthorne, *Bibliodiversity*, 46.
27.   International Alliance of Independent Publishers, *International Declaration of Independent Publishers 2014, To Promote and Strengthen Bibliodiversity Together*. Cape Town, 20 September, 2014, 7. http://www.alliance-editeurs.org/IMG/pdf/ international_declaration_of_independent_publishers_2014-6.pdf
28.   Simultaneously, we need to be cognisant of the appropriation of our ideas. Initially when 'fake news' was discussed it was generally used in relation to reporting by organisations of the Alt-right, such as Fox News and Breitbart. Donald Trump and the right now complain about being the victim of 'fake news', when in fact the news is simply accurate and fearless reporting.

questions is the result of many years of experience in the Third World (in India and Latin America) and involvement in women's struggles in Europe.[29]

The global publishing industry thrives on the subaltern or marginal voice because those existing on the margins have a new ideational energy. But the inclusion of such voices in mainstream publishing is often short-lived, either because it becomes subject to fashion, exoticised, swept up and spat out,[30] or because the new perspectives unearthed are too shocking and so too risky for the dominant culture to endure. More challenging is the possibility of those same marginal people taking over the means of production. As the publisher of a feminist press, that is exactly our intent. While in large publishing houses women play significant roles in editorial and marketing, it is less common to find women in leadership roles, or in charge of areas such as production, shipping, distribution, warehousing, digital technology and sales.

For a genuine fair speech to become a part of the production of books and the spread of ideas, we must squarely tackle the obstacles to justice and the vagaries of fashion in publishing. In Australia, multinational publisher Hachette is currently publishing a number of Indigenous writers and other writers from non-Anglo-Celtic backgrounds, but unless they know of the history of feminist publishing and independent publishing this venture into bibliodiversity will be temporary at best. The history of the mainstream publishing industry's dalliances with diversity does not bode well for a future change of management and direction.

Feminist and Indie Publishing Strategies

The very significant national and international events and magazines, and the wealth of feminist publishers and booksellers active during the last quarter of the twentieth century, represented the height of feminist publishing through traditional channels.[31] As one indicator, the quarterly *Feminist Bookstore News* (*FBN*) was essential reading for any feminist in the book industry during that period.

29.   Maria Mies, Veronika Bennholdt-Thomsen and Claudia von Werlof, *Women: The Last Colony* (New Delhi: Kali for Women, 1988), 1–2.
30.   Hawthorne, 'The Politics of the Exotic'.
31.   Hawthorne, *Bibliodiversity*, 4–8.

Carol Seajay, a lesbian feminist organizer, began the *Feminist Bookstore News(letter)* in 1976 to provide a means of connecting feminist booksellers, printers and publishers. The idea was the result of the 1976 Women In Print conference. *FBN* was widely considered the *Publisher's Weekly* for the feminist book trade with book news, business news, inspirational features, and a forum for sharing the problems faced by and the successful strategies employed by other publishers and bookstores. The final issue was Summer 2000.[32]

The rise and eventual demise of *FBN* also reflects the shift from analogue to digital which took place from the mid-1990s to 2000. In this period, while there was email, social media had not yet appeared. In spite of this, good communication flows between feminist printers, publishers and booksellers were already established, and *FBN* was critical to this. One can see that the International Feminist Book Fairs occurred squarely in the middle of this period (1984–1994). During this time there were also nationally based Feminist Book Fortnights, which occurred in the UK following the First International Feminist Book Fair in London, until the early- to mid-1990s. Australia had two Australian Feminist Book Fortnights, in 1989 and 1991, with hundreds of events in metropolitan areas of every state and 'from Broome to Burnie'. In Aotearoa/New Zealand the *Listener* Women's Book Week took place in the 1990s, and in the United States a feminist publishers' catalogue was produced. Each of these national events was associated with the production of catalogues. For example, in Australia, a catalogue of feminist titles published in Australia was printed and distributed nationally (by Penguin in 1989 and by Random House in 1991) to bookshops, which were encouraged to have window displays of books in the catalogue and to have events which promoted the work of feminist writers and their publishers. It was a well thought out and structured system for the promotion of writers, publishers and booksellers. A Top Twenty list was also selected, and posters of these book covers were included with the catalogues.

In Germany and Austria, BücherFrauen (the German equivalent of Women in Publishing) holds regular meetings, and every year at the Frankfurt Book Fair a woman is announced as the annual BücherFrau – the 'book woman of the year'. This role has been awarded to women from

32.   '*Feminist Bookstore News* Records, 1976–2000' (San Francisco Public Library) Online Archives of California, www.oac.cdlib.org

a range of roles: publishers, translators, booksellers, reviewers, agents, critics, librarians and authors. The organisation's purpose is to provide a platform for women in the field to support one another through information exchange, mentoring, training and recognition of service to the book industry. The organisation Women in Publishing exists in a number of English-speaking countries, including the UK, Hong Kong and Australia. It is more professionally oriented than the original Women in Print organisation in the United States, which had clearly defined political goals.

Much of what was done in the feminist book industry network has been copied by others (e.g. the Books Alive campaign in Australia) or adapted to the digital era. The International Alliance of Independent Publishers, based in Paris, was established in 2002, and its first meeting was held in Dakar, Senegal, in that year. International meetings have been held subsequently in Guadalajara, Mexico, in 2005; Paris, France, in 2007; and Cape Town, South Africa, in 2014. The Alliance has a permanent secretariat with several employees and, compared to the feminist organisations, considerably more funding (although its funding base is often under threat). It is structured around language groups that have their own meetings. The Alliance's English-language network has met in Paris (2007), Delhi (2008), Frankfurt (2013) and Istanbul (2015). There have also been a number of cross-language meetings, such as the one at Frankfurt (2013) for a meeting of social science publishers. The Alliance has a website detailing its history, declarations, policy and activities, and a list of member publishers represented by up to three published titles; and, since 2014, the organisation has had a presence on Facebook which enables publishers to communicate across language groups. 21 September has been announced as the International Day of Bibliodiversity, and language networks and publishers promote the ideas that inform the Alliance on this day though short videos, posters and memes. There is also a journal, *Bibliodiversity*, which publishes both academic and professional papers about independent publishing.

The most important aspect of the Alliance is networking, and the opportunities for co-publishing and translations. It is also an arena where publishers can compare experiences, such as problems around censorship and distribution, or simply share political and creative ideas. It is often only other independent publishers who really understand the challenges involved in surviving in the book industry. The Alliance is more focused on publishers than the feminist publishing networks were: the latter insisted that authors and booksellers should be involved.

Among the policy orientations of the Alliance for 2015–2018 is a focus on the 'Strengthening of inter-professional sharing (authors, librarians, booksellers, diffusers-distributors, digital actors, etc.): inter-professional meetings, joint lobbying'.[33]

Ostensibly more international and multilingual, the feminist book fairs were held not only in English-speaking countries (including the UK, Canada and Australia) but also in French-speaking cities (Montréal, in Canada, for instance), and in Oslo, Norway (1986), Barcelona (in the Catalan-speaking area of Spain) and the Netherlands, and another was proposed to take place in Brazil in 1996. However, cross-linguistic information-sharing is more formalised in the Alliance than in the feminist networks. There remain a number of publishers who have participated in both the feminist and the indie networks, including publishers from India, South Africa, Mexico and Australia.

Political and Creative Friendship

Friendship is rarely spoken about in business circles, but the book industry is about more than just business and money. It is about ideas, passions and politics. And, especially in the feminist and indie sectors, it's about what is inside the book: the creativity, structure and imagination.

So, unsurprisingly, the feminist and indie publishing scenes also depend heavily on friendship. We publishers want to work with people who share our approach. In the case of feminist publishing, not every press that calls itself 'feminist' will be a partner, while with others there is an immediate rapport. I can report that in the indie sector this variability of shared approaches and connections is also evident.

The occasions on which we meet can offer more than simply the opportunity to work on co-productions or translations. They can also draw out interesting ideas and perspectives. And when this happens, it is far more likely that we will keep in touch and work on a number of projects together. Indie and feminist publishers thereby develop a depth and breadth through working with others. A publisher in Chile, India, Turkey, South Africa or Syria connects with a book or an approach. This happens because, in this context, politics matters, as does a creative

33.   'Orientations, 2015–2018', International Alliance of Independent Publishers, accessed 25 November 2017, https://www.alliance-editeurs.org/orientations-2015-2018,1061?lang=en.

approach to publishing. There are a number of publishers with whom we have worked for a decade or even two, and this is fulfilling because we develop trust in one another, and this makes it possible to sometimes take on risky books, or for others to publish our books in their territory.

Knowing that the publisher on the other side of the table approaches the sale or purchase of rights from an ethical standpoint means that authors and publishers gain from the relationship. While money changes hands in these dialogues, friendship is the thing that outlasts all transactions.

WHAT KNOWLEDGE FOR DECOLONISING THE PHILOSOPHY OF TECHNOLOGY?

Ahmed Ansari

Invisible Knowledge & Knowing

Over the last few years, I've found myself spending a large chunk of every short academic break in my home city of Karachi, searching for books that can't be found easily in the United States. Usually, considering how niche my interests are, I find excellent books almost by accident – for example, this past year, while standing at the checkout counter of a local bookshop, my eye caught the religious section, and specifically a small stack of Amina Raquib's *Islamic Ethics of Technology* on the bottom shelf in a nondescript corner. Naturally, I bought a copy right away – but I was only the third person to have done so. Islamic technology studies books apparently don't have the same appeal as *101 Shining Stars of Islamic History* or *A Collection of Favorite Moral Tales*. On another occasion, I was shown Waqar Husaini's *Islamic Thought in the Rise of Islamic Technological Culture* by a vendor, after having requested another book – I silently thanked the local practice whereby booksellers try to sell you books they think are close to what you want when they don't have the book you asked for.

A look at the publishers of the above two titles also reveals something about the economy of scholarly publication and distribution in Pakistan. Raquib's book — based on her PhD dissertation, which was undertaken at the University of Queensland — was published in Kuala Lumpur, while Husaini's book was published in New Delhi. They can't be bought in American bookstores. While they can be found in Pakistan, they are admittedly not widely distributed: it is easier to find a copy of Martin Heidegger's *Being and Time* or Bijker and Pinch's *The Social Construction of Facts and Artefacts* than it is to find one of the most comprehensive studies of the political economy of technology in Pakistan, Ghulam Kibria's *Technology Acquisition in Pakistan*, which is sold only at its publisher's store in Karachi.

I cite these examples because they reveal a peculiar problem about the construction of disciplinary knowledge today. In the age of the internet, when one can assume that almost any kind of information can be found online, no matter how obscure, through the mechanisms of digital search engines and their consistently self-improving algorithms, in digital libraries, databases, or archives. And yet none of these books can be bought or downloaded online. No digital versions exist – the only reference, for example, to Mr. Kibria's book is in the form of a review of it by Prabir Purkayastha in 2001. And I think that this is important because it raises important questions about the perceived lack of scholarship on technology in Pakistan, for at the outset it seems as if there is little to none – and we haven't even accounted for the possibility that there might be scholars working in Urdu and other languages that are completely invisible to the English-speaking world.

What does this mean for technology studies in Pakistan and abroad? Do any scholars read these books, apart from those working in the incredibly niche field of Pakistani technology studies? Why aren't these books part of the curricula of the few programs that study technology critically in Pakistan? Is there important work that has been done in languages other than English? Does the lack of visibility for scholars working in countries like Pakistan mean that their work is doomed to obscurity, relegated to marginality unless it can find an audience with, or relate to the output of, work being produced in the Anglo-European sphere? And, most importantly, what does this mean for the constitution of what we can claim to 'know' about technology or technicity (the condition of being technological beings) both locally and globally? Why is the canon of the philosophy of technology, from Martin Heidegger to Lewis Mumford to Bernard Stiegler, so disturbingly homogenous?

As the anthropologist Arturo Escobar notes, in the general climate of anxiety about the Anthropocene and the waning of Western civilisation, new and interdisciplinary 'transition discourses' are emerging to propose ways of moving from the unsustainable structure of contemporary global capitalism towards new, plural ways of imagining life on the planet.[1] The 'pluriverse', as Escobar and other decolonial scholars including Walter Mignolo have called it, stands in contrast to the universalist paradigms of development, freedom, democracy, etc., that define the agendas of global institutions today. The pluriverse is characterised by multiple and different alternatives coming from different cultures and different parts of the world:

Hermeneutics, in the Western genealogy of thoughts, names a type of reflection on meaning and interpretation within one cosmology, Western cosmology. When you have to deal with two or more cosmologies, as I did in *The Darker Side of the Renaissance*, you need a pluritopic hermeneutics.[2]

1.   Arturo Escobar, 'Sustainability: Design for the pluriverse', *Development* 54, no. 2 (2011): 137–140.
2.   Walter Mignolo, 'On pluriversality', accessed 31 January 2018, http://waltermignolo.com/on-pluriversality/.

As Mignolo argues, as the political and economic hegemony of the West gives way to the growing multipolarity of a world in which Brazil, Russia, India, China and South Africa (the 'BRICS' nations) are coming into their own, the epistemic hegemony of the West also needs to be questioned. And as I have attempted to indicate, the present structure of our global knowledge systems leaves much to be desired.

This short essay examines why and how new knowledges must be generated in technology studies. Through the lens of decolonial theory, I attempt to trace connections between, on the one hand, the global distribution of indigenous texts on technology and, on the other hand, the structure of knowledge in the history and philosophy of technology, in order to propose ways to decolonise modern knowledge systems. I focus on the theoretical foundations of such a project, I define the problem of knowledge and pluriversality from a decolonial perspective, and I propose two projects relevant to the task of decolonising technology studies.

There is an urgent reason why I believe such a move is necessary. We no longer live on a planet that can sustain the current lifestyles of vast populations of people. While I do not believe that ecological catastrophe will spell the extinction of all life on earth, or even *human* life on earth, it will mean the end of modern civilisation as we know it. Technology has a crucial role to play in this – the technological foundations of modern life are the basis for the unsustainability of our present condition. Therefore, regardless of whether or not one is invested in a decolonial politics, i.e., whether one thinks from the centre of Anglo-European hegemony or from the margins of non-Western indigenous discourses, thinking ecologically entails that we strive to develop alternative ways of thinking about technology and technicity.

The Problem of (Modern) Knowledge

Modernity has a specific character. It encapsulates within it ideas, logics and paradigms, as well as institutions, practices, subjects and, of course, technologies. Democracy and the sovereign nation state, capitalism and the global market economy, development and industrialisation, the media and the art and entertainment industries, the courts and modern ideas of law and justice, globalisation, and so on, all fall under the rubric of modernity. Together, these comprise what Immanuel Wallerstein and Janet Abu-Lughod, in their macro-historical analyses of civilisations, would classify as the modern *world-system*.[3] As Wallerstein and Abu-Lughod showed, the roots of the present world-system lay in the expansion and growth of European civilisation through colonisation from the sixteenth century onwards. Colonisation was brutal and efficient: through a combination of genocide, enslavement and subjugation,[4] the Europeans swept through the Americas, Africa and Asia, displacing and replacing older political, economic and social systems, and establishing new loci, new centres and peripheries, of power.[5] Where prior to the sixteenth century there had been many continent-spanning empires but no single hegemonic power, the new world-system was unprecedented in the history of humanity in the sense that it was the first truly global and totalising civilisation.

This world-system is still in place, as decolonial scholars including Anibal Quijano, Ramon Grosfoguel and Walter Mignolo have recognised. Formal processes of decolonisation began in the decades following World War II, since European nations were unable to continue their imperial projects after the war. Yet, the new world order continued the colonial project: the hyper-industrial West, led by the superpowers of the Cold War era, the US and the USSR, continued to set both the terms and the content of global political and economic agendas. This happened, if not by approval, then by coercion:

Under the spell of neo-liberalism and the magic of the media promoting it, modernity and modernization, together with democracy, are being sold as a package trip to the promised land of happiness... yet, when people do not buy the package willingly or have other ideas of how economy and society should be organized, they become subject to all kinds of direct and indirect violence.[6]

3.   Immanuel Wallerstein, *The modern world-system: Capitalist agriculture and the origins of the European world-economy in the sixteenth centenary* (New York: Academic Press, 1974); Janet L. Abu-Lughod, *Before European hegemony: the world system AD 1250–1350* (New York and Oxford: Oxford University Press, 1991).
4.   Sven Lindqvist, *'Exterminate All the Brutes': One Man's Odyssey into the Heart of Darkness and the Origins of European Genocide*, trans. Joan Tate (New York: The New Press, 1996).
5.   Anibal Quijano, 'Coloniality of Power, Eurocentrism, and Latin America', *Nepantla: Views from South* 1.3 (2000): 533–580.
6.   Walter Mignolo, 'Delinking: The rhetoric of modernity, the logic of coloniality and the grammar of decoloniality', *Cultural Studies* 21, nos. 2–3 (2007): 450.

However, the decolonial critique of modern civilisations does not end with observations of relative power dynamics and dependencies between the West and the rest. The continued dominance of the West relied upon the ex-colonies continuing to hold onto their colonial legacies, tying their subsequent development and growth to the ideas, ideals and institutions that Western modernity espoused. This meant buying into market capitalism as the continued dominant mode of production, into industrialisation, automation and mass production as the dominant enablers of growth and development, and into globalisation and Western lifestyles, values and norms as ideals for social and cultural imaginaries. Thus, even after decolonisation, *coloniality* — the logic specific to colonialism — continued to exist as the dominant logic of modernity.

This logic was and is characterised by the subsumption or replacement of non-Western ways of thinking and being by western ones, and by the creation of new hierarchies of power not native to colonised populations. This meant, for example, the constitution of the idea of *race* as genealogical purity by the Spaniards and Portuguese over the course of the invasion of the Americas, its introduction into cultures where it had hitherto been unknown as a concept, restructuring their sense of identity, and its implementation as the basis for the classification of peoples as a justification for genocide, slavery and subjugation.[7] Eurocentric ways of knowing and interpreting the world replaced indigenous ways, and this rupture has continued to haunt the psyches of ex-colonised peoples to this day, whereby the identity of the colonised can only be defined in relation to their ex-colonisers:

> I was responsible at the same time for my body, for my race, for my ancestors. I discovered my blackness, my ethnic characteristics; and I was battered down by tom-toms, cannibalism, intellectual deficiency, fetishism, racial defects, slaveships, and above all else, above all: 'Sho' good eatin'.'[8]

Coloniality, therefore, as the underlying logic behind Western hegemony, is an implacable, omnipresent force. It is a totality, one that 'negates, exclude, occlude the difference and the possibilities of other

7.   Quijano, 'Coloniality of Power, Eurocentrism, and Latin America'.

8.   Frantz Fanon, *Black skin, white masks* (London: Pluto Press, 1986), 84–85.

totalities'.[9] As a part of continuing modernity, it continues to suppress other forms of knowledge and knowing, wherever they may be found. This would mean that colonial logic underlies modern academia, the site of new knowledge production in the world: colonialism underlies the structure of the modern school and university, the siloing of disciplines, pedagogical, research and publishing practices, and the various systems and platforms for knowledge distribution and dissemination.

This raises important questions about the production and dissemination of knowledge: *who* produces knowledge, *where* and *why*, to what ends and for whom? Who has access to it and who doesn't? Whose institutions and platforms are the primary sites for the dissemination of knowledge? How knowledge is distributed, its forms and mediums, become crucial matters to consider, especially to those for whom a project of creating alternatives matters. And yet, as we have seen, following the colonial rupture, a pure access to non-Western epistemologies is impossible, with the exception of perhaps a few small indigenous populations, relatively undisturbed or only recently exposed, scattered throughout the world. One could go so far as to say that knowledge has forever been tainted by Eurocentric bias, therefore we are doomed to be modern. Whatever access the ex-colonised have to pre-colonial ways of knowing and being will always be through the lens of modernity. How does one *delink*, to use Mignolo's term, from modernity, and think from the margins of the world-system? How does one practice 'thinking from the borders'?[10] How does one decolonise knowledge?

'Other' Genealogies of Technics, '(An)Other' Internet(s)?

I would like to begin to explore this question by underscoring the distinction between the coloniality of knowledge production and that of dissemination, because they produce slightly different, though interrelated, methodological issues. The first has to do with the structure of knowledge itself — in other words, the question of *what* knowledge is, which is tied to questions surrounding who produces it and where it is produced, its history and genealogy, and the ends to which it might be put. George G. Joseph makes a connection between misconceptions

9.   Mignolo, 'Delinking', 451.
10.   Walter Mignolo, 'Geopolitics of sensing and knowing: on (de) coloniality, border thinking and epistemic disobedience', *Postcolonial studies* 14, no. 3 (2011): 273–283.

about the history of mathematics, which in most standardised school textbooks is a largely Eurocentric history that marginalises the significant contributions made by non-Western civilisations, and structural biases within the global practice of mathematics as discipline:

There is a widespread acceptance of the view that mathematical discovery can only follow from a rigorous application of a form of deductive axiomatic logic, which is perceived as a unique product of Greek mathematics. As a consequence, 'intuitive' or empirical methods are dismissed as of little relevance in mathematics.[11]

Questioning the genealogy of thought in mathematics, to decentre it from its Anglo-European core, is necessary in order to open up the question of what mathematics is and what it could be. The same is true of the study of technology and technicity. As scholars from many disciplines have long argued, from philosophy to sociology to design studies, epistemes and epistemologies cannot be separated from materiality and artifice. We perceive and know the world through the mediation of tools and technologies,[12] and the world we engage with today is itself artificial.[13] Modernity also cannot be separated from modern technicity, and from its historical roots in the Industrial Revolution, as thinkers as far back as Marx attempted to show. However, there are hardly any accounts in decolonial scholarship of the role of technics in shaping the modern world-system, or the role that technologies play in shaping and moulding decolonial subjects and subjectivities.

So that we might be able to design for pluriversal ways of knowing and being, technology studies must first theorise technicity in relation to modernity, as a means to theorise what could be beyond modernity: *to theorise beyond modernity is also to theorise technicity and artifice as other than what it could be.* If unsustainability is intrinsic to technology today, but if technology determines the character of contemporary life, then the project of decolonising the history and philosophy of technology is vital in order to develop alternative technological foundations that

11.   George Ghevarughese Joseph, 'Foundations of Eurocentrism in mathematics,' *Race & Class* 28, no. 3 (1987): 22–23.

12.   Peter-Paul Verbeek, *What things do: Philosophical reflections on technology, agency, and design* (Pennsylvania: Penn State Press, 2005).

13.   Tony Fry, Clive Dilnot and Susan C. Stewart, *Design and the Question of History* (London: Bloomsbury Publishing, 2015).

might lead to a more sustainable existence. This project of decolonising philosophical thought needs to begin with an assessment of what modern technology is.

So far, there has been considerable interest generated within the Anglo-European sphere of thinking beyond modern technicity. For example, the German philosopher Peter Sloterdijk proposes a *homeotechnological* project, in which humanity would learn to cooperate on a global scale and would turn care for both the planet and ourselves into a collective project, in order to turn the earth into a 'global co-immunity structure' that will both protect and nurture human existence and allow non-human life to thrive.[14] He proposes this because, for the first time in our history, human beings across the planet are connected in a vast, global network of communication and knowledge. This means that there is the possibility to cultivate a global sense of crisis and use the immense reach of our connecting technologies to embark upon social and geo-engineering projects of a global scale. Similarly, Bernard Stiegler believes that the solution to the destructiveness of modern technology lies within the technology itself: invoking the idea of the *pharmakon*, which he borrows from Jacques Derrida, modern technicity is both poison and cure. Stiegler argues that the design of the next generation of technologies must deal explicitly with the problem of how we can have a freer, more open relation to the information we produce, overcoming an economisation of knowledge and desire.

There are two issues with both positions. Firstly, both Sloterdijk and Stiegler are trying to find a way out of our present unsustainability by finding a way *through* it: the underlying idea is that the foundations of modern technicity are in themselves not totally problematic, so they could be moulded into less oppressive and less destructive forms. In other words, mass production, mass consumption and mass connectivity are so inherently part of the human condition now that we cannot go back, or find another way – the only way to deal with the technological crisis is to reorient these very things to new purposes. They are both, in my opinion, conservative projects. Secondly, through a decolonial lens, both are rooted in the universalising project of Eurocentric thought, whereby possible alternatives to modern technology founded in different knowledges, values and imaginaries are entirely precluded. Both start

14.　　Peter Sloterdijk, *You must change your life* (Chichester: John Wiley & Sons, 2014).

with an analysis of modern technology and end up proposing the same kinds of projects that modern technology enabled and was enabled by – this is also true of the vast majority of other philosophers of technology. And so we must look elsewhere for alternative proposals, to work being done outside of the Anglo-European sphere, by thinkers on the margins of the world-system.

In his recent book *The Question Concerning Technology in China*, the Chinese philosopher Yuk Hui tackles the difficult task of reconstructing a genealogy of Chinese thought on technology by considering Confucian and Daoist philosophy (the nod to Heidegger's seminal work in the title is not incidental). Hui starts his book with an analysis of one of the most common and widely cited origin stories of how humans received the gift of being-technological: the myth of Prometheus and how he brought fire to humans. He then raises the provocation:

> In assuming a universal Prometheanism, one assumes that all cultures arise from *techne*, which is originally Greek. But in China we find another mythology concerning the creation of human beings and the origin of technics, one in which there is no Promethean figure.[15]

He then proceeds to trace a chronology of philosophical thought in China throughout history, parallel to the development of technological thought in Western civilisation, from Laoxi and Confucius through to the present day.

What Hui shows us – as Watsuji Tetsuro, Jun'ichiro Tanizaki and other scholars from philosophy and the arts in the Eastern traditions have also done – is that since the analysis of modern technology that Heidegger initiated has its roots in the Greek *techne* and Latin *ars*, we must look to concepts and histories that non-Western genealogies of technology might draw from. A decolonising of the philosophy of technology is necessary in order to meet the conditions of pluriversality outlined above – we must not accept that there is only one form of technicity, that which belongs to the West.

This brings us to the second issue, namely: how might one begin constructing such genealogies, and if such projects were successful, to whose benefit would they be? This is precisely where the current

---

15. Yuk Hui, *The Question Concerning Technology in China* (Falmouth: Urbanomic, 2016), 14.

ways in which knowledge is carried and disseminated globally becomes problematic. As I pointed out at the start of this essay, the lack of accessible work online by non-Western scholars can mean one of two things, either that no work in Urdu exists in the philosophy of technology, or that it is simply invisible.

If we consider the second possibility, it leads us to the conclusion that scholars like Mignolo have arrived at, i.e., that the internet and its various platforms are racialised. In our increasingly hyper-digitised age, where everything becomes the object of online surveillance and documentation, and where the trend is to bridge the gap between the real and the virtual by translating the real into information (including the human subject, where the 'real' subject becomes increasingly answerable and reducible to the 'virtual' subject), both the careers of academics and the continued production of academic knowledge is increasingly contingent on what can be seen and accessed virtually. In this case, the preferred course of action might seem to be to bring more non-Western scholars onto the internet, something that corporations with the necessary computational power like Google have committed themselves to – as Anne Wil-Harzing points out, Google Scholar now dwarfs other scholarly search engines like Scopus and Web of Science in terms of representation.[16]

And yet the problem with such a direct approach is that the internet is a global knowledge platform that not only excludes but also *totalises* — it totalises all sensible human experience and thought into information. As such, it is inextricably part of the technological foundations of the global world-system. This leads us to a necessary reassessment of the uses of knowledge in the twenty-first century. The matter in question, then, is not the representation of non-Western scholarship, but the ends that its representation serves, since all information that becomes accessible knowledge is also subject to the taxes that global capitalism exacts from the individual seeking knowledge, and to the exactions of the academic-industrial complex and its institutions.

Today's capitalism should be called the information economy. Information has become wealth to be extracted and accumulated...

16.   Anne Harzing, 'Do Google Scholar, Scopus and the Web of Science speak your language?', *Harzing.com*, accessed 31 January 2018, https://harzing.com/publications/white-papers/do-google-scholar-scopus-and-the-web-of-science-speak-your-language.

Cybernetic capitalism develops so as to allow the social body, devastated by Capital, to reform itself and offer itself up for one more process of accumulation.[17]

If to be present within the world-system is to circulate within its mechanisms, then how is one to break out of it? Here, two strategies present themselves. Tiqqun, in their polemical manifesto *The Cybernetic Hypothesis*, observe that the structure of the World Wide Web was designed in such a way that it could survive the destruction of the majority of its nodes, but would collapse if a small number of core nodes were targeted in incisive strikes by hackers – Tiqqun were motivated by the scenario of a disintegration of the whole global system by 'guerilla warfare'. I do not think that such a scenario, as commendable as its aims may be, is realistic. However, another scenario presents itself – that of creating spaces that are both accessible and not. To delink — recalling Mignolo and other decolonial scholars — is not to disappear. Invoking Derrida's figure of the *pharmakon*, not in the Stieglerian sense of making the technology more open and casting a wider net over the hidden world of academic publishing, but in an opposite way, we might create sites and spaces of knowledge that are accessible and yet reside outside of the monopolistic confines of the digital world-system. I posit that this is entirely possible, by way of archives that operate as collaboratively constructed communities. An example of this would be the internet repository AAAARG, which started as a small community of scholars uploading, sharing and curating open collections of texts and grew over a decade into one of the largest member-driven collections of academic texts online, providing an alternative to the heavily gated paid platforms.

As Janet Abu-Lugodh pointed out in *Before European Hegemony*, the world-system prior to the rise of Europe had no single superpower or civilisation at its centre – instead, power was shared between many different, regionally bound societies and cultures, many of them in contact with each other, sharing resources and information in syncretic, rich ways. The model of the pre-colonial world could be a model for the global knowledge economy and its platforms today, where localised archives might also serve as sites for the creation of alternative genealogies, and canons in disciplines like technology studies could be

---

17.   Tiqqun, *The cybernetic hypothesis*, accessed 31 January 2018, https://theanarchistlibrary.org/library/tiqqun-the-cybernetic-hypothesis.pdf, 22-24.

the basis for a flowering of non-Western thought and its distribution. Perhaps there could be other ways of structuring the internet that do not follow its increasingly centrally governed trajectory of today, and so the challenge for the architects at the margins of the future web would be to imagine what new possibilities and visions for the internet could emerge: new knowledges sustained by new platforms in new, plural realms of the digital.

README.md

Sean Dockray & Benjamin Forster

Introduction

How might we ensure the survival and availability of community libraries, individual collections and other precarious archives? If these libraries, archives and collections are unwanted by official institutions or, worse, buried beneath good intentions and bureaucracy, then what tools and platforms and institutions might we develop instead?

While trying to both formulate and respond to these questions, we began making Dat Library and HyperReadings:

Dat Library distributes libraries across many computers so that many people can provide disk space and bandwidth, sharing in the labour and responsibility of the archival infrastructure.

HyperReadings implements 'reading lists' or a structured set of pointers (a list, a syllabus, a bibliography, etc.) into one or more libraries, *activating* the archives.

Installation

The easiest way to get started is to install Dat Library as a desktop app,[1] but there is also a programme called 'datcat',[2] which can be run on the command line or included in other NodeJS projects.

Accidents of the Archive

The 1996 UNESCO publication 'Lost Memory: Libraries and Archives Destroyed in the Twentieth Century' makes the fragility of historical repositories startlingly clear.[3] '[A]cidified paper that crumbles to dust, leather, parchment, film and magnetic light attacked by light, heat humidity or dust' all assault archives. 'Floods, fires, hurricanes, storms, earthquakes' and, of course, 'acts of war, bombardment and fire, whether deliberate or accidental' wiped out significant portions of many hundreds of major research libraries worldwide. When expanding the scope to consider public, private and community libraries, that number becomes uncountable.

1.   http://dat-dat-dat-library.hashbase.io/ and https://github.com/e-e-e/dat-library

2.   http://github.com/sdockray/dat-cardcat

3.   http://www.stephenmclaughlin.net/ph-library/texts/UNESCO%201996%20%20Lost%20Memory_%20Libraries%20and%20Archives%20Destroyed%20in%20the%20Twentieth%20Century.pdf

Published during the early days of the World Wide Web, the report acknowledges the emerging role of digitisation ('online databases, CD-ROM, etc.'), but today we might reflect on the last twenty years, which has also introduced new forms of loss.

Digital archives and libraries are subject to a number of potential hazards: technical accidents like disk failures, accidental deletions, misplaced data and imperfect data migrations, as well as political-economic accidents like defunding of the hosting institution, deaccessioning parts of the collection and sudden restrictions of access rights. Immediately after library.nu was shut down on the grounds of copyright infringement in 2012, Lawrence Liang wrote of feeling 'first and foremost a visceral experience of loss'.[4]

Whatever its legal status, the abrupt absence of a collection of 400,000 books appears to follow a particularly contemporary pattern. In 2008, Aaron Swartz moved millions of US federal court documents out from behind a paywall, resulting in a trial and an FBI investigation. Three years later, he was arrested and indicted for a similar gesture, systematically downloading academic journal articles from JSTOR. That year, Kazakhstani scientist Alexandra Elbakyan began Sci-Hub in response to scientific journal articles that were prohibitively expensive for scholars based outside of Western academic institutions.[5] The repository, growing to more than 60 million papers, was sued in 2015 by Elsevier for $15 million, resulting in a permanent injunction. Library Genesis, another library of comparable scale, finds itself in a similar legal predicament.[6]

Arguably one of the largest digital archives of the 'avant-garde' (loosely defined), UbuWeb is transparent about this fragility. In 2011, its founder Kenneth Goldsmith wrote: 'by the time you read this, UbuWeb may be gone. [...] Never meant to be a permanent archive, Ubu could vanish for any number of reasons: our ISP pulls the plug, our university support dries up, or we simply grow tired of it.'[7] Even the banality of exhaustion is a real risk to these libraries.

The simple fact is that some of these libraries are among the largest in the world yet are subject to sudden disappearance. We can only

4.   https://kafila.online/2012/02/19/library-nu-r-i-p/
5.   https://en.wikipedia.org/wiki/Sci-Hub
6.   See https://www.memoryoftheworld.org for further analysis and an alternative approach to the same issues. ('When everyone is librarian, library is everywhere.')
7.   http://www.ubu.com/resources/

begin to guess at what the contours of 'Lost Memory: Libraries and Archives Destroyed in the Twenty-First Century' will be when it is written ninety years from now.

Non-Profit, Non-State Archives

Cultural and social movements have produced histories which are only partly represented in state libraries and archives. Often they are deemed too small or insignificant or, in some cases, dangerous. Most frequently, they are not deemed to be anything at all — they are simply neglected. While the market, eager for new resources to exploit, might occasionally fill in the gaps, it is ultimately motivated by profit and not by responsibility to communities or archives. (We should not forget the moment Amazon silently erased legally purchased copies of George Orwell's *1984* from readers' Kindle devices because of a change in the commercial agreement with the publisher.)[8]

So, what happens to these minor libraries? They are innumerable, but for the sake of illustration let's say that each could be represented by a single book. Gathered together, these books would form a great library (in terms of both importance and scale). But to extend the metaphor, the current reality could be pictured as these books flying off their shelves to the furthest reaches of the world, their covers flinging open and the pages themselves scattering into bookshelves and basements, into the caring hands of relatives or small institutions devoted to passing these words on to future generations.

While the massive digital archives listed above (library.nu, Library Genesis, Sci-Hub, etc.) could play the role of the library of libraries, they tend to be defined more as sites for biblioleaks.[9] Furthermore, given the vulnerability of these archives, we ought to look for alternative approaches that do not rule out using their resources, but which also do not *depend* on them.

Dat Library takes the concept of 'a library of libraries' not to manifest it in a single, universal library, but to realise it progressively and partially with different individuals, groups and institutions.

8.   http://www.nytimes.com/2009/07/18/technology/companies/18amazon.html
9.   https://www.jmir.org/2014/4/e112/

Archival Properties

So far, the emphasis of this README has been on *durability*, and the 'accidents of the archive' have been instances of destruction and loss. The persistence of an archive is, however, no guarantee of its *accessibility*, a common reality in digital libraries where access management is ubiquitous. Official institutions police access to their archives vigilantly for the ostensible purpose of preservation, but they ultimately create a rarefied relationship between the archives and their publics. Disregarding this tendency toward preciousness, we also introduce *adaptability* as a fundamental consideration in the making of the projects Dat Library and HyperReadings.

To adapt is to fit something for a new purpose. It emphasises that the archive is not a dead object of research but a set of possible tools waiting to be activated in new circumstances. This is always a possibility of an archive, but we want to treat this possibility as desirable, as the horizon towards which these projects move. We know how infrastructures can attenuate desire and simply make things difficult. We want to actively encourage radical reuse.

In the following section, we don't define these properties but rather discuss how we implement (or fail to implement) them in software, while highlighting some of the potential difficulties introduced.

Durability: In 1964, in the midst of the 'loss' of the twentieth-century, Paul Baran's RAND Corporation publication 'On Distributed Communications' examined 'redundancy as one means of building ... highly survivable and reliable communications systems',[10] thus midwifing the military foundations of the digital networks that we operate within today. While the underlying framework of the Internet generally follows distributed principles, the client–server/request–response model of the HTTP protocol is highly centralised in practice and is only as durable as the server.

Capitalism places a high value on originality and novelty, as exemplified in art, where the ultimate insult would be the label 'redundant'. Worse than being derivative or merely unoriginal, being redundant means having no reason to exist — a uselessness that art can't tolerate. It means

10.   https://www.rand.org/content/dam/rand/pubs/research_memoranda/2006/RM3420.pdf

wasting a perfectly good opportunity to be creative or innovative. In a relational network, on the other hand, redundancy is a mode of support. It doesn't stimulate competition to capture its effects, but rather it is a product of cooperation. While this attitude of redundancy arose within a Western military context, one can't help but notice that the shared resources, mutual support and common infrastructure seem fundamentally communist in nature. Computer networks are not fundamentally exploitative or equitable, but they are used in specific ways and they operate within particular economies. A redundant network of interrelated, mutually supporting computers running mostly open-source software can be the guts of an advanced capitalist engine, like Facebook. So, could it be possible to organise our networked devices, embedded as they are in a capitalist economy, in an anti-capitalist way?

Dat Library is built on the Dat Protocol,[11] a peer-to-peer protocol for syncing folders of data. It is not the first distributed protocol (BitTorrent is the best known and is noted as an inspiration for Dat),[12] nor is it the only new one being developed today (IPFS, or the Inter-Planetary File System, is often referenced in comparison),[13] but it is unique in its foundational goals of preserving scientific knowledge as a public good. Dat's provocation is that by creating custom infrastructure it will be possible to overcome the accidents that restrict access to scientific knowledge. We would specifically acknowledge here the role that the Dat community — or any community around a protocol, for that matter — has in the formation of the world that is built on top of that protocol. (For a sense of the Dat community's values, see its code of conduct.)[14]

When running Dat Library, a person sees their list of libraries. These can be thought of as similar to a torrent,[15] where items are stored across many computers. This means that many people will share in the provision of disk space and bandwidth for a particular library, so that when someone loses electricity or drops their computer, the library will not also break. Although this is a technical claim — one that has been made in relation to many projects, from Baran to BitTorrent — it is more importantly a social claim: the users and lovers of a library will share the

11.   https://github.com/datproject/docs/blob/master/papers/dat-paper.md
12.   https://en.wikipedia.org/wiki/BitTorrent
13.   https://ipfs.io/
14.   https://github.com/datproject/Code-of-Conduct/blob/master/CODE_OF_
CONDUCT.md
15.   https://en.wikipedia.org/wiki/Torrent_file

library. More than that, they will share in the work of ensuring that it will continue to be shared.

This is not dissimilar to the process of reading generally, where knowledge is distributed and maintained through readers sharing and referencing the books important to them. As Peter Sloterdijk describes, written philosophy is 'reinscribed like a chain letter through the generations, and despite all the errors of reproduction — indeed, perhaps because of such errors — it has recruited its copyists and interpreters into the ranks of brotherhood (sic)'.[16] Or its sisterhood — but the point remains clear that the reading/writing/sharing of texts binds us together, even in disagreement.

Accessibility: In the world of the web, durability is synonymous with accessibility — if something can't be accessed, it doesn't exist. Here, we disentangle the two in order to consider *access* independent from questions of resilience.

Technically Accessible: When you create a new library in Dat, a unique 64-digit 'key' will automatically be generated for it. An example key is 6f963e59e9948d14f5d2eccd5b5ac8e157ca34d70d724b41cb 0f565bc01162bf, which points to a library of texts. In order for someone else to see the library you have created, you must provide to them your library's unique key (by email, chat, on paper or you could publish it on your website). In short, *you* manage access to the library by copying that key, and then every key holder also manages access *ad infinitum*.

At the moment, this has its limitations. A Dat is only writable by a single creator. If you want to collaboratively develop a library or reading list, you need to have a single administrator managing its contents. This will change in the near future with the integration of hyperdb into Dat's core.[17] At that point, the platform will enable multiple contributors and the management of permissions, and our single key will become a key chain.

How is this key any different from knowing the domain name of a website? If a site isn't indexed by Google and has a suitably unguessable domain name, then isn't that effectively the same degree of privacy? Yes, and this is precisely why the metaphor of the key is so apt (with

16.   https://rekveld.home.xs4all.nl/tech/Sloterdijk_RulesForTheHumanZoo.pdf
17.   https://github.com/mafintosh/hyperdb

whom do you share the key to your apartment?), but also why it is limited. With the key, one not only has the ability to *enter* the library, but also to completely *reproduce* the library.

Consenting Accessibility: When we say 'accessibility', some hear 'information wants to be free' — but our idea of accessibility is not about indiscriminate open access to everything. While we do support, in many instances, the desire to increase access to knowledge where it has been restricted by monopoly property ownership, or the urge to increase transparency in delegated decision-making and representative government, we also recognise that Indigenous knowledge traditions often depend on ownership, control, consent and secrecy in the hands of the traditions' people.[18] Accessibility understood in merely quantitative terms isn't able to reconcile these positions, which this is why we refuse to limit 'access' to a question of technology.

While 'digital rights management' technologies have been developed almost exclusively for protecting the commercial interests of capitalist property owners within Western intellectual property regimes, many of the assumptions and technological implementations are inadequate for the protection of Indigenous knowledge. Rather than describing access in terms of commodities and ownership of copyright, it might be defined by membership, status or role within a community, and the rules of access would not be managed by a generalised legal system but by the rules and traditions of the people and their knowledge.[19] These rights would not expire, nor would they be bought and sold, because they are shared, i.e., held in common.

It is important, while imagining the possibilities of a technological protocol, to also consider how different *cultural protocols* might be implemented and protected through the life of a project like Dat Library. Certain aspects of this might be accomplished through library metadata, but ultimately it is through people hosting their own archives and libraries (rather than, for example, having them hosted by a state institution)

18.	Terri Janke, 'Managing Indigenous Knowledge and Indigenous Cultural and Intellectual Property', in *Australian Indigenous Knowledge and Libraries*, edited by Martin Nakata and Marcia Langton (Sydney: UTSePress, 2006), 83, accessed 2 February 2018, https://epress.lib.uts.edu.au/system/files_force/Aus%20 Indigenous%20Knowledge%20and%20Libraries.pdf
19.	Jane Hunter, 'The Role of Information Technologies in Indigenous Knowledge Management', in *Australian Indigenous Knowledge and Libraries*, edited by Martin Nakata and Marcia Langton (Sydney: UTSePress, 2006), 101–102, accessed 2 February 2018, https://epress.lib.uts.edu.au/system/files_force/Aus%20 Indigenous%20Knowledge%20and%20Libraries.pdf.

that cultural protocols can be translated and reproduced. Perhaps we should flip the typical question of how might a culture exist within digital networks to instead ask how should digital networks operate within cultural protocols?

Adaptability (Ability to Use/Modify As One's Own): Durability and accessibility are the foundations of adoptability. Many would say that this is a contradiction, that adoption is about use and transformation and those qualities operate against the preservationist grain of durability, that one must always be at the expense of the other. We say: perhaps that is true, but it is a risk we're willing to take because we don't want to be making monuments or cemeteries that people approach with reverence or fear. We want tools and stories that we use and adapt and are always making new again. But we also say: it is through use that something becomes invaluable, which may change or distort but will not destroy — this is the practical definition of durability. S.R. Ranganathan's very first Law of Library Science was 'BOOKS ARE FOR USE', [20] which we would extend to the library itself, such that when he arrives at his final law, 'THE LIBRARY IS A LIVING ORGANISM', [21] we note that to live means not only to change, but also to live *in the world*.

To borrow and gently distort another of Raganathan's concepts, namely that of 'Infinite Hospitality', it could be said that we are interested in ways to construct a form of infrastructure that is infinitely hospitable. [22] By this we mean infrastructure that accommodates the needs and desires of new users/audiences/communities and allows them to enter and contort the technology to their own uses. We really don't see infrastructure as aimed at a single specific group, but rather that it should generate spaces that people can inhabit as they wish. The poet Jean Paul once wrote that books are thick letters to friends. Books as infrastructure enable authors to find their friends. This is how we ideally see Dat Library and HyperReadings working.

20.   S. R. Ranganathan, *The Five Laws of Library Science* (Madras: The Madras Library Association, 1931), 1, accessed 2 February 2018, https://babel.hathitrust.org/cgi/pt?id=uc1.$b99721;view=1up;seq=37
21.   Ibid., 382.
22.   http://www.dextersinister.org/MEDIA/PDF/InfiniteHospitality.pdf

Use Cases

We began work on Dat Library and HyperReadings with a range of exemplary use cases, real-world circumstances in which these projects might intervene. Not only would the use cases make demands on the software we were and still are beginning to write, but they would also give us demands to make on the Dat protocol, which is itself still in the formative stages of development. And, crucially, in an iterative feedback loop, this process of design produces transformative effects on those situations described in the use cases themselves, resulting in further new circumstances and new demands.

Thorunka: Wendy Bacon and Chris Nash made us aware of *Thorunka* and *Thor*. *Thorunka* and *Thor* were two underground papers in the early 1970s that spewed out from a censorship controversy surrounding the University of New South Wales student newspaper *Tharunka*. Between 1971 and 1973, the student magazine was under focused attack from the NSW state police, with several arrests made on charges of obscenity and indecency. Rather than ceding to the charges, this prompted a large and sustained political protest from Sydney activists, writers, lawyers, students and others, to which *Thorunka* and *Thor* were central.

The campaign contested the idea of obscenity and the legitimacy of the legal system itself. The newspapers campaigned on the war in Vietnam, Aboriginal land rights, women's and gay liberation, and the violence of the criminal justice system. By 1973 the censorship regime in Australia was broken. Nearly all the charges were dropped.[23]

Although the collection of issues of *Tharunka* is largely accessible via Trove,[24] the subsequent issues of *Thorunka*, and later *Thor*, are not. For us, this demonstrates clearly how collections themselves can encourage modes of reading. If you focus on *Tharunka* as a singular and long-standing periodical, this significant political moment is rendered almost invisible. On the other hand, if the issues are presented together, with commentary and surrounding publications, the political environment becomes palpable. Wendy and Chris have kindly allowed

23.   http://107.org.au/event/tharunka-thor-journalism-politics-art-1970-1973/
24.   http://trove.nla.gov.au/newspaper/page/24773115

us to make their personal collection available via Dat Library (the key is: 73fd26846e009e1f7b7c5b580e15eb0b2423f9bea33fe2a5f41fac0d db22cbdc), so you can discover this for yourself.

Academia.edu alternative: Academia.edu, started in 2008, has raised tens of millions of dollars as a social network for academics to share their publications. As a for-profit venture, it is rife with metrics and it attempts to capitalise on the innate competition and self-promotion of precarious knowledge workers in the academy. It is simultaneously popular and despised: popular because it fills an obvious desire to share the fruits of one's intellectual work, but despised for the neoliberal atmosphere that pervades every design decision and automated correspondence. It is, however, just trying to provide a return on investment.

Gary Hall has written that 'its financial rationale rests ... on the ability of the angel-investor and venture-capital-funded professional entrepreneurs who run Academia.edu to exploit the data flows generated by the academics who use the platform as an intermediary for sharing and discovering research'.[25] Moreover, he emphasises that in the open-access world (outside of the exploitative practice of for-profit publishers like Elsevier, who charge a premium for subscriptions), the privileged position is to be the one 'who gate-keeps the data generated around the use of that content'. This lucrative position has been produced by recent 'recentralizing tendencies' of the internet,[26] which in Academia's case captures various scattered open-access repositories, personal web pages and other archives.

Is it possible to redecentralise? Can we break free of the subjectivities that Academia.edu is crafting for us as we are interpellated by its infrastructure? It is incredibly easy for any scholar running Dat Library to make a library of their own publications and post the key to their faculty web page, Facebook profile or business card. The tricky — and interesting — thing would be to develop platforms that aggregate thousands of these libraries in direct competition with Academia.edu. This way, individuals would maintain control over their own work; their peer groups would assist in mirroring it; and no one would be capitalising on the sale of data related to their performance and popularity.

25.   http://www.garyhall.info/journal/2015/10/18/does-academiaedu-mean-open-access-is-becoming-irrelevant.html
26.   http://commonstransition.org/the-revolution-will-not-be-decentralised-blockchains/

We note that Academia.edu is a typically centripetal platform: it provides no tools for exporting one's own content, so an alternative would necessarily be a kind of centrifuge.

This alternative is becoming increasingly realistic. With open-access journals already paving the way, there has more recently been a call for free and open access to citation data.[27] The Initiative for Open Citations (I4OC) is mobilising against the privatisation of data and working towards the unrestricted availability of scholarly citation data.[28] We see their new database of citations as making this centrifugal force a possibility.

Publication Format: In writing this README, we have strung together several references. This writing might be published in a book and the references will be listed as words at the bottom of the page or at the end of the text. But the writing might just as well be published as a HyperReadings object, providing the reader with an archive of all the things we referred to and an editable version of this text.

A new text editor could be created for this new publication format, not to mention a new form of publication, which bundles together a set of HyperReadings texts, producing a universe of texts and references. Each HyperReadings text might reference others, of course, generating something that begins to feel like a serverless World Wide Web.

It's not even necessary to develop a new publication format, as any book might be considered as a reading list (usually found in the footnotes and bibliography) with a very detailed description of the relation-ship between the consulted texts. What if the history of published works were considered in this way, such that we might always be able to follow a reference from one book directly into the pages of another, and so on?

Syllabus: The syllabus is the manifesto of the twenty-first century. From 'Your Baltimore "Syllabus"',[29] to '#StandingRockSyllabus',[30] to 'Women and gender non-conforming people writing about tech',[31] syllabi are being produced as provocations, or as instructions for reprogramming

27.   https://www.insidehighered.com/news/2017/12/06/scholars-push-free-access-online-citation-data-saying-they-need-and-deserve-access
28.   https://i4oc.org/
29.   https://apis4blacklives.wordpress.com/2015/05/01/your-baltimore-syllabus/
30.   https://nycstandswithstandingrock.wordpress.com/standingrocksyllabus/
31.   https://docs.google.com/document/d/1Qx8JDqfuXoHwk4_1PZYWrZu3mmCs
V_05Fe09AtJ9ozw/edit

imaginaries. They do not announce a new world but they point out a way to get there. As a programme, the syllabus shifts the burden of action onto the readers, who will either execute the programme on their own fleshy operating system — or not. A text that by its nature points to other texts, the syllabus is already a relational document acknowledging its own position within a living field of knowledge. It is decidedly not self-contained, however it often circulates as if it were.

If a syllabus circulated as a HyperReadings document, then it could point directly to the texts and other media that it aggregates. But just as easily as it circulates, a HyperReadings syllabus could be forked into new versions: the syllabus is changed because there is a new essay out, or because of a political disagreement, or because following the syllabus produced new suggestions. These forks become a family tree where one can follow branches and trace epistemological mutations.

Proposition (or Presuppositions)

While the software that we have started to write is a proposition in and of itself, there is no guarantee as to *how* it will be used. But, when writing, we are imagining exactly that: we are making intuitive and hopeful presuppositions about how it will be used, presuppositions that amount to a set of social propositions.

The Role of Individuals in the Age of Distribution: Different people have different technical resources and capabilities, but everyone can contribute to an archive. By simply running the Dat Library software and adding an archive to it, a person is sharing their disk space and internet bandwidth in the service of that archive. At first, it is only the archive's index (a list of the contents) that is hosted, but if the person downloads the contents (or even just a small portion of the contents) then they are sharing in the hosting of the contents as well. Individuals, as supporters of an archive or members of a community, can organise together to guarantee the durability and accessibility of an archive, saving a future UbuWeb from ever having to worry about their 'ISP pulling the plug'. As supporters of many archives, as members of many communities, individuals can use Dat Library to perform this function many times over.

On the Web, individuals are usually users or browsers — they use browsers. In spite of the ostensible interactivity of the medium, users are kept at a distance from the actual code, the infrastructure of a website, which is run on a server. With a distributed protocol like Dat, applications such as Beaker Browser or Dat Library eliminate the central server,[32] not by destroying it, but by distributing it across all of the users. Individuals are then not *just* users, but also hosts. What kind of subject is this user-host, especially as compared to the user of the server? Michel Serres writes in *The Parasite*:

> It is raining; a passer-by comes in. Here is the interrupted meal once more. Stopped for only a moment, since the traveller is asked to join the diners. His host does not have to ask him twice. He accepts the invitation and sits down in front of his bowl. The host is the satyr, dining at home; he is the donor. He calls to the passer-by, saying to him, be our guest. The guest is the stranger, the interrupter, the one who receives the soup, agrees to the meal. The host, the guest: the same word; he gives and receives, offers and accepts, invites and is invited, master and passer-by... An invariable term through the transfer of the gift. It might be dangerous not to decide who is the host and who is the guest, who gives and who receives, who is the parasite and who is the *table d'hote*, who has the gift and who has the loss, and where hospitality begins with hospitality.[33]

Serres notes that *guest* and *host* are the same word in French; we might say the same for *client* and *server* in a distributed protocol. And we will embrace this multiplying hospitality, giving and taking without measure.

The Role of Institutions in the Age of Distribution: David Cameron launched a doomed initiative in 2010 called the Big Society, which paired large-scale cuts in public programmes with a call for local communities to voluntarily self-organise to provide these essential services for themselves. This is not the political future that we should be working toward: since 2010, austerity policies have resulted in 120,000 excess deaths in England.[34] In other words, while it might seem as though *institutions* might be comparable to *servers*, inasmuch as both are centralised infrastructures, we should not give them up or allow them to be dismantled under the assumption that those infrastructures can simply be distributed and

32.   https://beakerbrowser.com/
33.   Michel Serres, *The Parasite* (Baltimore and London: The Johns Hopkins University Press, 1982), 15–16.
34.   http://bmjopen.bmj.com/content/7/11/e017722

self-organised. On the contrary, institutions should be defended and organised in order to support the distributed protocols we are discussing.

One simple way for a larger, more established institution to help ensure the durability and accessibility of diverse archives is through the provision of hardware, network capability and some basic technical support. It can back up the archives of smaller institutions and groups within its own community while also giving access to its own archives, so that those collections might be put to new uses. A network of smaller institutions, separated by great distances, might mirror each other's archives, both as an expression of solidarity and positive redundancy and also as a means of circulating their archives, histories and struggles.

It was the simultaneous recognition that some documents are too important to be privatised or lost to the threats of neglect, fire, mould, insects, etc., that prompted the development of national and state arch-ives.[35] As public institutions, they were, and still are, tasked with often competing efforts to house and preserve while simultaneously also ensuring access to public documents. Fire and unstable weather understandably have given rise to large fire-proof and climate-controlled buildings as centralised repositories, accompanied by highly regulated protocols for access. But in light of new technologies and their new risks, as discussed above, it is compelling to argue now that, in order to fulfil their public duty, public archives should be distributing their collections where possible and providing their resources to smaller institutions and community groups.

Through the provision of disk space, office space, grants, tech-nical support and employment, larger institutions can materially support smaller organisations, individuals and their archival afterlives. They can provide physical space and outreach for dispersed collectors, gathering and piecing together a fragmented archive.

But what happens as more people and collections are brought in? As more institutional archives are allowed to circulate outside of institu-tional walls? As storage is cut loose from its dependency on the corporate cloud and into forms of interdependency, such as mutual support net-works? Could this open up spaces for new forms of not-quite-organi-sations and queer-institutions? These would be almost-organisations that uncomfortably exist somewhere between the common categorical

35.   See: Beredo, B. C., 'Import of the archive: American colonial bureaucracy in the Philippines, 1898–1916', PhD diss., University of Hawaii at Manoa, Honolulu, 2011, http://hdl.handle.net/10125/101724

markings of the individual and the institution. In our thinking, it's not important what these future forms exactly look like. Rather, as discussed above, what is important to us is that in writing software we open up spaces for the unknown, and allow others agency to build the forms that work for them. It is only in such an atmosphere of infinite hospitality that we see the future of community libraries, individual collections and other precarious archives.

A Note on This Text

This README was collaboratively written, and is still being collaboratively written, in a Git repository.[36] Git is a free and open-source tool for version control used in software development. All the code for HyperReadings, Dat Library and their numerous associated modules are managed openly using Git and hosted on GitHub under open-source licenses. In a real way, Git's specification formally binds our collaboration as well as the open invitation for others to participate. As such, the form of this README reflects its content. Like this text, these projects are, by design, works in progress that are malleable to circumstances and open to contributions, for example by opening a pull request on this document or raising an issue on our GitHub repositories.

36.   See: https://en.wikipedia.org/wiki/Git and https://en.wikipedia.org/wiki/Repository_(version_control). You can view the repository containing this text at https://github.com/sdockray/hyperreadings.

DISTRIBUTED SITUATEDNESS

Patricia Reed

Feminists have to insist on a better account of the world; it is not enough to show radical historical contingency and modes of construction for everything.[1]

The failure to change the world may not be unrelated to the failure to understand it.[2]

Knowledge claims have historically been idealised from an Archimedean viewpoint – an imaginary vantage point that would allow one to observe reality from an objective distance. Since the 1970s, however, feminist theories of knowledge have challenged this particular framing of objectivity from a distance. The legacy of feminism's incursion into epistemology has been, rather, to situate knowledge claims by insisting on the significance of the socio-normative contexts that underpin the production of all knowledge. Although there is no singular feminist epistemology, what feminist epistemologies highlight through their various lenses is the *politicity* of epistemology itself, namely the entanglements of knowledge claims with matters of gender, class, race, age and social status. Feminist perspectives on epistemology thereby 'reconfigure the borders between epistemology, political philosophy, ethics [...] as we come to see the interrelationships and inseparability of heretofore disparate issues'.[3] In this essay, I argue for the extrapolation of situated knowledge, by both updating it in view of distributed cognition (pluri-situatedness) and examining how knowledge works back upon us, effectively *resituating* us in the process. Only in this way might we better grasp the complexity of our interdependent world that increasingly eludes us in an effort to find traction and forge modes of maximal political mobility *within* it.

In tandem with the rise of feminist epistemologies, the late 1970s also saw the emergence of Science & Technology Studies (STS), a discipline focusing on the bidirectional ways in which socio-cultural conditions affect scientific research and technological development, and vice

1. Donna Haraway, 'Situated Knowledges: The Science Question in Feminism and the Privilege of Partial Perspective', *Feminist Studies* 14, no. 3 (Autumn 1988): 575–599.
2. Ray Brassier, 'Concepts and Objects', in *The Speculative Turn: Continental Materialism and Realism*, ed. L. Bryant, N. Srnicek and G. Harman (Melbourne: re.press, 2011), 47–65.
3. Linda Alcoff and Elizabeth Potter, 'Introduction: When Feminisms Intersect Epistemology', in *Feminist Epistemologies*, ed. Linda Alcoff and Elizabeth Potter (New York: Routledge, 1993), 3.

versa.[4] Together, these late twentieth-century critiques of epistemic practices bore two important achievements: (1) the dismantling of the purported 'neutrality' of scientific activity, emphasising instead the social conditions that shape the construction of knowledge;[5] and (2) the shattering of the paradigm of perspective-free, 'bodyless' knowledge production, so that the standpoint of the knower can no longer be universally generalisable, but must always be viewed as historically contingent. This means that all knowing substantively involves the material situation (mind, body and instruments) of particular knowers. These developments also served to deprivilege the traditional hierarchies within epistemology that championed propositional knowledge (knowing *that*) over materialist knowledge practices (knowing *how*).[6] As interventions go, these critiques did not seek to obliterate objectivity entirely (by relativising or localising scientific knowledge to such a degree as to equate it with personal beliefs or religious doctrines), but rather they sought to ground theories of knowledge in relation to socio-cultural and material practices so as to deny the facile separation of the objective and the subjective.[7]

Of Caricatures and Deadlocks

The tendency toward epistemic relativism that subsequently swept across much of the humanities, often under the rubric of 'post-structuralism', did not sit well for many in the scientific community. Perspectives that emphasised a socially and linguistically constructed world, which often deployed the word 'reality' in scare quotes only, were deemed especially problematic. The 'science wars', as they were called, began after the polemical publication of *Higher Superstition: The Academic Left and Its Quarrels With Science* (1994) by the biologist Paul R. Gross and the mathematician Norman Levitt, but these 'wars' were made public by the Sokal affair, after an article by the physicist Alan Sokal was accepted for the journal *Social Text,* entitled 'Transgressing

4.   STS often intersects with feminist epistemologies, albeit with little acknowledgement.

5.   This claim is/was more widely held by non-scientists than by scientists themselves.

6.   Vrinda Dalmiya and Linda Alcoff, 'Are "Old Wives' Tales" Justified?', in *Feminist Epistemologies*, ed. Linda Alcoff and Elizabeth Potter (New York: Routledge, 1993), 217-244.

7.   For an elaborate account of the historical co-relation between the ideal of objectivity and the construction of selfhood (the binarisation of which can only be traced back to the mid-nineteenth century), see Lorraine Daston and Peter Galison, *Objectivity* (New York: Zone Books, 2007).

the Boundaries: Towards a Transformative Hermeneutics of Quantum Gravity' (submitted in 1994, published in 1996).[8] In a subsequent text for the magazine *Lingua Franca*, Sokal revealed the article to be a hoax, suggesting that it had only been accepted because '(a) it sounded good and (b) it flattered the editors' ideological preconceptions'.[9] The elaborate prank created much buzz – it was picked up in major media outlets in both the United States and France – but it served only to widen the chasm between the 'two cultures' of the hard sciences and the humanities,[10] falsely reducing the terms of the squabble to pro-science or anti-science, pro-reason or anti-reason. While it is undeniable that there have been dubious appropriations of scientific terms and concepts within the humanities (and this continues to occur, as we currently see in many 'critiques' of AI, for example), there have also been some very broad caricatures painted by 'hard' scientists who have lumped together diverse thinkers into a monolithic 'leftist academic culture'. Debilitating reductions and misapprehensions have flown in both directions, but this essay is not about adjudicating the dispute. Instead, I want to look at what was sacrificed in this exercise of mutually annihilating reductionism, and at how our understanding of epistemology, along with its inherent political ramifications, ought to orient itself today.

Twenty years after the science wars, the popular cultural climate (primarily on the right, but also sometimes on the left) has taken the 'constructivist' understanding of the creation of knowledge to the extreme, typically in pursuit of political, economic and religious agendas, such as climate change denial, anti-vaccination campaigns and creationism. This has led some of the founders of STS to question their role in highlighting the social aspects of knowledge construction in scientific practices, and to reconsider their analyses as an enabler for the proliferation of private interests or beliefs.[11] In these warped instances, the relativisation of epistemology has been so distorted as to negate its initial and ongoing import. This tendency does a disservice to the hard sciences and the

8.   Alan Sokal, 'Transgressing the Boundaries: Towards a Transformative Hermeneutics of Quantum Gravity', *Social Text* 46/47 (Spring/Summer 1996): 217–252 available at: http://www.physics.nyu.edu/sokal/transgress_v2/transgress_v2_singlefile.html. For a discussion of the hoax, see: Steven Weinberg, 'Sokal's Hoax', *The New York Review of Books*, XLIII, no. 13 (8 August, 1996): 11–15, available at: http://www.physics.nyu.edu/sokal/weinberg.html
9.   Ibid.
10.   C.P. Snow, *The Two Cultures and the Scientific Revolution: the Rede Lecture 1959* (Cambridge: Cambridge University Press, 1959).
11.   Bruno Latour, 'Why Has Critique Run Out of Steam? From Matters of Fact to Matters of Concern', *Critical Inquiry* 30 (2004): 225–248.

humanities alike. Results in the sciences can be cherry-picked and funded on ideological grounds or out of self-interest, or used to stall action when labelled as 'inconclusive' for the same reasons. The humanities similarly seek to rigorously analyse techno-scientific procedures without undermining their enterprise absolutely, or remaining critical without falling into debilitating pitfalls of strict techno-scientific pessimism. It's important to recall that these incapacitating exaggerations of relativisation were never the ambition of feminist epistemologies, which were in fact concerned with *bolstering* the scope of epistemology through the integration of formerly disregarded or unrecognised knowledges and knowledge practices, thereby correcting omissions that have served only to *limit* our understanding of the world.[12] Beyond the divide between so-called 'hard' and 'soft' knowledges (and what each can do respectively), the more ambitious question is not reducible to pro- or anti-science. Rather, we should ask: how might we augment our definitions of epistemology, so that they are not exclusively bound to Western scientific procedures? Who and what are the stakeholders in knowledge production? And how can we open up knowledge and its *instrumentalisation* to public scrutiny?

Worlds In Common vs Preference Worlds

In its extreme, unintended deployment, epistemic relativisation has contributed *less* to the desired multiplication of knowledges, a deeper sea of knowers and a more robust grasp of reality, and more to a climate of fractured, destabilised, *irreal* worlds.[13] In this scenario, partly fuelled by the positive feedback loops of algorithmic automation and online personalisation, a complex *world in common* has been forsaken for the simplicity, conformity and reassurance of *preference worlds*. What we experience in our preferential, techno-homophilic chambers is simultaneously a barrage of confirmation bias and outrage at the 'biased' other who is publicly mocked *ad infinitum*, so we make no headway on a shared account of reality. The temptation to react to this scenario by attempting to *purify* it by purging bias and falsehood echoes those debunked ideali-

12.   Linda Alcoff and Elizabeth Potter, 'Introduction: When Feminisms Intersect Epistemology', *Feminist Epistemologies*, ed. Linda Alcoff and Elizabeth Potter (New York: Routledge, 1993), 6.
13.   In Metahaven's film *The Sprawl* (2016), an argument is put forth (along with upside-down film footage) that contemporary propaganda is no longer about persuading people, but about deconstructing the opposing side, disrupting dominant narratives, and undermining the provability of truths.

sations of science as a neutral arbitrator of an objective reality with which we can *all* concur. So where does that leave us? How can we escape the reductive deadlock of the with-us-or-against-us negative lesson from the science wars that has leaked into our present? How can we account for situated (relativised and localised) knowledge that is tethered to historical and geographic particularities whilst remaining vigilant in the collective pursuit of an account of reality as such?[14] Because knowledge can never be severed from its makers or the conditions of its making, the stakes are inherently political – especially, to repeat, as epistemologies become instrumentalised. This requires us to move from the plane of 'world-denying constructivism',[15] as a *parody* of 'situatedness', which forecloses any claim on reality (even if always subject to fallibility), to a 'world-*affirming* constructivism', so that we might be able to account for situated, local variations *and* distributed, planetary coherency – a world in common.

The Cold World and Our Existential Situation

It is understandable that we might be tempted to retreat into bubbles of automated familiarity, confirming particular known knowledges, but this is utterly inadequate to the demands of our time. We need a *better account of reality*, one that measures up to the increasingly complex, abstract, insensible and distributed qualities of our world in common. (The task is made more arduous still by the fact that this world contains many human and non-human *worlds* within it.)[16] To transform our accounts of reality is to enable novel perspectives through which to manoeuvre and relate anew, where this reorientation allows us to better speculate on collective political navigation, rather than resorting to what was, what is, or what we (think) we know. The world in common overflows and overwhelms us – but when the possibility for changing it is bound to our capacity to better understand it, operating in a mode of complexity withdrawal by emphasising only the here-and-now of our concrete situation leaves us cognitively and instrumentally enfeebled.

14.   Donna Haraway posed a very similar query in her 1988 essay 'Situated Knowledges: the Science Question in Feminism and the Privilege of Partial Perspective', *Feminist Studies* 14, no. 3 (Autumn 1988): 575-599, wherein she grapples with the dilemma between the poles of objectivity and partial perspectives.
15.   Fabio Gironi, 'Science-Laden Theory: Outlines of an Unsettled Alliance', *Speculations* 1 (2010): 9-46.
16.   Achille Mbembe draws on Edouard Glissant's concept of an 'all-world' to describe this phenomenon of a totality composed of all worlds in his epilogue of the *Critique of Black Reason*, entitled 'There Is Only One World', (Durham, NC: Duke University Press, 2017), 179-183.

The expression 'cold world'[17] has been used to describe this overwhelming moment, namely 'the alienation that we experience in relation to the complex world of big data, hyper capitalism, and the apparent impossibility of fathoming or understanding what this world is'.[18] Importantly, the term 'cold world' refers not only to the complex world 'out there' that confounds epistemic traction (our account of reality), but also to our generic *exis-tential* crisis as humans within the world (our collective situatedness). The term describes the paradoxical condition of a world that humans have fabricated, but also a world in which the diverse constructed 'bits' have been amassed into an intricate amalgam (intentionally or otherwise) that no human brain can grasp, despite the fact that 'we' built it. Some human minds and bodies have intervened in the world to the degree of permeating and remoulding its geological core, but at the cost of becoming impotent as individuals and as a species *because of* our dominance over the world. This is in stark contrast to the narrative once presumed to be evidence of our 'mastery', which saw nature pictured as a mere backdrop for our actions. (The 'we' evoked here is of course only a partial one, whose particular formulation is that of the Western logic that underpins current hegemonic conditions.) This existential crisis of the human in the face of our 'unfathomable' world (at both a local and a planetary scale) forces us to contend with an augmented, politically oriented, multi-scalar demand for a concept of 'situatedness' that would account not only for a *particular* condition but for a *generic* 'human' situatedness as well, and also for the ways in which these two modes are entwined. This is important for two reasons.

Firstly, 'objects' of our time that require substantial episto-political mobilisation are distributed and complex, meaning that although they produce empirical, *local* or *situated* effects (that can be sensed, like weather), they only come into existence as a systemic whole via procedures of averaging (like climate). A plethora of types of knowledge is required to co-construct a diagram of this reality – a reality that is abstract and pluri-situated across bodies, materials and knowledge practices, yet is coherent, nonetheless. The type of cognition required for better

---

17.   For an account of how the experiential dejection of our condition can be transformed into a source for forging other life-worlds, see Dominic Fox, *Cold World: The Aesthetics of Dejection and the Politics of Militant Dysphoria* (London: Zero Books, 2009).

18.   Amanda Beech, 'Cold World and Neocon Noir', in *Cold War Cold World*, ed. Amanda Beech, Robin Mackay and James Wiltgen (Falmouth: Urbanomic, 2017), 33–54.

understanding these complex systems is itself distributed, composed of 'multiple humans and objects [that] can do things individual humans cannot', requiring one to go beyond the 'cognitive-science analysis of the individual bounded by the skin'.[19] This boils down to a need for epistemology to elaborate a concept of 'distributed situatedness' in order to adequately grasp the complexity of our reality, and for complexity not to be dismissed through a romantic framing as sublime impenetrability. We must seek to better diagram our reality in order to strategise better political purchase.

Secondly, the mega-structural scales through which computational and material procedures drive and organise our contemporary condition have resituated the human animal. We are no longer the radiant centre of activity from which reality unfolds, is constructed or is determinedly controllable.[20] This plight, known as a Copernican humiliation, carries with it the possibility of remapping human self-understanding *in* and *with* the world, in order to draw out other epistemological and logical approaches. The conceptual integration of this humiliation is an important example of our 'exceptional unexceptionalism': through our rather exceptional capacities for reasoning and self-reflection, we come to realise we can be unexceptionally 'carved up into chemicals and atoms and DNA, in the end not so far away from a piece of fruit'.[21] (This formula extends into our unexceptional boundedness to evolutionary processes, wherein extinction is more a norm than an anomaly, so our survival is far from guaranteed.) This second point amounts to the capacity of human reason to reach for 'something that may cause the human itself to be displaced'. This new, *generically* situated human self-image opens conceptual and material pathways for navigating the world otherwise, departing as it does from an altogether different perspective.

While 'situated knowledge' teaches us that epistemology cannot be divorced from socio-environmental contexts, perhaps more crucial is the question of how knowledge permeates and *resituates* us through this activity of thinking. Such is the principle of the 'inhuman',[22] as articulated

19.   Donald MacKenzie, *Material Markets: How Economic Agents are Constructed* (Oxford: Oxford University Press, 2009), 16.
20.   Benjamin Bratton, *The Stack: On Sovereignty and Software* (Cambridge: MIT Press, 2015).
21.   Nina Power, 'Inhumanism, Reason, Blackness, Feminism' *Glass-Bead*, Site 1: Logic Gate, Politics of the Artefactual Mind (2017). http://www.glass-bead.org/article/inhumanism-reason-blackness-feminism/?lang=enview
22.   See Negarestani's founding essay, in which his elaboration on the term is mapped out: 'The Labor of the Inhuman' *e-flux* 52 (February 2014), available at: http://www.e-flux.com/journal/52/59920/the-labor-of-the-inhuman-part-i-human/

by Reza Negarestani – a humanism pushed to a logical end, insofar as it 'perennially reopens itself to the universe and produces knowledge that potentially undercuts what it means to be human at any given historical moment'.[23] Inhuman situatedness is not fully determined, nor bound to a fixed point, but is subject to mobility via the interpolation of knowledge. Mobile situatedness proceeds by way of generative alienation: from one situation to another, via encounters with the strange, where our understanding of what *is* and where we stand within it is enduringly reframed, including our relations with each other and with non-humans. This mobility creates new vistas of interrogation, while disabling others. The inhuman capacity for the revision of knowledge, and for the transformation of self-understanding and values based on new knowledge, is wholly contingent upon confrontations with the unknown. Fallibility is a powerful driver of this revisionary capacity, and not a signal of intellectual weakness. We therefore need cultural-institutional frameworks that care for this fallibility as a generative force, instead of conceiving of it as a shameful ineptitude, as is too often the case in academia today, driven by imperatives of authorial dominance. Fallibility is rather an indispensable property of knowledge co-creation. To reject or wilfully neglect the unfamiliar, or to disincentivise revision, is to render situatedness immobile, amounting to a misapprehension of situated knowledge that carries no possibility of exceeding its situation. As discussed above, the challenge of creating a better account of our complex, interdependent reality today supersedes the capacities of any single heroic human actor. Knowing our world – a knowing that can admittedly never be total or complete – can only be the result of bit-part intelligences, requiring massive collaborative efforts at an unprecedented scale; the crises of our times are too acute for us to shy away from this challenge. As such, humility and the capacity for conceptual revision are key ingredients. We must be able to actively integrate alien epistemologies, not only with regard to human transdisciplinary and transcultural necessities, but also with regard to non-human considerations that increasingly throw into question our presumed human monopoly on intelligence itself.[24]

23.   Power, 'Inhumanism, Reason, Blackness, Feminism'.
24.   In his 'The Inclosure of Reason', *Technosphere Magazine* (Berlin: Haus der Kulturen der Welt, 2017), Anil Bawa-Cavia maps out a brilliant case study of Artificial Intelligence (Machine Learning) in relation to Inhuman Reasoning. Available at: https://technosphere-magazine.hkw.de/article1/6aefb210-0ee6-11e7-a253-d9923802c14e

It must be possible to think, in a world, what does not appear within the world.[25]

Inexistent Humanness

The words 'human' and 'inhuman' have been used above as if self-evident, as blanket terms that universalise 'us' into a common category, presumably with collective agency. This, however, is too great a rhetorical leap to be politically useful, and this is one reason why the legacy of 'situating knowledge' remains of utmost relevance. While 'human' as a generic category is today essential, it is far from functionally, ethically and pragmatically given. The planetary scale of something like climate change demands a response from a collective agent of a comparable scale – the generic 'human' – but we cannot neglect the historical and continuing exclusivity of such categorical designations. Socially and politically, we cannot suddenly become 'universalised' simply because we are now confronted with a species-wide threat, despite the scientific designation of us all as *Homo sapiens sapiens*. Are we now conveniently all supposed to be universally human, just because we are facing a threat of mass extinction? If the capacity for reasoning is taken as the central property of the human, replete with its persistent *inhuman* drives, then political exclusion is nothing less than an act of wilful dehumanisation. In view of the history of material and epistemological struggles around the category of the human, it would be misguided to imagine a sudden manifest sense of solidarity amongst members of this scientific category, even though we desperately need it. The category of 'human' may hold scientifically, but the universality of this scientific classification is not commensurate with the long-running political battles over the scope of its enclosure.

Although there is an entrenched disconnect between the *universal* scientific framing of the 'human' and the non-uniform *partiality* of its manifestation, we should not abandon this critical category. Our socio-environmental circumstances today require a stereoscopic integration of the generic category of 'human' buttressed by inhuman drives to collectively resituate us. This is a conflict between *ontological* and *logical* classifications. On an ontological view, the category 'human' exists, and all humans

25. Alain Badiou, *Logics of Worlds: Being and Event II*, trans. Alberto Toscano (London: Bloomsbury, 2009), 122.

scientifically count in this view. On the logical view, 'which is the legislation of appearing'[26] or *counting* in the world, most humans have been historically omitted from measure. Those bodies and concepts that ontologically belong to the world but logically do not count are deemed *inexistent*. The category of 'inexistence', drawn from Alain Badiou, refers to a degree of existence that is not nothing, but which operationally approaches zero (a kind of bare-life, minimal being without counting).[27] For the 'human' to live up to its ontological reality, the collective battle is that of the transition from inexistence (simply being) to existence (appearing and counting). It is on this plane that we must fight for the coming into (logical) existence of the (universal) human, if this category is to gain political weight. It is only then that we could be said to *exist in what we know* (where epistemology is augmented beyond a purely propositional realm of simply *knowing that*). Without this logical becoming, we will remain bound to the 'inexistent human', a situation of generic humanity that is politically intractable, and ensnared in a quagmire of merely 'knowing that we know' the human is a collective category.[28] While the category 'human' is politically urgent and ontologically true, it will remain a veil for idealised, ahistorical claims without consequence until it becomes *logically* manifest – that is, until it becomes politically integrated.

The call for a stereoscopic synthesis that could bridge the distinctions between the *scientific* image of the world (abstract knowledge) and the *manifest* image of it (how humans conceptualise themselves in the world) has been central to the philosophical project of Wilfrid Sellars.[29] The manifest image is not a naïve entity subordinate to the scientific image,[30] but concerns the shared domain of norms in action, leading to the claim that 'if man had a radically different conception of himself, he would be a radically different *kind* of man'.[31] This crucial difference entails a broader question wherein the manifest image contextualises our activity in mundane and epistemic registers alike, namely: what kind of

26. Ibid., 156.
27. Ibid., 324.
28. Ibid., 427.
29. Wilfrid Sellars, 'Philosophy and the Scientific Image of Man', in *Science, Perception and Reality* (Atascadero: Ridgeview Publishing Company, 1991), 7-40. (Lecture delivered in 1962.)
30. Sellars uses the term 'image' in a 'usefully ambiguous way', not to deny it the status of reality. On the one hand, image denotes the contrast between an object and its projection onto a plane, like a shadow, so the image exists but is dependent on an object. On the other hand, 'image' is used to evoke the imaginary, which may or may not actually exist, but the imagination of it certainly does exist.
31. Wilfrid Sellars, 'Philosophy and the Scientific Image of Man', my emphasis.

world in common ought to be constructed from the vantage point of this inhuman resituation? When a defining step of political reconstruction is predicated on 'understanding and imagining what ought to be done in our world from the perspective of the postulated possible world',[32] we need to begin by imagining the otherworldly consequences that a resituated inhuman image might entail. This otherworld is *inexistent* insofar as it exists only as a possibility; it is not empirically available to us: it is accessible only by way of hypothesis, by way of carefully reasoned narrative constructions that exceed our known and accounted-for reality.

We must demand a better account of reality from *any* epistemic project, but such work must also be extended into a hypothetical dimension. An epistemic project must be able to speculate on what is not yet accounted for, if knowledge is to forge pathways beyond the here and now of existing perspectives and critical deconstruction towards what could be otherwise. In other words, an epistemic project should be focused not just on the situatedness of knowledge, but also on *how* the apprehension of knowledge works upon us, transforms us and resituates us, constituting new possibilities for relation as a result. Planetary-scale crises that intersect multiple disciplines, material practices, cultures and social ecosystems necessitate distributed cognition at an unprecedented scale, yet tackling these crises hinges on an inhumanist drive to resituate the human, contesting its dehumanising borders. It is through this supplementary dimension of inhuman reasoning that we might mobilise for an inexistent otherworld foreclosed in our existing account of the world in common – a reality that is partially constructed by us, but which is also, humblingly, indifferent and invariant to us.

32.	Reza Negarestani, 'Antinomies of Experience and the Question of the Transcendental Struggle', *Résistance(s)*, lecture at LUMA Foundation, New York, February 2017.

THE PARADOX OF DISSEMINATION

Justin Clemens

Similar crypto-analyses must become universal and mechanical in the chaos of codes that begins with the world-historical dismissal of everyday language in favor of a universal discrete machine.[1]

The German media theorist Friedrich Kittler has pointed out that, with the development and domination of the Internet, not only do we have – for the first time in history – a real-time integrated system of absolute knowledge founded upon a universal binary code capable of transcribing and disseminating any possible message globally with vast volumes of other data at essentially the speed of light, but one which thereby renders absolutely anything any individual human can think, know, or say, utterly irrelevant.[2] No wonder Kittler invokes G.W.F. Hegel's 'absolute knowledge' as not only now possible, but also as having been accomplished. If such knowledge is, to use Hegel's terminology, both finally 'in-and-for-itself', it is also definitively 'not-for-us'.[3]

The consequences – epistemological, existential and environmental – couldn't be more extreme. First, nothing anyone can say any more will be either true or false. Second, nothing anyone can say any more is in principle distinguishable from anything 'said' by a robot: we have ourselves been integrated into the system as minor components; the projected supplantation of humans by Artificial Intelligence (AI) is not a dystopian future, but an achieved (and banal) actuality.[4] Third, there is no longer any message, or even vast aggregates or sets of messages, that will enable any further significant transformation in the system of knowledge. Yet, fourth, as Kittler immediately adds, one crucial message will forever remain to be delivered: the apocalypse itself. This 'message about the message' doesn't simply mean that 'the revolution will not be televised' (of course it won't). It rather means: the only message that can affect the system is foreclosed from the circuits of the system itself; the message can only be received with and as the system's obliteration,

1. Friedrich Kittler, 'Protected Mode', in *Literature, Media, Information Systems: Essays*, ed. and intr. by John Johnston (Amsterdam: OPA, 1997), 168.
2. See, for instance, Kittler, *Literature, Media, Information Systems*, passim.; Friedrich Kittler and John Armitage, 'From Discourse Networks to Cultural Mathematics: an Interview with Friedrich A. Kittler', *Theory, Culture & Society* 23, no. 7-8 (2006): 17–38.
3. See G.W.F. Hegel, *Phenomenology of Spirit*, trans. A.V. Miller, analysis and foreword J.N. Findlay (Oxford: Oxford University Press, 1977).
4. As Kevin Kelly put it: 'Like all utilities, AI will be supremely boring, even as it transforms the Internet, the global economy, and civilization', 'The Three Breakthroughs That Have Finally Unleashed AI on the World', *Wired*, 27 October 2014, https://www.wired.com/2014/10/future-of-artificial-intelligence/.

even as the system continues to transmit right up to the very nanosecond before impact.

This is therefore a decisive paradox, or, perhaps, one of the great revelations of contemporary media dissemination: the more powerful the means of distribution, the weaker the messages thereby distributed – except for the ultimate message itself, the one that bears upon the totality of the system as such. Part of the uniqueness of the Internet as a 'discourse network' (another Kittlerian term, adapted from the paranoid-schizoid visions of Judge Schreber) is that its powers of representation are patently immeasurably in excess of the content it can represent. No wonder everybody always seems to feel that they're 'under-represented' whenever they consider where they are in the field of representation. Because they are; but they aren't, too. The feeling isn't only mutual, but mandatory. It's also essentially correct, if not in the sense that people usually seem to give it.

Rather, to repeat, under the current conditions of digital media, the content as well as the impact of the content of any message tends towards zero. The epitome of a contemporary message is that it has minimal content and minimal qualities – indeed, these tend towards the absolutely infinitesimal – although its mere circulation produces hitherto-unprecedented volumes of further information. In other terms, this is what the Italian philosopher Giorgio Agamben considers the exposure of the essence of communicability – and not just communication. For the first time in human history, at the very 'end' of this history, we are confronted by a communicability that is itself incommunicable.[5] Or, as the French linguist Jean-Claude Milner puts it, there is no name of the name.[6]

There are, accordingly, very many ways of phrasing the difficulties, each almost as dissatisfactory as the others. Accomplished 'accelerated' distributivity entails the evacuation of meaning, indistinguishable from a chaos, or chaosmos, of meanings. Because any proposition regarding the putative context under which any meaning can be established is itself subject to another context which exceeds that proposition's delimitations – if one wishes one could refer to the familiar paradoxes of self-reference, or to decision problems, or to the reentry-of-the-form-into-the-form, or

5.   See, inter alia, Giorgio Agamben, *Language and Death: The Place of Negativity*, trans. Karen E. Pinkus with Michael Hardt (Minneapolis, MN: University of Minnesota Press, 1991).
6.   See Jean-Claude Milner, *Les noms indistincts* (Paris: Seuil, 1983).

whatever[7] – it turns out that only the end of all things can constitute a stable enough referent for such an establishment.[8] Until then, the difference between so-called 'metadata' and 'data' will remain utterly unstable – and only the aforementioned apocalypse will stop this abyssal and truth-corrosive precession of metas.

In the meantime – or at least in what James Joyce called 'the pastime of past time' – we can while away the hours with speculative archaeologies. Here and there, drawing on some of the familiar authorities, such as Marshall McLuhan and Jacques Rancière, regarding the status of the distributivity of modern media regimes, let's enumerate some basic affordances of our own media situation that literally demolish – or, perhaps, 'remolish' – the received architectures of production and kinds of address, hierarchy and transmission. When all media have become subject to a single über-medium, that of 'the Internet', media themselves disappear.[9] In a nutshell, we are no longer subject to 'the distribution of a-medium-in-dominance', nor to 'regimes of the sensible', but to a dissemination of the distribution of insensibles.

One can certainly hear McLuhan's ghost rattling its chains in these various statements (not forgetting that 'ghosts' in such a context have to be considered as dissimulating traces of older media situations, lingering as attenuated figures amidst the broken realities of the new). As McLuhan famously phrased it, 'The medium is the message', before adapting this to 'The medium is the massage'.[10] Media don't merely convey information, but constitute regimes of existence for humans; that is, they not only establish the limits of reality as such, but thereby also provide forms of psycho-physiological therapy. As such, all media systems are also remedial.[11] And they are so in a number of senses. They are remedial because they remedy or supplement physical and psychical deficiencies, and do so by providing their so-called 'users' with doses

7.   Here, I think of the penchant of some contemporary logicians for saving appearances by affirming true contradictions, e.g., the 'dialethism' of Graham Priest in *One: Being an Investigation into the Unity of Reality and of its Parts, including the Singular Object which is Nothingness* (Oxford: Oxford University Press, 2014), a book which, despite its ingenuity, doesn't know that its knowing is dependent upon its unknowing of our media situation.
8.   See on this point Ray Brassier, *Nihil Unbound: Enlightenment and Extinction* (New York: Palgrave Macmillan, 2007).
9.   As Adam Nash and I have argued, following indications of Jean Baudrillard, in 'Digital Ontology after the Event of the End of Media', *The Fibreculture Journal* 24 (2015): 6–32.
10.   Marshall McLuhan and Quentin Fiore, *The Medium is the Massage: an Inventory of Effects* (New York: Simon & Schuster, 1989).
11.   See also Jay David Bolter and Richard Grusin, *Remediation: Understanding New Media* (Cambridge, MA: MIT, 2000).

of information that are at once anxiety-inducing and pleasure-giving. In a different-if-related context, Jacques Derrida drew a word from Plato to nominate this double effect as that of the *pharmakon*, simultaneously poison and cure; for his part, Jacques Lacan spoke of the scraps of 'surplus-pleasure', or *jouissance*, that humans convulsively seek to squeeze from their subjection to media.[12] This irrevocable human submission to media creates a kind of 'Narcissus-narcosis': that is, the druggy, self-loving affects that media users experience in using their preferred media, for the most part unable to even suspect that the limits of the medium are the limits of their world. For McLuhan, we are all narcoleptic narcissists, except at those rare moments when the emergence of a new medium shocks us all into a momentary recognition that our ways of thinking are programmed by media – before we settle back again into the next generation of self-confirming narcoses. Aside from anything else, this means that media are not, whatever the claims made for them, primarily epistemic; they are rather affective.

Yet this remedial quality in the sense of sensorial therapeutics is doubled by another key structural feature for McLuhan: the 'content' of any medium is always another medium, or media. A medium is also re-medial in this sense. Media never ratify any particular viewpoint, but render any particular viewpoint relative to their own operations; indeed, they drive the proliferation of competing viewpoints in the service of their own dissemination. In other words, media are always correlated with a mass-age, in that they not only give our cerebra a nice buffing, buffeting and buffering, but effectively produce masses of anonymous persons who, despite not knowing each other at all, start to act without knowing it in coordinated ways precisely because they are all subject to the same medium or media. Today, we are ourselves now submitted to the contemporary narcosis of the Internet and its accompanying technologies... and in a way that is impossible for us to 'think' or 'feel' our way out of.

McLuhan called the 'Gutenberg Galaxy' the material restructuring required for the new interstellar vistas opened up by the early modern print revolution.[13] For McLuhan, the linearity, anonymity and mass-production of print have certain consequences for the human

12.   See Jacques Derrida, *Dissemination*, trans. Barbara Johnson (Chicago: University of Chicago Press, 1981); Jacques Lacan, *The Seminar of Jacques Lacan. Book 17, the Other Side of Psychoanalysis*, trans. Russell Grigg (New York: Norton & Norton, 2007).
13.   Marshall McLuhan, *The Gutenberg Galaxy* (Toronto: The University of Toronto Press, 2011).

sensorium, including the suppression of orality-aurality in favour of vision, the *in*-dividuation of persons and social segmentation. The 'visual homogenizing of experience' and the functional differentiation of modern social systems is an effect of the dominance of a particular medium, print, a dominance that is now at best residual. For McLuhan, it was the new audio-visual mayhem ushered in by television that gave 'Gutenberg Man' his most serious shock; today, what we call 'the Internet' has swallowed even the TV in its infinite maw.

Since what you are now reading is technically an essay concerning the possibilities for creative work according to the vicissitudes of contemporary mediatic distribution, I would like to offer, along the lines of the French philosopher Jacques Rancière's thesis of three 'regimes of distribution of the sensible', a minimal schematic of three regimes of the arts underpinning our current situation. For Rancière, as is now well known, considers that there have been three significantly different ways of treating the realm of *aesthesis*, at once the science of sense-perception, of what counts and what cannot count as treatable by the human sensorium, and of the role played by something like the technical or design object under these regimes.[14] Rancière calls the first of these the 'ethical' regime, because, à la Plato, what is subject to knowledge is to be separated entirely from the simulacra that cover over and pervert it. In this regime, there is, strictly speaking, no real art or design at stake; rather, there is an epistemic cut into the hierarchy of the relation between copies and simulacra. The second of Rancière's regimes is identified with the name of Aristotle: here, the principle of mimesis, or 'imitation' or 'representation', is at stake. Mimesis separates various forms of art in order to enable their evaluation internally and their comparison externally. Finally, we have the regime of the aesthetic, a fully modern regime in which art is separated from and conjoined with non-art according to a novel paradox: on the one hand, art is now recognisable by not having any particular distinguishing features; on the other, precisely to the extent that this radical indistinction operates within every singular presentation, art itself becomes linked to the problematic of truth.

For Rancière, crucially, 'design' becomes a feature of our 'modernity' in an unprecedented way in the aesthetic regime. In his studies of the unexpected links between Stéphane Mallarmé, one of the most radical

14.   See, for instance, Jacques Rancière, *Dissensus: On Politics and Aesthetics*, ed. and trans. S. Corcoran (London and New York: Continuum, 2010).

and influential of experimental poets, and the engineer Peter Behrens, involved with the design of industrial utilitarian equipment, Rancière notes that: 'Between Mallarmé and Behrens, between the pure poet and the functionalist engineer, therefore exists this singular bond: a single idea of simplified forms and a single function attributed to these forms – to define a new texture of common life'.[15] This 'new texture' means that there is now a certain 'equivalence' drawn between 'graphics' and 'plastics': that is, there is no longer any hierarchy nor principle nor practice that will a priori enable any stable distinction to be drawn between the media that support aesthetic differentiation of practices into plausibly demarcated genres.

While presuming the remedial nature of media, and their bearing upon the regimes of the sensible in the paradoxical forms I have briefly outlined from Kittler-McLuhan-Lacan-Derrida, let me now rerun Rancière's triple according to slightly different criteria: that is, according to the status of creative producers. The descriptions generated from the history of metaphysical doctrines, and the sociological accounts of functional revaluations wreaked by transformations in the forces and relations of media production, can here be usefully supplemented by attending to the situation of workers themselves. Like all generalisations, it will be eminently dissatisfactory and seething with exceptions. Nonetheless, it hopefully enables a useful orientation towards the problematic of creativity under the conditions of the contemporary. My own triplet can be summarised according to the relative dominance in a regime of the artisan, the artist or the designer. It's also worth mentioning that this is not a hierarchical or evaluative discrimination, only a heuristic and descriptive typology. Its value – if it has one – is merely to illuminate little conceptual cracks in the sequence of historical media situations. Moreover, it is also necessary to underline that the features that constitute the aforementioned 'relative dominance' change dramatically across regimes. Finally, this also means that if ethical idealism, mimetic typology and veridical aesthesis – Rancière's triple typology – at once remain available positions and practices within our media situation, not one of them functions as a control for the others. Why not? Because the new distributivity of the Internet reconfigures the relationships between producer and product in such a way that every existing structuring of

15.   J. Rancière, *Le destin des images* (Paris: La Fabrique-éditions, 2003), 111. See also 'Art, Life, Finality: The Metamorphoses of Beauty', *Critical Inquiry* 43 (2017): 597–616.

the relation between the making of creative works becomes itself only a non-determining option within a system that exceeds it. Indeed, radical distributivity entails the dispersion of human creative programmes into a virtual whole that forecloses the very element, the 'end', that would enable semantic and syntactic closure.

What I will call 'the artisanal regime' is clearly pre-modern or, at least, pre-industrial. The artisan made functional objects (even if that function was ultimately to be decorative or ritual), embodied specialised technical skills and worked according to stringent canons of production and association. The distribution of tasks of any artisan is specialised and differentiated according to its materials (e.g., leather, iron, stone), its techniques (the particular modes of treating such materials), its inheritances (e.g., its transmission through institutions such as guilds) and its economies (e.g., of the local markets for the products).

By contrast, the modern artist, exemplarily the avant-garde experimenter, emerging in a post-Renaissance situation that is also one of nascent mass-production of commodities and de-localised markets, becomes, strangely, someone whose value derives from their rupture from existing market routines: the modern artist is, to draw from current marketing jargon, the very paradigm of a 'disrupter' (or is it 'disruptor'?), who intervenes by producing 'critical' – that is, crisis-bearing – objects redolent of potential futures. By the way, this is one way of grasping just how retrograde and reactionary are the entrepreneurs who today proclaim the absolute value of 'disruption'; avant-gardism in art fell into desuetude over half a century ago, to the benefit of design, which, if it is indeed interested in making interventions into the contemporaneity of a symbolic economy, no longer does so on the basis of such avant-gardism. Whether you wish to follow the testimony of the avant-gardists themselves (e.g., the Dadaists or Surrealists), the accounts of the contemporaneous critics (e.g., Clement Greenberg's account of the media-specific radicality of the modern painter) or the retrospective accounts of our own times (e.g., Rancière's thesis, already invoked above, concerning the 'indistinction' of modern art), the 'objects' that the paradigmatic avant-gardist character produced are no longer simply beautiful, functional or even exchangeable objects.

But the designer is neither artisanal nor artistic, according to the operations of these prior regimes. Certainly, coterminous with the 'aesthetic regime' of the avant-garde artist, industrial capitalism marks the moment at which 'design' and 'production' come to be sharply differentiated; and whereby, moreover, each stage of production is subdivided and specialised until no single person is capable of comprehending and competing with the quantity of an assembly line. This is not to say that design did not exist as a recognisable, delimited practice prior to this, but industrial capitalism marks the moment at which, in the Smithian segmentation of the production process, design – as an abstract schema of selection, combination and transformation of ele-ments without any necessary particular connection to material labour – becomes clearly identified as an important subset of applied intellectual labour.

The modern crystallisation of the designer as an engineer of schematics of everyday life found correlates in contemporaneous metaphysics. Here, the first *Critique* of Immanuel Kant stands as a monument, anticipation and theorisation of the dynamics of such a system.[16] For in Kant we find that all human experience is synthetic, in the sense of being produced by artificial operations of unification upon multiples of different kinds of information. Kant famously asks, 'how are synthetic judgments possible a priori?' and answers by means of the transcendental sources of sense apprehension, re-productive imagination and re-cognitive apperception. Though all phenomena have their ultimate source in the noumenal, that is a source about which we must remain forever ignorant. Although the philosophical disputes regarding what the noumenal 'actually' 'is' will undoubtedly continue interminably, its key function in Kant is simply to ensure that, as the bedrock of whatever we call reality, we can't know anything about what it is 'in itself'. All phenomena we can sense or know must derive from the noumenal, but, of this source of all phenomena, we can be assured of nothing. The noumenal is a zone subtracted from every possible knowledge: it 'ex-sists', perhaps as a retrofitted and void presupposition of the system, perhaps as the real-as-impossible.

It is the synthesis of imagination – for Kant, the faculty of 're-production' between intuition (which provides sense data according to the forms of space and time) and understanding (which provides the concepts with which to think such data) – that functions precisely *schematically*. The imaginative schemata of Kant produce nothing new themselves, but enable both the archiving and montage of the already-

16.   If there are now of course very many competing translations of this
philosophical classic, the most famous remains Immanuel Kant's *Critique of Pure
Reason*, trans. Norman Kemp Smith (London: Macmillan, 1929).

given. In doing so, such schemata also offer the possibility of what Kant calls a 'hypotyposis' of the unrepresentable: the reinscription in graphic, visual or plastic terms of elements that are, strictly speaking, too abstract to acquire any adequate representation, but, in being so schematised, create possibilities for both knowledge and action that would otherwise be impossible. So it is no surprise that when contemporary theorists attempt to speak of our media situation the problem of schemata re-emerges with a vengeance.

Take the work of Luciano Floridi, whose theories of information remain in a Kantian frame. In a recent essay, Floridi proposes to outline what he calls 'the *conceptual logic* of design of a system'.[17] For Floridi, such a programme is epistemological, not ontological, given that it bears merely and modestly upon 'the logic of the model of a system', and not on the being of the system itself. The problem with this account is that, à la Kant, it excludes the real problem that is in fact the problem of the real: it's not just a reference 'about' that characterises contemporary (let's say: post-computational) design, but the fact that contemporary design is made from the very data that it is itself about. The diverse and pressing issues of material specificity that concerned both artisan and artist, even if they were engaged in transforming such materials into new things, are subordinated in such a space to external considerations managed by design. Not that materiality is therefore irrelevant to design – rather the contrary. But materials themselves become elements of selection on the basis of operatory concerns, rather than determining limits, constraints or essences with an independent resistance.

What does this mean? It means that materials have themselves now acquired a plasticity that they previously did not have, as well as contingent formal implications that are to be exposed and deformed in and by their very deployment. Whether we are dealing with technical innovations such as translucent concrete or black-that-is-blacker-than-black ('unmeasurable by spectrometers'!), new technological capacities enable the submission of materials to design. Rather than 'truth to materials' (which of course remains an option for contemporary design), there is a potential to generate surprising, interesting or unprecedented deployments that push materials beyond traditional limits as part of the

17.   Luciano Floridi, 'The Logic of Design as a Conceptual Logic of Information', *Minds and Machines* 27 (2017): 496. Italics are Floridi's.

effects and ends of the design itself. The subjacent logic is to create Unlimited Inc. from limited ink.

Floridi's own imagery is (unconsciously) revealing: 'compare the conceptual logic of a watch with the conceptual logic of the design of a watch', he says. But a watch is exemplarily an eighteenth-century mechanical timepiece, whereas the logic of contemporary design, no matter its level of abstraction or, indeed, whatever its alleged materiality, is that it is still only information about information. This means that the opposition Floridi offers, between that of modelling a system (epistemological) and that 'the logic of a model of a system is the logic of the system' (ontological), is false or, at least, insufficient. Even as Floridi asserts the insufficiency of Kantian and Hegelian systems-modelling for contemporary computing – 'transcendental' and 'dialectical' approaches, respectively – he repeats the basic Kantian operation that insists upon an absolute breach between all possible schemata and the world they are 'about'. So when he gives his own proposal – 'a design logic of future conditions of feasibility of a system' – it simply repeats one, derivative aspect of the modern design engineering approach. Floridi presumes that epistemic features are primary in design systems, and that there is an irreducible distinction between schema and world that governs all human endeavours. Yet, at the very moment he draws on the Kantian division of phenomena from noumena, he occludes the Kantian problematic of hypotyposis.

But the primacy of distributivity in the digital computational system of absolute knowledge that reigns today says 'No!' to this position; or, more precisely, 'yes, but... and but... and but...' Another, better proposition would be that 'the logic of a model of a system is included in the system of which it is a model'. So affect, not knowledge, is more decisive for any modelling of the system within the system. The contemporary designer, in a sense that goes beyond the restrictions of Floridi and Rancière, properly assumes her dominance with the current virtualisation of labour and the deterritorialisation of culture.[18] The 'modern' designer may or may not be identifiable with the engineers of schemata or the artists of everyday life, as these writers seem to maintain, but the contemporary designer is no longer a creature of such a regime.

18.   See Michael Hardt and Antonio Negri, *Empire* (Cambridge, MA: Harvard University Press, 2000).

For there's been a regime change. 'Design' in the regime of networked digital computing designates the fact, first, that 'nature' has entirely disappeared or revealed itself as always already shaped by human forces (this is what we now regularly call 'the Anthropocene'); second, that there is a necessity to assume organised, conscious and technical control over the artificial environments occupied by human beings (and we can see avatars of this 'will' in every domain of existence, whether in the 'nudge theory' of Nobel economists or in the filter bubbles produced for their subscribers by the great data entrepreneurs); third, it presumes the persistent differentiation and interference of disparate cultural markets, simultaneously proprietorial and appropriative, constantly attempting on the one hand to retract certain phenomena from distribution according to IP concerns, whether corporate or cultural, and, on the other, to reinject what has been withdrawn back into radical distribution. Moreover, fourth, design presumes an indefinite surplus of trans-substantial objects; it is only when the struggle to eat and breed is basically assured that such concerted attention can be directed towards the tiniest and previously unnoticed or indiscernible aspects of everyday life. Design is, moreover, inherently trans-identitarian because of its distributivity: it works in the zone opened up by the systematic convergence of technical, commercial and aesthetic exigencies, and the concomitant destabilisation of every traditional strut of personal identity.

But if we tally up the consequences of this situation, we find something historically and conceptually unprecedented. The total absorption of human action into the inhuman electric distributivity of the Internet means that there is no information that does not circulate or, rather, is not constituted a priori by such distributivity. As such, following the brief discussion above of the rigours to which the contemporary designer is submitted, every position once assigned to communication comes to its point of dissolution. With the virtual digitisation of all possible information, the alleged 'sources' of information become irreducibly multiple, and the alleged 'receivers' likewise. These multiples are, for the most part, 'insensible', in that they have no possible particular sense inherent to them, and nor can they for the most part cross the thresholds of sensation. The designer as assembler-retransmitter of such information becomes primarily a synthesiser of informatic-affect doses, and not a vector of illumination. Nobody wears a watch to tell the time anymore; or, rather, there are so many ways of telling the time available that wearing a watch at all is at the very least a decision regarding a self-performance of preferences. As it's probably even impossible today in metropolitan first-world cultures to avoid having the time told to you by many devices simultaneously, the primacy of affect in design is clearly more crucial than that object's nominal use.

Any representation or model of this system can therefore be, at best, hypotypotic, in the Kantian sense. In being so, however, this means that 'the distributions of the sensible', or sequences of epistemes, now take place within a system that at once enables their subsistence and ensures their irrelevancy. The designer is the last avatar of an in-human figure of creativity remaining to the system, constantly remodelling fragments of information according to local directives whose specific raisons d'être tend to vanish in their very transmission. This distributivity which conditions contemporary design should alert us to the fact that we are no longer subject to any distributions of the sensible, but to the dissemination of the distribution of insensibles. Until, that is, the final, un-designable message arrives, one which we will never receive, as, as...

Biographies

Ahmed Ansari

Ahmed Ansari is a PhD candidate in Design
Studies at Carnegie Mellon University
(CMU). His present research looks at
the intersection between decolonial
theory and the philosophy of technology,
focusing on recovering and deriving 'other',
non-Western philosophies of technics,
specifically those of pre-colonial India and
China. He is also a founding member of the
Decolonising Design platform, and teaches
courses in systems thinking, cultural
theory and the history and philosophy of
technology at CMU.

Neil Arthur

Neil Arthur is best known as the frontman
of synth-pop band Blancmange. In 1982,
Blancmange signed to London Records and
released their first album *Happy Families*,
followed by *Mange Tout* in 1984. The band
played a farewell concert at the Royal Albert
Hall in 1986. As a solo artist, he released his
first album *Suitcase* in 1994 on Chrysalis
Records. In 2011, he reformed Blancmange
and released *Blanc Burn*. Their most recent
release is *Unfurnished Rooms* (2017).

Stuart Bertolotti-Bailey

Stuart Bertolotti-Bailey is a graphic designer,
writer and publisher based in Liverpool
and currently working as Head of Design
at the Institute of Contemporary Arts in
London. He is one half of artist duo Dexter
Sinister, along with David Reinfurt, and one
third of archiving/publishing platform The
Serving Library, along with Reinfurt and
Francesca Bertolotti-Bailey. He co-founded
and co-edited the left-field arts journal *Dot
Dot Dot* in 2000 and continues to edit
its successors, *Bulletins of The Serving
Library* (since 2011) and *The Serving Library
Annual* (since 2017), both of which are fully
archived at www.servinglibrary.org.

David Blamey

David Blamey is a London-based artist and
proprietor of the independent imprint Open
Editions. His work encompasses several
activities, including teaching, publishing
and exhibiting, which overlap to form a
multi-dimensional practice that defies
conventional categorisation. To this end,
his projects are positioned consciously
within a range of public situations, both
inside and beyond the art gallery. His recent
activities include releasing a record, *Rural*
(2015); a book, *Specialism* (2016); and a film,
Rice (2017), that premiered at the Mumbai
International Film Festival (2018). He curated
Learning To Listen for Bang & Olufsen
and *Short Bursts of Concentrated Joy* for
Houghton Festival (2017) and will launch
a new online sound project called *British
Earways* in 2018.

Justin Clemens

Justin Clemens writes on psychoanalysis, European philosophy and Australian poetry. His books include *Psychoanalysis is an Antiphilosophy* (Edinburgh University Press, 2013), *Minimal Domination* (Surpllus, 2011) and *The Mundiad* (Hunter, 2013). He is also the co-editor of a number of scholarly collections, such as *What is Education?* (Edinburgh University Press, 2017) and *Badiou and His Interlocutors* (Bloomsbury, 2018). He teaches at The University of Melbourne.

Alex Coles

Developing themes initially explored in the books *DesignArt* published by the Tate in 2005 and *Design and Art* by MIT Press/Whitechapel in 2007, Alex Coles is currently developing two series of books with Sternberg Press, Berlin: The Transdisciplinary Studio and EP. The first volume of EP was devoted to the Italian avant-garde 1968–1976, the second volume focused on design fiction, and the soon-to-be-released third volume examines the notion of post-craft. Coles is currently Professor of Transdisciplinary Studies at the University of Huddersfield.

David Cross

David Cross is an artist and academic, engaging with the contested ideal of sustainability. From 1991, when he left the Royal College of Art, until 2014, he collaborated with Matthew Cornford as Cornford & Cross, making context-specific art projects that address critical issues to activate social agency. Perceiving a conflict between his internationalism and environmentalism, David stopped using jet travel in 2005. As a Reader at UAL, David works for education as a public good, combining transformative pedagogy with constructive institutional critique. With students at UAL, he campaigned successfully for UAL to divest £3.9 million from fossil fuels.

Neil Cummings

Neil Cummings was born in Wales and lives in London. He is a Professor at Chelsea College of Arts and is on the editorial board of Documents of Contemporary Art. Neil has made projects with museums, central banks, galleries, archives, auction houses, places of education, department stores and enthusiasts. These projects, although diverse, have consistently engaged directly with the institutions that designate and exhibit art, and the increasingly devolved experience of art, to its publics. Neil is currently working on The Anthropocene Atlas: London.

Sean Dockray

Sean Dockray is an artist, writer and programmer living in Melbourne. From 2005 to 2013, he was a co-director with Fiona Whitton of the Los Angeles non-profit, Telic Arts Exchange. Sean initiated the knowledge-sharing platforms AAAARG. ORG in 2004 and The Public School in 2007. The Public School has offered more than 500 reading groups, workshops, tours and lectures on subjects ranging from knot theory to student occupations. His publications include 'Fake News, Artificial Intelligence, and Data Visualization' (2017) in *ArtLink*, 'Sharing Instinct: An Annotation of the Social Contract Through Shadow Libraries' (2015) with Lawrence Liang as part of the e-flux Supercommunity, and an upcoming essay commission for Triple Canopy.

Benjamin Forster

Benjamin Forster does not have any pets. He was a professional artist for many years. Now he is somewhat unconcerned with professionalilty except as a concept. He has a number of formal papers, like an Honours degree in Visual Arts from the Australian National University, a Graduate Diploma in Library Science from Curtin University, and a soon-to-expire learner driver's license from the NSW Roads and Maritime Services. In 2016, he co-founded Frontyard Projects in Marrickville, where he helps to hold public space open and continues to care for the decommissioned Australia Council for the Art's research library.

Susan Hawthorne

Susan Hawthorne has worked in the publishing industry for more than thirty years as Senior Editor at Penguin Books and co-founder of the independent feminist press Spinifex. She is the author of *Bibliodiversity: A Manifesto for Independent Publishing*, which has been translated into Arabic, French, German and Spanish. From 2012 to 2016, she was English Language Co-ordinator for the International Alliance of Independent Publishers. In 2015, she received the George Robertson Award for Service to the Publishing Industry; in 1991, the Pandora New Venture Award, Women in Publishing International for Spinifex Press (UK); and in 1989, the Florence James Pandora Award for Outstanding Contribution to Women's Publishing. She is Publisher at Spinifex Press and Adjunct Professor in the College of Arts, Society and Education at James Cook University, Townsville. In addition to her work in publishing, she is a poet and novelist, and her latest book *is Dark Matters: A Novel* (2017).

Brad Haylock

Brad Haylock is a designer, publisher and academic. He is an Associate Professor of Design at RMIT University, Melbourne, where he manages the Master of Communication Design programme, and he is founding editor of Surpllus, an independent, para-academic imprint focusing on critical and speculative practices across art, design and theory.

Robert Hetherington

Robert Hetherington is a writer and designer whose work explores questions surrounding the position of the text. He examines the lifespan of information as it shifts and morphs through multiple forms and meanings, moving between authors and readers, focusing on the points at which one process ends and the next begins and how, ultimately, in a digital age, these lines of demarcation become increasingly blurred. Robert completed his MA at the Royal College of Art in 2015. Since then, he has lectured regularly in the School of Communication at the RCA and on the Graphic Design programme at Camberwell College of Art. He has contributed to a number journals and publications, with articles published by *Design Observer* and *Icon Magazine*, amongst others.

Jonathan Lindley

After working with the bands Enter Shikari and Drumcorps, Jonathan Lindley began to research post-subcultural theory, particularly the development of 'neo-tribes', at The University of Huddersfield in 2015. As a major part of his research, he relaunched Sunbird Records in 2012, an independent record label in

Darwen, Lancashire, which has now evolved into a cross-disciplinary community actively encouraging a diverse, sometimes extreme, collective of artists and musicians spanning the worlds of established and alternative music styles. In 2016 Lindley opened his own music venue in Darwen as an incubator for local activity.

Gareth Long

Gareth Long's work offers space for a constantly movable host of subjects: copying, seriality, amateurism, translation and collaboration. Within his diverse practice, these topics are engaged both as thematic concerns and as methods of production. Interested in questioning and dismantling notions of authorship, his work functions to extend and compact, reframe and refabricate grand narratives through processes of reading, re-reading and misreading.

Jens Maier-Rothe

Jens Maier-Rothe writes, edits and makes exhibitions. He has realised exhibitions internationally, including collaborations with the Van Abbemuseum, Stedelijk Museum, Lisson Gallery and Kadist Art Foundation. From 2008 to 2011 he directed the curatorial platform Sonic Thinking and from 2012 to 2015 he was founding co-director of the art initiative and exhibition space Beirut in Cairo. Maier-Rothe regularly writes on contemporary art and culture for journals such as *Camera Austria International*, *Ibraaz* and *Ocula*. His latest book publications include *Mass Effect* (MIT Press/New Museum, 2015), *Cave 1 – Territories* (Sternberg Press, 2016), *Future Imperfect* (Sternberg Press, 2016) and *White Paper* (Valiz, 2016).

Markus Miessen

Markus Miessen is a Berlin-based architect and writer, and he is a Professor at the Academy of Design, University of Gothenburg, Sweden. He received his PhD from the Centre for Research Architecture at Goldsmiths, London. The initiator of the *Participation* tetralogy, his work revolves around questions of critical spatial practice, institution building and spatial politics. Miessen has previously taught at the Berlage Institute (Rotterdam) and the Architectural Association (London). Amongst many other books and writings, Miessen is the author of *The Nightmare of Participation* and *Crossbenching* (both Sternberg Press, Berlin). His Berlin-based practice, Studio Miessen, is currently working on a strategic redesign of Martin-Gropius-Bau in Berlin, as well as projects for and with Artsonje Center (Seoul) and Kunsthalle Vienna, and for the artists Omer Fast, Flaka Haliti and Hito Steyerl. The studio's largest project to date is a strategic framework design for a former NATO military site in Germany, which is currently being transformed into a cultural centre.

Billie Muraben

Billie Muraben is a writer, editor and lecturer. Her work focusses on the broader context of (and surrounding) art and design practice, as well as forays into satire, geopolitics, science fiction and considering what we can learn from Las Vegas. Recent work includes pieces on exhibitions at the Fondazione Prada and Ditchling Museum of Art & Craft, a feature on Eduardo Paolozzi's time as a tutor at the Royal College of Art and a review of the first academic collection on the study of ghost signs. She teaches on the BA and MA programmes in Graphic Communication Design at Central Saint Martins.

Rathna Ramanathan

Rathna Ramanathan is a graphic designer whose practice is situated around and inspired by the contexts of culture, language, typography and publishing. Based in London and Chennai, Rathna specialises in the research, design and curation of marginalized content and endangered practices within intercultural publishing with South Asia as the site of investigation. Themes that resonate in her work include the relevance of tangible and intangible heritages in contemporary design and dialogues of people, politics and place. She runs her own studio minus9 and has a PhD in Typography and Graphic Communication from the University of Reading. Rathna has taught in India and in the UK and heads Visual Communication at the Royal College of Art. Her work with Tara Books has received multiple international awards.

Patricia Reed

Patricia Reed is an artist, writer and designer based in Berlin. As an artist, selected exhibitions include those at The Museum of Capitalism (Oakland), Homeworks 7 (Beirut), Witte de With (Rotterdam), HKW (Berlin) and Württembergischer Kunstverein (Stuttgart). Recent writings have been published in *e-flux Architecture*, *_AH Journal, Cold War Cold World* (Urbanomic), *Reinventing Horizons* (Tranzitdisplay), *Moneylab #2* (Inst. of Networked Cultures) and *The Neurotic Turn* (Repeater Books). With Victoria Ivanova, she co-curated the *1948 Unbound: Tokens* session as a performative symposium with the House of World Cultures team, Berlin (2017), and she is currently a theory researcher for Public Art Munich 2018. Reed is also part of the Laboria Cuboniks (techno-material feminist) working group.

Adrian Shaughnessy

Adrian Shaughnessy is a designer, writer, educator and publisher. He co-founded the design group Intro, an early adopter of digital technology and a pioneer of digital motion graphics. He writes regularly for many of the leading design journals and hosts an occasional radio show on ResonanceFM called *Graphic Design on the Radio*. In 2009, he was awarded a Visiting Professorship at the Royal College of Art. He lectures extensively around the world. He is co-founder of the publishing imprint Unit Editions, which boasts a non-traditional distribution model for its books. Shaughnessy is the author of numerous books on design.

Martine Syms

Martine Syms uses video and performance to examine representations of blackness and its relationship to American situation comedy, Black vernacular, feminist movements and radical traditions. Her artwork has been exhibited and screened extensively, including presentations at the Museum of Modern Art, the New Museum, The Studio Museum in Harlem, the Hammer Museum (Los Angeles), The Museum of Contemporary Art (Los Angeles) and the Institute of Contemporary Art (London). She has lectured at Yale University, SXSW, University of Chicago, Johns Hopkins University and MoMA PS1, among other venues. Syms' recent exhibitions include *Projects 106* (Museum of Modern Art), *The Easy Demands* (Sadie Coles), *Borrowed Lady* (SFU Galleries, Vancouver), *Fact and Trouble* (ICA, London) and *COM PORT MENT* (Karma International, Los Angeles). She runs Dominica Publishing, an imprint dedicated to exploring blackness in visual culture. She is a faculty member in the Art Department at the California Institute of the Arts.

Jake Tilson

Jake Tilson is an artist, graphic designer and author. His work is held in museums worldwide including the Tate Gallery and Museum of Modern Art. Tilson founded the influential arts magazine, *Atlas* (1984) and was an early web pioneer with his award-winning website *TheCooker* (1994), featured in *New Media in Late 20th Century Art*, Thames & Hudson (1999). His first cookbook, which he also designed, *A Tale of 12 Kitchens* (2006), won the Gourmand World Cookbook Award and was shortlisted for both the Andre Simon Award and Glenfiddich Award. He is currently working on a book about the typography of Venice, and a large-scale exhibition on the Tsukiji Fish Market in Tokyo.

Pip Wallis

Pip Wallis is Curator of Contemporary Art at the National Gallery of Victoria, Melbourne, where she has organised exhibitions by Helen Maudsley and Hito Steyerl, and performances by Paulina Olowska, Adam Linder and Simone Forti, and she co-edited 'Body', *NGV Triennial 2017*, with Hannah Black. She was previously Managing Editor of *X-TRA Contemporary Art Quarterly* (Los Angeles); Curator-in-Residence at Chisenhale Gallery, London, where she curated a performance work by Brian Fuata; and Curator at Gertrude Contemporary, Melbourne,where she curated exhibitions by Kate Newby, Claire Lambe and Atlanta Eke. She edited *un Magazine* (volume 9, 2015), was visiting curator at The Irish Museum of Modern Art (Dublin, 2015) and has presented at Take On Art Symposium(New Delhi, 2017) and Woman, Art and Feminism Conference (Melbourne, 2018).

Eva Weinmayr

Eva Weinmayr is an artist based in London. She runs AND Publishing in collaboration with Rosalie Schweiker and collaborates with Andrea Francke on The Piracy Project, an exploration of the philosophical, legal and practical implications of book piracy, which questions common sense assumptions about ownership, authorship and the implications policy development has had on the current debate around intellectual property. Institutions she has worked with include SALT (Istanbul), The Showroom (London), Kunstverein Munich and MayDay Rooms (London), among others. Recent publications include *Pause: 21 scenes concerning the Silence of Art in Ruins* (Occasional Papers, London) and *Downing Street* (New Documents, Los Angeles). In 2016, she co-convened Let's Mobilize: What is Feminist Pedagogy?, a three-day investigation of queer and feminist pedagogies at Valand Academy Gothenburg, where she is conducting a PhD in artistic research.

Acknowledgments

The editors would like to thank each other. Thank you Brad for your diligence and for maintaining a cheery demeanour during our skype meetings that, because of the time difference between northern and southern hemispheres, took place at anti-social times of day. Thank you David for the short ride in a fast machine, for your pragmatism and for conceding that 'epistemology' mightn't be a dirty word after all. We are particularly grateful to all our contributing writers, whose generosity and passion for the subject under examination has created such a kaleidoscopic and thought-provoking picture. Special thanks to Cathy Johns for her sharp-eyed copy-editing. Thank you to Joe Pochodzaj for laying out the book so efficiently, to Jon Hares for its beautiful design and to Laurence Soens for overseeing its physical manifestation as a printed product for distribution in our material world.

Patricia Reed would like to extend thanks to Brad Haylock for his invaluable edits and comments.

Series Editor
David Blamey

Editors
David Blamey
Brad Haylock

Copy-editor
Cathy Johns

Design
Jonathan Hares

Design Layout
Joseph Pochodzaj

Font
Stephan Müller
Unica Neue Regular & Light

Cover Paper
Neenah Lahnstein
Neobond 200gsm

Publisher
Open Editions

E-orders:
Open Editions
orders@openeditions.com
+44 (0)20 7830 9779